Battle-Pieces and Aspects of the War

CIVIL WAR POEMS

Herman Melville

A sketch for the painting *Jane Jackson, Formerly a Slave* by Elihu Vedder, which Melville viewed at the 1865 exhibition of the National Academy of Design. The painting inspired Melville's poem "Formerly a Slave."

Battle-Pieces and Aspects of the War

CIVIL WAR POEMS

Herman Melville

Foreword by
James M. McPherson

Introduction by
Richard H. Cox and Paul M. Dowling

Interpretive Essays by
Helen Vendler, Rosanna Warren,
Richard H. Cox, and Paul M. Dowling

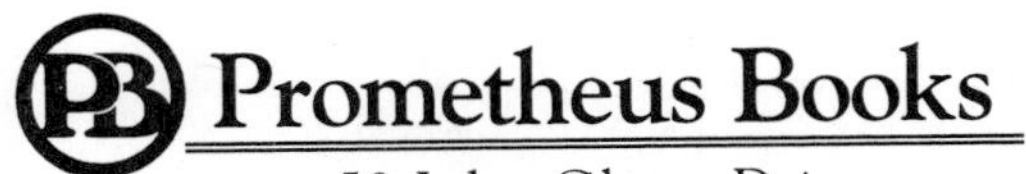

59 John Glenn Drive
Amherst, New York 14228-2197

LITERARY CLASSICS

Published 2001 by Prometheus Books

Inquiries should be addressed to
Prometheus Books
59 John Glenn Drive
Amherst, New York 14228–2197
VOICE: 716–691–0133, ext. 207
FAX: 716–564–2711
WWW.PROMETHEUSBOOKS.COM

05 04 03 02 01 5 4 3 2 1

Battle-Pieces and Aspects of the War originally published:
New York: Harper & Brothers, 1866.

Library of Congress Cataloging-in-Publication Data

Melville, Herman, 1819–1891.
Battle-pieces and aspects of the war : Civil War poems / Herman Melville ; foreword by James M. McPherson ; introduction by Richard H. Cox and Paul M. Dowling ; interpretive essays by Helen Vendler . . . [et al.]
p. cm. — (Literary classics)
Includes bibliographical references.
ISBN 1–57392–893–3 (pbk. : alk. paper)
1. United States—History—Civil War, 1861–1865—Poetry. 2. War poetry, American. I. Vendler, Helen Hennessy. II. Title. III. Literary classics (Amherst, N.Y.)

PS2384 .B3 2001
811'.3—dc21 00–054866

Printed in the United States of America on acid-free paper

Prometheus's Literary Classics Series

Henry Adams, *Esther*

Aristophanes, *Assembly of Women (Ecclesiazusae)*

Charles Brockden Brown, *Wieland, or The Transformation*

Samuel Butler, *Erewhon*

Lewis Carroll, *Phantasmagoria*

Anton Chekov, *Stories of Men*

Anton Chekov, *Stories of Women*

Kate Chopin, *The Awakening*

Stephen Crane, *Maggie, A Girl of the Streets*

George Eliot, *Scenes of Clerical Life*

Harold Frederic, *The Damnation of Theron Ware*

Frank Harris, *My Life and Loves*

Nathaniel Hawthorne, *The Scarlet Letter*

Henry James, *The Turn of the Screw* and *The Lesson of the Master*

Ring Lardner Jr., *The Ecstasy of Owen Muir*

Sinclair Lewis, *Main Street*

Jack London, *The Star Rover*

The Love Songs of Sappho
Translated with an essay by Paul Roche. Introduction by Page duBois

Herman Melville, *Battle-Pieces and Aspects of the War*

Herman Melville, *The Confidence Man*

John Neal, *Rachel Dyer*

Edgar Allan Poe, *Eureka: A Prose Poem*

Seasons of Life
Compiled by Nigel Collins. Edited by Jim Herrick and John Pearce

Upton Sinclair, *The Moneychangers*

Henry David Thoreau, *Civil Disobedience*, *Solitude*, and *Life without Principle*

Mark Twain, *The Diaries of Adam and Eve*

Mark Twain, *The Mysterious Stranger*

Walt Whitman, *Leaves of Grass*

Émile Zola, *Lourdes*

HERMAN MELVILLE was born the second son of a wealthy merchant in New York City on August 1, 1819. Only twelve when his father died bankrupt, the young Melville worked as a bank clerk and a schoolteacher before signing on a packet ship bound for Liverpool in 1839 to try his fortune as a sailor. In 1841 Melville sailed on the whaling ship *Acushnet* bound for the South Pacific; the following year, the *Acushnet* anchored in the Marquesas islands, where Melville deserted ship. He made his way to Tahiti and then to Hawaii, finding employment with an English merchant. Melville returned to the United States in 1844 as an ordinary seaman aboard the *United States*, landing in Boston, where he was honorably discharged.

His sea adventures furnished the material for Melville's successful first novels, *Typee* (1846) and *Omoo* (1847). Following the publication of *Mardi* (1849), *Redburn* (1849), and *White-Jacket* (1850), Melville began work on his masterpiece, *Moby-Dick* (1851).

In 1850 Melville moved with his wife and family to a farm in Pittsfield, Massachusetts. Unable to earn a living from the farm, Melville was forced to borrow money from relatives; he also received some income from stories and sketches published in popular magazines. These pieces, including the now acclaimed "Bartleby, the Scrivener," were later collected in the *Piazza Tales* (1856).

After 1850, however, Melville's literary success faded: *Moby-Dick* was both a critical and commercial failure; the complexity of this and Melville's next work, *Pierre* (1852), could not rekindle the interest readers had in his early adventure stories. The final novel Melville published before abandoning prose altogether was *The Confidence Man: His Masquerade* (1857), a satirical and allegorical tale which baffled reviewers condemned at its appearance as "misanthropical," but which is now considered to be among Melville's best works. Thereafter, Melville turned to poetry; his *Battle Pieces* (1866), *Clarel* (1876), and *John Marr and Other Sailors* (1888) were published in small, privately subsidized editions.

In 1863 Melville sold his farm and moved back to New York

City, where, to support his family, he became a customs inspector, a position he held from 1866 to 1885, when some unexpected legacies made it possible for him to retire. Herman Melville died, all but forgotten, in New York City on September 28, 1891. The manuscript of *Billy Budd*, now Melville's best known work after *Moby-Dick*, was found in his desk after his death; it remained unpublished, however, until 1924.

Contents

Acknowledgments

The genesis of this book was a Liberty Fund Colloquium devoted entirely to Melville's *Battle-Pieces*. We are grateful to the Board and Fellows of Liberty Fund for support of that colloquium, and to the participants in the colloquium for their reflections, and thus to both for their roles in inducing us to bring to the reading public this reprint of Melville's book along with essays about its worth.

We also wish to thank William A. Williams Jr. for having produced a Web site concordance to *Battle-Pieces* (it may be found at www.concordance.com); the editors of *Raritan* and the *Southern Review* for permission to reprint the Warren and Vendler essays; and George W. Carey, editor, and John M. Vella, managing editor, of the *Political Science Reviewer*, for permission to draw upon materials previously published in our review in that journal.

Foreword

James M. McPherson

Herman Melville is not one of America's nineteenth-century authors that we associate with the Civil War. Several of his contemporaries achieved prominence with their writings about the war and its context: James Russell Lowell with his two series of *The Biglow Papers* (1848 and 1864), his editorship of *Atlantic Monthly* and *North American Review*, and his "Ode Recited at the Harvard Commemoration, July 21, 1865"; John Greenleaf Whittier with his many antislavery and war poems; Walt Whitman with his war poetry and prose writings and his work as a volunteer nurse in army hospitals; or Harriet Beecher Stowe whose *Uncle Tom's Cabin* reportedly caused Abraham Lincoln to say, when he met her in 1862: "So you're the little woman who wrote the book that made this great war." Even Mark Twain, who wrote little about the Civil War, offered a memorable appraisal of its impact in *The Gilded Age*: the war, he said, "uprooted institutions that were centuries old, changed the politics of a people, transformed the social life of half the country, and wrought so profoundly upon the entire national character that the influence cannot be measured short of two or three generations."

By contrast, Melville wrote little and published nothing about the war while it lasted. The fall of Richmond on April 3, 1865, however, inspired him to produce seventy-two poems—his first effort in this genre—which he published in 1866 as *Battle-Pieces and Aspects of the War*. Reviewers were not kind to this volume, and readers did not rush to buy it—only 525 copies sold during the decade after publication. Long out of print, *Battle-Pieces* was virtually forgotten until rediscovered in the 1960s. It is now made newly available in this splendid edition with an introduction by the editors and several essays by scholars that help make these profound but difficult poems more accessible.

One reason for the long obscurity of Melville's war poems was their lack of triumphalism. Most of the writings by other authors of note celebrated, in one degree or another, the triumph of Union and freedom by Northern victory. Melville certainly approved this outcome. But his poems plumbed the existential depths of the human tragedy and suffering wrought by the war. The dominant theme in many of these short poems is tragic irony: the contrast between "Young soldiers marching lustily/ Unto the wars" and the "Death in rosy clime" that "Would come to thin their shining throng."

A sign of the growing modern appreciation of Melville's *Battle-Pieces* is the inclusion of thirteen of the poems (more than those of any other author except Whitman) in *The Columbia Book of Civil War Poetry*, published in 1993. Significantly, of the seven thematic categories in which this anthology groups the poems, the only one in which Melville is not represented is "Moral Fervor." Melville's ironic and tragic vision precluded one- or two-dimensional fervor. But for a deeper understanding of the war, we need his three-dimensional vision. And this volume will help us to see it.

Introduction

Poetry and Politics

Richard H. Cox & Paul M. Dowling

While Herman Melville is acknowledged to have written America's greatest novel and some of its greatest short stories, he is virtually unknown as a poet; and when known, it is usually as a failed poet. Indeed, his poetry is in a limbo of the kind inhabited by his great prose fiction a century ago, when almost no one read him. Yet this great writer spent roughly thirty of his mature years writing books of poetry: *Battle-Pieces and Aspects of the War* (1866), *Clarel: A Poem and Pilgrimage in the Holy Land* (begun in 1856 and published in 1876), *John Marr and Other Sailors* (1888); and *Timoleon* (1891).

The purpose of this volume is to introduce—or reintroduce—to both scholars and ordinary citizens the first of his books of poetry, his book on the American Civil War. The relatively small handful of writers who have paid some attention to *Battle-Pieces and Aspects of the War* generally have tended to focus either on its unconventional poetry or on its problematic politics.[1] But we shall argue that these judgments are inadequate for they do not view the book as Melville intended: as a peculiar, and peculiarly intricate, marriage of literary form and military-political history and thought, which is to say, of poetry and politics.

We are aware, however, that such a linking may appear paradoxical or misleading. Paradoxical because poetry, according to some of its modern practitioners, transcends the paltry business of politics while the poet inhabits the realm of the apolitical artist. And misleading because other modern poets are committed to progressive policies of equality and social justice, with verse in the service of partisanship. Neither of these possibilities attracted Herman Melville.

For our poet, the fate of his country, caught up in the convulsions of the Civil War and its terrible aftermath, mattered profoundly. Indeed, it is virtually impossible, as we shall argue, to separate his patriotism from his poetry. Hence, he writes in the "Supplement" to *Battle-Pieces* in reference to the grave problem of Reconstruction of the Union: "the times are such that patriotism—not free from solicitude—urges a claim overriding all literary scruples" [259].* On the other hand, his patriotism is a thoughtful attachment to the American Founders' notion of a self-governing republic, based on the fundamental documents of the regime. Such an allegiance mediated between an optimistic progressivism about mankind on the one hand and a pessimistic cynicism on the other. Hence in "The House-top," although the New York draft riots of July 1863 undermine the faith that man is naturally good, Melville equally rejects the belief in the "cynic tyrannies of honest kings." Between these extremes lay the American experiment in self-government. That experiment is vividly symbolized by references in five of the seventy-two poems to the "Dome" of the Capitol, the seat of the deliberative, legislative branch of our government, and the only symbol of that government ever to be mentioned in his book.

In this introduction, we begin the argument for viewing Melville as a peculiar kind of political poet and do so in three stages. First, we sketch his times and two of his writings prior to the Civil War, a sketch which emphasizes the importance of the political. Second, we sketch the initial reception of *Battle-Pieces*

---

*See "Note on the Text," page 39.

and of the editions of the book which have thus far been published. Third, we present summaries of the four interpretive essays which follow the text of Melville's book, each, in its way, viewing Melville's poetry as a marriage of literature and political history.

MELVILLE AND THE ANTEBELLUM POLITICAL BACKGROUND TO THE CIVIL WAR: *MOBY-DICK* AND *BENITO CERENO*

Born in 1819 in New York City, Melville grew to manhood there and in Albany, New York, at a time when expansion of the American Republic aggravated the great issue of chattel slavery. For the admission of new states inevitably raised the question whether they would be permitted to enter the Union as either "free" or "slave"; and the institution itself repeatedly raised the question of its relationship to the ultimate premises of the two most fundamental of America's "organic laws,"[2] the Declaration of Independence and the Constitution.

The ultimate premise of the Declaration is that there are natural rights, which are manifest in "self-evident" truths. None is more explosive politically than the very first, that which recognizes that "all men are created equal." The ultimate premise of the Constitution is that "we the people," as is our right by nature, intend to found a polity which will, through the Constitution, secure the fundamental ends articulated in the Preamble: "a more perfect Union," "Justice," "domestic tranquility," "common defense," "general Welfare," and, perhaps most encompassing, "the blessings of liberty." The institution of chattel slavery, rooted as it is in the denial of the natural right of equality of all men, proves on reflection to be in essential conflict with every one of these ends.

The nation's dedication to both fundamental "organic laws" is revealed in congressional enactments. In 1788, Congress, operating under the Articles of Confederation, passed a resolution by which "congress would, in a body, attend divine worship . . . to return thanks for the divine mercy, in supporting the independence of the states." In 1814, Congress authorized publication of an official compilation of the statute laws of the United States, and stipulated that the text of the statutes should be preceded by the Declaration as well as the Constitution and the Articles of Confederation. In 1845, Congress authorized a newer compilation of the statutes. Again, the three "organic laws" stand at the head of the statutes as a noble preamble. This version of the laws remained in place all during the sectional crisis which eventuated in the Civil War and during the war itself.

That increasingly dangerous crisis was the political background to the formative and mature years of Herman Melville. The year after he was born, Congress enacted the Missouri Compromise: Maine was to enter the Union as a free state, Missouri as a slave state, and slavery was henceforth to be excluded from the portion of the Louisiana Purchase north of the line 36 degrees 30 minutes. When Melville was eight years old, in 1827, and living in New York City, New York State abolished slavery, an event celebrated on July 5 with an Emancipation Day parade in the city. When he was thirty-one years old and in the course of finishing *Moby-Dick*, Congress made still another attempt to resolve the burgeoning conflict over the extension of slavery in the series of bills called the Compromise of 1850. The single most fateful provision of this legislation was the enactment of the principle called "popular sovereignty": majority vote of the citizens would legally decide whether new states to be formed in the territories of New Mexico and Utah would be admitted as "slave" or "free." The undermining of the first principle of the Declaration of Independence was by now far advanced, but in the name of the people's indefeasible right to choose whether to found new slave-based polities.

When Melville was nearing thirty-five, in May 1854, the problem of the extension of slavery was reopened with Congress's passage of the Kansas-Nebraska Act. Most crucial, the act applied the principle of "popular sovereignty" to the organization of the two territories, and, even more ominously, repealed the Missouri Compromise. Popular sovereignty now increasingly appeared to mean that whatever the majority decided was right must simply become law, even if it was in profound conflict with the Republic's fundamental principles as those are articulated in the Declaration and the Constitution.

In October 1854, Abraham Lincoln, deeply troubled by the ascendancy of untrammeled "popular sovereignty" as *the* fundamental political principle in the American regime, gave his famous "Peoria Speech." He attacked the Kansas-Nebraska Bill, denounced the repeal of the Missouri Compromise, and forthrightly opposed any extension of slavery into the territories. He held that to do so would be subversive of both the Declaration of Independence and the Constitution. In so arguing, he appealed from "popular sovereignty" to the principles of natural right as articulated in the Declaration.

In 1856, Melville published his novella *Benito Cereno*. Its writing and publication took place against the backdrop of the small-scale civil war over the extension of slavery which was going on in Kansas and Nebraska. "Bloody Kansas" was to prove a harbinger of the full-scale Civil War to come. We shall see presently what Melville seeks to do in his fictional portrayal of a Yankee captain's suppression of a slave rebellion on a Spanish ship.

The preceding sketch of political events shows that by the time that the Civil War erupted in 1861, Melville had long been witness to the fundamental conflict of the American regime. We shall now argue that he reflected upon what he witnessed; that he introduced his reflections into *Moby-Dick* and *Benito Cereno*; and that the reflections in these works anticipate his rhetorical stance as well as the substance of his political thought in the book of poetry on the Civil War. In what follows, we can but sketch the bare bones of an argument in support of this view, but it is sufficient to form the background to his treatment of the violent resolution of the conflict in *Battle-Pieces*.

Moby-Dick

Moby-Dick (1851) appears at first to have little to do with an America troubled by a conflict over slavery. Indeed, the novel seems an escape from that conflict into a whaling expedition, which is set forth in a narrative memoir about the interlocking of two monomaniacal pursuits: Ahab, captain of the *Pequod*, engages in what at first appears to be the monomaniacal pursuit of an enormous white whale called "Moby Dick"; Ishmael, a crew member, engages in the monomaniacal pursuit of all possible knowledge concerning whales. The novel traces both pursuits in great detail. It ends with Moby Dick's destruction of the *Pequod*, bringing sudden violent death to Ahab and all members of his crew, save for Ishmael. The epilogue has this epigraph from the book of Job: "And I only am escaped alone to tell thee" (Job 1.15–19). At the end of his epilogue Ishmael reveals that he was accidentally saved by a ship called the *Rachel*, in search of "her missing children [crew men lost overboard]." In the last word of his memoir—a work he seems to have been saved from death above all in order to write—he calls himself an "orphan."

On its surface, as the preceding sketch so perceives it, *Moby-Dick* seems to say nothing about chattel slavery. And yet, as one ponders Melville's intention in constructing so remarkable an edifice in the midst of the deepening crisis in the American political regime around 1849–51, one cannot help but notice that scattered all through Ishmael's memoir are tantalizing references and allusions to ancient and modern political philosophers: Aristotle, Bacon, Pierre Bayle, Descartes, Hobbes, Locke, Montaigne, Plato, Rousseau, and Socrates, among others.[3] These references and allusions are perplexing, not least because Ishmael's use of them is not only seemingly casual but also deeply ironical. Consider just this example: At one point in his memoir, Ishmael offers a nugget of sage advice to ship-owners of whalers who may chance to read his book. "Beware of enlisting in your vigilant fisheries any lad with lean brow and hollow eye; given to unreasonable meditativeness; and who offers to ship with Phaedon instead of Bowditch in his head."[4] Ishmael's deft contrast between *Phaedo*, Plato's great dialogue on the immortality of the soul, and Nathaniel Bowditch's *New American Practical Navigator* (1802), is but one indication of Melville's juxtaposition of the philosophical problem of how to understand the nature of the soul, and the utterly practical problem of how to navigate the vast expanses of the ocean back to the safe shelter of political society.

Katherine Zuckert has taken careful notice of this philosophical dimension of *Moby-Dick*.[5] She argues that Melville causes Ahab and Ishmael, the two main foci of the novel, to leave the settled protection of the Constitution and statute laws of American political society in order to venture into the untrammeled and highly dangerous "state of nature" represented by the vast oceans of the world. Following Zuckert's general lead, we proffer two examples of "political philosophy in novel form" as the mode of political thought that is intricately articulated in *Moby-Dick*. Both treat the fundamental question of the relationship between nature and convention, that issue (as Melville's comments suggest) which underlies the conflict over chattel slavery. The first treats that question in the form of the relationship between natural and conventional claims to rule, as it is sketched in chapter 54, "The Town-Ho's Story (As it is told at the Golden Inn)." The second treats that question in the form of the relationship between the natural and the conventional claims to the acquisition and possession of property, as it is sketched in chapters 89 and 90, "Fast-Fish and Loose-Fish" and "Heads or Tails." Both these treatments ultimately bear decisively on the great question of the rightness of the institution of slavery, even though that is not immediately apparent on the surface of the novel.

In chapter 54, Ishmael tells a story focusing on two men: Radney, who is the mate; and Steelkilt, who is a crewman. Radney comes from Nantucket, the main port of American whalers, thus is of the elite of whaling's commonwealth; Steelkilt hails from the frontier of inland America, Lake Erie and Buffalo, thus is of the pioneers living on the edge of the land version of "the state of nature." Radney's contempt for Steelkilt in part reflects his pride in his origins.

Radney legally exercises the conventional rule of a ship's officer, in spite of the fact that he is a man of deeply flawed character: harsh, unfair, and highly sensitive to criticism. Steelkilt is ordinarily willing to obey conventional shipboard rule, but is also aware of his superiority in character, looks, and ability to Radney, hence in principle more suited by nature to rule. Ishmael depicts the conflict thus:

> Now, as you well know, it is not seldom the case *in this conventional world of ours* [emphasis added]—watery or otherwise; that when a person placed in command over his fellow-men finds one of them to be very significantly his superior in general pride of manhood, straightway against that man he conceives an unconquerable dislike and bitterness; and if he have a chance he will pull down and pulverize that subaltern's tower, and make a little heap of dust of it. (ch. 54, 245–46)[6]

As the story unfolds, Radney hears Steelkilt, who is strenuously manning a pump, make some critical remarks about Radney's lack of character. The mate spitefully orders Steelkilt to sweep the deck and, worse still, to remove pig droppings—base work on board ship ordinarily performed only by boys. Steelkilt's refusal leads at last to open conflict. The potent spiritedness of each man—his passionate sense of being unjustly treated—produces a crisis of rule. The captain, quite properly legally siding with Radney—"justice demanded it"—seeks to reduce Steelkilt and some who join him to submission to authority. He at length succeeds. But the captain also most unwisely does not intervene to prevent Radney from spitefully, in an act of sheer vengeance, applying the lash to Steelkilt, though the latter had warned the mate that were he so to act it would lead to the mate's death. Steelkilt then contemplates the murder of Radney at an opportune moment, yet would make it appear an accident. But, perhaps providentially, Steelkilt is saved from having to perform that illegal and vengeful act by the remarkable denouement: Radney is crushed to death in the jaws of Moby Dick during a vain attempt to kill the great whale. Whether justice is thus done, and whether, if so, it is providential, with Moby Dick as the instrument of Providence, remains for the reader to decide, for Ishmael is but the teller of the story.

But one must also reflect on this further question: May not Ishmael's story suggest that as Steelkilt is in a fundamental sense the natural ruler of Radney, so he, Ishmael, is at bottom the natural ruler of Ahab? Still further: If these two particular actual relations of superiors to inferiors in rank are based on conventional not natural faculties and abilities of the men involved, what is one to think of the even more troubling relation of American white master to American Negro slave? That question, suggested but not explicitly articulated by Ishmael's grand memoir, was the deepest problem of the American Republic at the time Melville composed *Moby-Dick*. What is more, it is but a particular historical version of the more fundamental problem whether slavery is always and everywhere only conventional, or can sometimes be considered natural. We have no way of knowing if Melville had read, for example, Aristotle's immensely thoughtful discussion of that question in the first book of his *Politics*. But we strongly suspect that he was very aware, given his attentiveness to the progress of events as the crisis loomed, that one of the staples of many Southern defenses of slavery was an argument for the natural superiority of whites to Negroes, hence of the naturally just character of the rule of white masters over Negro slaves.

Now the difficulty of resolving this question in practice, especially in the American Republic in the 1850s and 1860s, given the deep and persistent passions and interests involved on both sides, was very great. For it turns on the still larger and more difficult political question of the degree to which human reason, pure and simple, is capable of ordering the positive laws of any given political society so as to bring them into accord with what is naturally right. A terse, pessimistic, paradoxical formulation of the general problem is contained in an undated and little-known poem by Melville, "A Reasonable Constitution." The poet says:

> What though Reason forged your scheme?
> 'Twas Reason dreamed the Utopia's dream:
> 'Tis dream to think that Reason can
> Govern the reasoning creature, man.

Our second example of Melville's treatment of nature and convention focuses on Ishmael's treatment of this deeply troubling question: What are the principles, natural and conventional, pertaining to the acquisition and legal possession of material things of this world? In chapters 89 and 90, Ishmael lays down an answer. At first, his answer appears to apply simply to whales in the ocean, and is reducible to these two "laws": "I. A Fast-Fish belongs to the party fast to it. II. A Loose-Fish is fair game for anybody who can soonest catch it." But Ishmael soon claims that these two laws contain "the fundamentals of all jurisprudence." Indeed, as his account unfolds, we discover that his "jurisprudence" is much more concerned with possession of vacant land, of human beings, and more startling, of whole countries already under rule, than it is with that of whales taken in the state of nature. Listen to these questions posed by Ishmael: "What are the sinews and souls of Russian serfs and Republican slaves but Fast-Fish, whereof possession is the whole of the law?" This parallel of the condition of "Republican slaves" to "Russian serfs" can hardly be a comfort to American owners of slaves, should they fall upon Ishmael's memoir.

Nor is this all. "What to . . . Brother Jonathan [The United

States] is Texas but a Fast Fish?" asks Ishmael, warming to his subject. And as for ostensible "Loose-Fish," hear him on the discovery of America: "What was America in 1492 but a Loose-Fish, in which Columbus struck the Spanish standard [to claim it] for his royal master and mistress?" Finally, most ominous, is this question by Ishmael: "What at last will Mexico be to the United States? All Loose-Fish." The outcome of the Mexican War, recently achieved when Melville completed *Moby-Dick*, was to raise the question whether the United States might not extend itself well beyond Texas to the whole of Mexico. Such an expansion might well upset the balance of free and slave states in the Union.

Having ventured far in the realm of "jurisprudence," Ishmael at length advances the startling notion that "the rights of man" might themselves be understood as a kind of "Loose-Fish." With that notion in the immediate background, Ishmael opens chapter 90, "Heads or Tails," with an epigraph in Latin: *De balenver sufficit, si rex habeat caput, et regina caudam*. It is from Bracton's *De Legibus et Consuetudinibus Angliae*, the first systematic compilation of English law. This is the only one of the 135 chapters in *Moby-Dick* to open with an epigraph from a work of jurisprudence. The singularity of this chapter, especially given the gravity of the issue being treated, thus requires a few further remarks.

Ishmael jocularly renders Bracton's Latin thus: "that of all whales captured by anybody on the coast of that land [England], the King, as Honorary Grand Harpooner, must have the head, and the Queen be respectfully presented with the tail." Ishmael's satirical elevation of the King of England to the rank of "Honorary Grand Harpooner" introduces a further inquiry into the nature of law in relation to what is by nature just. For the pith of the chapter is an account of a notorious case of the application of the ancient law of England: Some "honest mariners" from an English port, having at great peril pursued a whale far out at sea, then killed and beached it, are at once confronted by an officer of the Crown. He carries Blackstone's *Commentaries* under his arm. Citing Blackstone, he compels the whalers to turn the whale over to the Duke of Wellington. For what reason? Why, the duke's claim is indefeasible and is found to be "delegated" from "the Sovereign." Ishmael turns Lockean political philosopher. He naughtily inquires what can possibly be the right of the Sovereign to a whale which has been captured by the labor of sailors operating in the state of nature. Then, even more naughtily adverting to Plowden, a writer cited by Blackstone, Ishmael finds that the whale belongs to the king and queen, rather than to those who use their labor to capture and kill it, "because of its superior excellence." This is Ishmael's pithy and devastating comment on the commentators: "And by the soundest commentators this has ever been held to be a cogent argument in such matters" (ch. 90, 401). One has but to transpose this episode into the context of the American debate whether whites are meant by nature to rule blacks because of the alleged "superior excellence" of the whites to see the explosive potential of Ishmael's ventures into "jurisprudence."

Nature versus convention: Is the conventional master the natural and thus rightful one? Is property naturally or only conventionally rightly possessed? Melville's double insertion of the nature-convention problem into the unfolding story of the pursuit of Moby Dick in the state of nature is but one of the many remarkable ways in which political philosophy takes novel form in his book. Let us next consider, then, how this mixed mode of *Moby-Dick* is deftly carried forward in Melville's novella *Benito Cereno*.

Benito Cereno

Like Harriet Beecher Stowe's *Uncle Tom's Cabin* (1852), Melville's *Benito Cereno* (1856) uses fiction to persuade antebellum Americans to oppose slavery. But we shall show their modes of persuasion differ. Showing the Negroes in his story to be fully human, Melville dramatizes the prejudices which prevent North and South from recognizing both that humanity and slavery's injustice.

Thus, unlike *Uncle Tom's Cabin*, nature's opposition to convention leads to tragedy.[7]

Melville's novella opens in 1799 off the coast of Chile, where an American merchant ship approached a ship flying no flag and apparently in some difficulty. Thinking to aid its crew, the American Captain (Amasa Delano) approaches what turns out to be a Spanish merchantman carrying slaves. Everywhere are signs of disorder and lack of discipline on the Spanish ship—the blacks (for instance) are unchained and appear hostile to the white Spaniards.Although disturbed by these signs, Delano remains uncertain of their cause, vacillating between suspicion that the Spanish Captain (Benito Cereno) plans some treachery against the American ship or that he is too weak to command his own ship properly. The American Captain cannot see the truth: that the slaves control this ship and are presenting a *trompe d'oeil* elaborately contrived by their leader, Babo. For the American believes Negroes naturally inferior and incapable of rule. When at length Delano discovers the truth, he forcefully retakes the Spanish ship and re-enslaves the blacks. Back on land, there is a trial wherein depositions by the Spaniards explain how the Negroes took over the ship and ruled it by terror, demanding passage to their native Senegal. The blacks, for instance, killed their former master (Don Alexandro Aranda), placed his skeleton on the ship's prow, and warned the whites: "Keep faith with the blacks from here to Senegal, or you shall in spirit, as now in body, follow your leader" (107). After the trial, at which Babo is condemned to death, there is a final meeting between Cereno and Delano. The Spaniard is a broken man, unable to forget the experience of being deceived by Babo; the American, by contrast, remains optimistic and wants to forget the experience.

Although Melville based this plot on Captain Amasa Delano's *A Narrative of Voyages and Travels* (1817), he made subtle and revealing changes in this narrative to suggest his own political design. In general, whereas the real-life Delano's narrative self-servingly highlights his own compassion and bravery, Melville focuses on Delano's prejudice and how it deceives him about the slave rebellion. Among specific details, Melville changes the months and the year of his novella to recall events in American Constitutional history.[8] His slave ship sails not in winter (as the real-life one did) but in summer, thus allowing Melville's slaves to gain their independence on July 4, the day America gained its independence. What is good for America, Melville seems to suggest, is good for Negroes. Again, Melville changed the year of the revolt from 1804 to 1799, the midpoint of the twenty year allowance for the slave trade in the U.S. Constitution. Likewise transformed is the slave ship. It is rechristened the *San Dominck* to recall the island where a 1799 slave rebellion occurred. Added to the ship is a carved figurehead of Christopher Columbus, the man who first brought slavery to the New World. One here cannot but recall Ishmael's sardonic reference to Columbus's "discovery" of America, and his claiming it for Spain—while bringing slavery into the new world.

Also suggesting the slavery controversy in antebellum America is the way Delano's miscomprehension of the true state of affairs on the *San Dominck* mimics the prejudices of Americans. Although Babo covertly rules by terror, Delano views Babo and his fellow blacks as one might charming household pets. When Babo, pretending to be Cereno's valet, shaves his supposed master, the Spanish captain is terrified with Babo's knife at his throat. But the uncomprehending American cheerfully muses upon the scene:

> There is something in the Negro which, in a peculiar way, fits him for avocations about one's person. Most Negroes are natural valets and hairdressers; taking to the comb and brush congenially as to castanets, and flourishing them apparently with almost equal satisfaction. There is, too, a smooth tact about them in this employment, with a marvelous, noiseless, gliding

> briskness, not ungraceful in its way, singularly pleasing to behold, and still more so to be the manipulated subject of. And above all the great gift of good humor. Not the mere grin or laugh is here meant. Those were unsuitable. But a certain easy cheerfulness, harmonious in every glance and gesture; as though God had set the whole Negro to some pleasant tune.[9]

Faced with cunning like Shakespeare's Iago with Othello, the American sees only Harriet Beecher Stowe's Topsy. Thus does Melville pierce the complacency of Northern opinion about blacks as shoe shiners and minstrel singers.

But Delano is not alone in miscomprehending. So also does Cereno in the final meeting with Delano. Even back on land, he remains terrified and indeed a man broken by the experience of Babo's evil treachery. When Delano tells Cereno to forget the past and renew himself as do the forces of nature, Cereno notes that these, having no memory, are not human. Although Cereno thereby evinces a more human response to the slave revolt than Delano's, he still does not apprehend Babo's humanity. In fact then neither white captain learns by the experience that blacks are unjustly enslaved.

Suggesting the whites' incomprehension of the humanity of the blacks is Melville's ambiguous ending to his story:

> Some months after [the trial], dragged to the gibbet at the tail of a mule, the black [Babo] met his voiceless end. The body was burned to ashes; but for many days, the head, that hive of subtlety, fixed on a pole in the Plaza, met, unabashed, the gaze of the whites; and across the Plaza looked towards St. Bartholomew's church, in whose vaults slept then, as now, the recovered bones of Aranda; and across the Rimac bridge looked towards the monastery, on Mount Agonia without; where, three months after being dismissed by the court, Benito Cereno, borne on the bier, did, indeed, follow his leader. (116–17)

The three last words of the story are ambivalent. At first, Cereno "follow[ed] his leader" into death, appears to mean he followed Aranda. As one reflects on the novella, however, in reality Babo seems Cereno's true leader, as indeed he is Delano's. For it is this subtle black who outwits the two white captains in the story, showing himself the natural ruler of these two conventional ones.

Babo, who could have explained his human superior and the humanity of the other blacks, refuses to speak after his recapture. As Melville writes, "His aspect seemed to say, since I cannot do deeds, I will not speak words" (116). Since the deeds of the blacks risking their lives for freedom could not convince whites of their humanity, what could words do? Hence Babo dies in resolute silence, his stillness resembling that of the uneducated Negro slave in America. Such men need a spokesman. This they receive in Herman Melville. The white captains in this story are too close to the experience to reflect upon it and thereby to rethink their prejudices. Not so is the reader of a fictional presentation of the story. He can discern, as whites in the story cannot, Babo's humanity and his natural rule.

Such a teaching about black humanity differs from that of Harriet Beecher Stowe. *Uncle Tom's Cabin* presents the Negro as good hearted but pathetic, to be pitied as a victim and cared for as a child. Although at the end Uncle Tom is killed by his evil owner Simon Legree, several other black slaves escape to Canada with the help of good whites. Thus Stowe's story is melodrama. *Benito Cereno*, by contrast, presents the blacks as something manly and cunning to be feared as an enemy. Babo is in fact the natural aristocrat of the story. But that human excellence ("the head, the hive of subtlety") is misperceived by whites. And thus Melville's story is tragic—indeed, tragic for both blacks and whites. In fact, Melville's view resembles both that of Alexis de Tocqueville in his prediction of a race war in America and that of Thomas Jefferson in his remark about white Americans threatened with slavery: "we have the wolf by the ears and we can neither hold him, nor safely let him go."[10]

Benito Cereno was Melville's final antebellum publication on the issue which led to the Civil War. Melville appears pessimistic about overcoming the problem of chattel slavery in America. The prejudices and resentments on the part of the two races make a solution seem unlikely. Indeed, this grave American problem appears in *Moby-Dick* and *Benito Cereno* as insoluble. Yet within a decade, the solution provided by the Northern victory in the Civil War created new and different difficulties for the American Republic, difficulties to which Melville turned in his *Battle-Pieces and Aspects of the War*.

ON *BATTLE-PIECES AND ASPECTS OF THE WAR*

When the Civil War erupted, like a volcano, Herman Melville was forty-two. The zenith of his fame as the author of exciting sea tales—*Typee*, *Omoo*, *Redburn*, and others—apparently had been reached nearly a decade earlier. *Moby-Dick* (1851) received mixed reviews both in England and America. Later short prose works, such as *The Piazza Tales* (1856), which includes *Benito Cereno*, were accorded but slight attention. *The Confidence Man: His Masquerade* (1857), a satire on hypocrisy and materialism found hardly any audience. In short, by the time of Fort Sumter, Melville's career as an author appeared simply to be at an end.

Ordinary citizens and literary luminaries were thus wholly unprepared for the publication on August 17, 1866, of *Battle-Pieces and Aspects of the War*. In fact, the *New York Herald* remarked, in announcing the book's forthcoming publication, "for ten years the public has wondered what has become of Melville."[11] What had become of him was soon evident with the appearance of *Battle-Pieces*, a small volume of 272 pages, containing seventy-two poems and a prose "Supplement."

Battle-Pieces was reviewed in twenty-seven Northern newspapers, few of which connected his politics with his poetry.

Although a few reviewers gave perfunctory praise to some of the contents, a number of the longer, more detailed reviews were often quite critical, on the one hand of Melville's political views, and on the other hand, of his poetry. After perfunctory praise of Melville's poetry ("not inappropriately rugged enough"), the *New York Herald* (September 3, 1866) spent considerable space praising the politics of proposed reconciliation set forth in Melville's "Supplement." By contrast, the reviewer for the *New York Times* concluded about the same "Supplement": "The use of such treasonable language as this shows a singular hardihood on the part of one who has studied and written about the ferocious inhabitants of the South Sea islands, who were accustomed, as we all know, to keep cold missionary on their sideboards." Others largely ignored Melville's politics and concentrated on his poetry, often critical of its ruggedly unconventional character. Thus the *Round Table* (New York) reviewer said: "His sense of melody is deficient . . . while some of his rhymes are positively barbarous." Again, the *New York Albion* (September 15, 1866) said, "Of verse as verse he knows little, seldom writing a stanza that is melodious throughout."[12] Given the tone of some of these reviews, it is perhaps not surprising that, by a whole decade after its publication, Melville's portrayal of the Civil War had sold 525 copies, this in a nation approaching forty million people.

Today, there are many editions of Melville's numerous prose works, and a huge body of commentary on virtually all those works, including even such less popular novels as *The Confidence Man*. In sharp contrast, his *Battle-Pieces and Aspects of the War* is still known but to a handful of scholars—mostly professors of literature and Civil War history—and to a stray interested citizen here and there. Not until 1963 was there a scholarly edition of the book, prepared by the late Hennig Cohen. It contains a careful introduction, many detailed notes, and, as a bonus, vivid illustrations reproduced from graphic art of the Civil War. Unfortunately, Cohen's fine edition has long been out of print; copies are available either from a few second-hand bookstores or in some libraries. Sidney Kaplan published an edition in 1972. It contains an introduction, a note on the text, a list of Melville's revisions, the text of several contemporary reviews, and a photographic reprint of the 1866 edition. This edition is also out of print. As we compose this essay, the only edition in print, thus readily available, is also a reprint of the 1866 edition, issued by Da Capo in 1995. It faithfully reproduces both the content and the look Melville intended. Best of all, it contains a perceptive and helpful introduction by Lee Rust Brown, a specialist in American literature. But it contains no supplementary materials or notes. In short, Melville's book on the Civil War, some one hundred thirty years after he published it, is largely terra incognita to most Americans, whether scholars or ordinary citizens, and is readily available only in a version which offers little help with the difficulties of the text, which are considerable.[13]

The Interpretive Essays

The present volume cannot hope to supply all that is needed to give proper respect to and appreciation of Melville's remarkable achievement in *Battle-Pieces*. Our more modest hope is to provide readers a way to understand Melville's poems, a way connecting literary form and political-military history. It is not that Melville had unconventional poetic views on the one hand and moderate political views on the other. It is not that his verse differs from that of Lowell and Whitman on the one hand and his politics differs from that of Radical Republicans on the other. Rather, Melville united poetry and politics in an intimate way. This the essays attempt to reveal.

The very title of Helen Vendler's "Melville and the Lyric of History" calls attention to this uncommon linkage. She argues the greatness of Melville's poems based not only on "the reflective thought in them" but also on the "most original method Melville discovered by which he could fold the epic matter of history into lyric. . . . " In contrast with usual lyric structure, Melville tends "to offer first an impersonal philosophical conclusion, next the narrative that has produced it, and last the lyric feeling accompanying it." "The March into Virginia" exemplifies this "back-to-front fashion" (256). Vendler, of course, acknowledges other qualities in Melville's "arresting and wholly original poetry" which render it "unassimable to his own epoch and to ours": the poet's stoic irony, his steely view of warfare, his insistence on the ambivalence felt by any spectator of war, his refusal to pronounce easily on the whole, and his invention of a species of epic lyric comprehensive enough to include metaphysics, narrative, panoramic tragedy, and individual pang" (267). Yet she concludes with the hope that Melville's book will finally achieve for him what he named "the belated funeral flower of fame" (268).

Like Helen Vendler, Rosanna Warren argues for Melville's belated fame by showing that his critics miscomprehended his poetry. Where critics found in this book "great crudities," Warren sees "a concentrated, elliptical art, which instead of delivering ready-made judgments [in the manner of Whitman or Lowell], forces readers to participate in the chiaroscuro process of arriving at judgment" (280). *Battle-Pieces* poetically dramatizes the dawning of cognition through struggle; his poems are "modes of action precipitating a provisional but tragic knowledge" (274). In "The Portent," for instance, "historical event [the hanging of John Brown] becomes event in the mind of the reader through the event in language" (275). Instead of immediately announcing its subject, this poem leaves the reader suspended in doubt until a parenthesis in the penultimate line of the first stanza. Eschewing the pro-Brown sentiments of Emerson or the anti-Brown ones of Hawthorne, "Melville's poem takes shape and life in the gap between these two . . ." (276). Further reflecting such uncertainty is the prosody: the first line of each stanza is catalectic or lacking a last, unstressed syllable, leaving readers hanging like Brown's corpse. Concerning such "great crudities" perceived by readers accustomed to the mellifluousness of Longfellow and Lowell, Warren concludes: "Only poetry of the highest order weaves its strands of sound so complexly into its semantic and syntactic orders, converting the arbitrary into the provisionally significant" (286).

Richard Cox's essay treats the question of how literary form—both that of the structure of the entire book and of certain aspects of its poetic diction—is related to the political framework of the Civil War and its aftermath. He focuses on two dimensions of that relationship: First, following the injunction of Ishmael, the narrator of *Moby-Dick*, that "There are some enterprises in which a careful disorderliness is the true method," he shows that what seems on the surface to be but a somewhat disorderly collection of poems on the Civil War is, in fact, an extraordinarily orderly structure falling into four main parts, each thematically related to the three others and each reflective of the political foundations of the conflict. He shows, second, that a singular device which Melville uses to indicate the precision of his orderliness and, in two crucial instances, his utterly precise deliberate disorderliness, is that of chronology. That chronology naturally focuses mainly on the actual period of the Civil War from 1861 to 1865. But it also treats events both before and after the war, suggesting that, in Melville's mind, our Civil War is not over. As T. S. Eliot remarks, "I question whether any serious civil war ever does end." What is most striking about the two instances of deliberate disorderliness as to chronology is that they evoke the memory of Abraham Lincoln. Cox suggests that "Melville seems to construe his own book as a poetic substitute for the great speeches of the magnanimous president who has been silenced by a bullet fired by hate-inspired John Wilkes Booth."

Finally, Paul Dowling begins with the disappointment readers express at the dispassionate character of Melville's poetry. He argues that the source or cause of Melville's emotional moderation of *Battle-Pieces* is not poetic weakness; rather, Melville chose moderation on both political and poetic grounds. Politically, "the poet composes *Battle-Pieces* in hopes of tempering extremes of passion both by omission and commission, by avoiding certain things and fabricating others" (330). Certain features of wartime leaders (Lincoln, Grant, and Lee) are either omitted or else fabricated. Lincoln (hated in the South) all but disappears from this book; Grant is recalled not for "unconditional surrender" but for generosity after triumph; Lee's victory at Chancelorsville is omitted, but Lee is given a fabricated speech urging Northern forgiveness of the South. Besides the political motive for his time, Melville had a poetical one for the ages: to respond to Plato's criticism of poetry by imitating Shakespeare's manner of finding a role for dispassionate wisdom in poetry. Which is to say, Melville sides with Socrates in the "old quarrel of philosophy and poetry" of Plato's *Republic*. As Dowling concludes, "*Battle-Pieces* disappoints readers because Herman Melville subordinated commercial popularity to his love of country and his love of wisdom" (347).

Notes

1. See the bibliography for various commentaries on *Battle-Pieces*.

2. The Declaration of Independence, the Articles of Confederation, the Northwest Ordinance of 1787, and the Constitution are "The Organic Laws of the United States of America." Virtually all of the time since 1878, they have stood, under that title, as a noble preamble to the statutes of the federal government. The latest version of those statutes is the *United States Code*. For a detailed historical analysis of the statutory basis of placing the "organic laws" at the head of the statutes, see *Four Pillars of Constitutionalism: The Organic Laws of the United States*, introduction by Richard H. Cox (Amherst, N.Y.: Prometheus Books, 1998), 9–71.

3. The most revealing treatment of the references and allusions to these, as well as many other authors, may be found in the detailed notes

in the bicentennial edition of the novel. *Moby-Dick, or, The Whale* by Herman Melville, ed. Luther S. Mansfield and Howard P. Vincent (New York: Hendricks House, 1952). See also: Mary K. Bercaw, *Melville's Sources* (Evanston, Ill.: Northwestern University Press, 1987); Merton M. Sealts, *Melville's Reading*, revised and enlarged edition (Columbia: University of South Carolina Press, 1988); and Gail H. Coffler, *Melville's Classical Allusions: A Comprehensive Index and Glossary* (Westport, Conn.: Greenwood Press, 1985).

4. *Moby-Dick, or The Whale* (Evanston and Chicago: Northwestern University Press and The Newberry Library, 1988), ch. 35, 158. Hereafter cited in parentheses by chapter and page.

5. Catherine H. Zuckert, *Natural Right and the American Imagination: Political Philosophy in Novel Form* (Savage, Md.: Rowman & Littlefield Publishers, Inc., 1990).

6. See also this statement by Ishmael: "For be a man's intellectual superiority what it will, it can never assume the practical available supremacy over other men, without the aid of some sort of external arts and entrenchments, always, in themselves, more or less paltry and base" (ch. 33, 147–48).

7. Our reading of Melville's novella is especially indebted to Catherine H. Zuckert's "Leadership—Natural and Conventional— in Melville's "Benito Cereno," *Interpretation: A Journal of Political Philosophy* 26, no. 2 (winter 1998): 239–56.

Melville's story might have recalled to its immediate readers two widely publicized United States court cases of slave rebellions on board ships: the *Amistad* in 1839 and the *Creole* in 1843. The former of these reached the U. S. Supreme Court where John Quincy Adams, arguing for the Africans, echoed the Declaration of Independence: under the "law of nations," the Africans were obliged to obey only the "law of Nature and Nature's God." Justice Joseph Story concurred: "We may lament the dreadful acts by which they asserted their liberty, and took possession of the Amistad, but they cannot be deemed pirates or robbers in the sense of the law of nations." *United States* v. *Amistad* 15 Peters 593 94, quoted in Zuckert, "Leadership," 241.

8. Melville's changes from his source were first noted by William Richardson, *Melville's "Benito Cereno": An Interpretation With Annotated Text and Concordance* (Durham, N.C.: Carolina Academic Press, 1987),

71–72. Richardson's volume also reprints the relevant portion of Amasa Delano's *Narrative of Voyages and Travels*, 95–122.

9. Quoted from *The Piazza Tales and Other Prose Pieces 1839–1860* (Evanston and Chicago: Northwestern University Press and The Newberry Library, 1987), 83. Further citations from this volume will be in parentheses in the text. This volume, like Richardson's, reprints the relevant part of Delano's *Narrative of Voyages and Travels*.

10. Alexis de Tocqueville's prediction of a race war between Negroes and whites appears in *Democracy in America* (Chicago: University of Chicago Press, 2000), 326, 611. For Jefferson, see his letter to John Holmes, April 22, 1820, in *Thomas Jefferson Selected Writings*, ed. Harvey C. Mansfield (Arlington Heights, Ill.: AHM Publishing Corp., 1979), 92. Diane J. Schaub makes a similar contrast between Melville's novella and Stowe's novel in her "Master and Man in Melville's 'Benito Cereno,' " in *Poets, Princes, & Private Citizens*, ed. Joseph M. Knippenberg and Peter Augustine Lawler (Lanham, Md.: Rowman & Littlefield, 1996), 54–55.

11. *The Battle-Pieces of Herman Melville*, ed. with introduction by Hennig Cohen (New York: Thomas Yoseloff, 1963), 11.

12. *Herman Melville: The Contemporary Reviews*, ed. Brian Higgins and Hershel Parker (Cambridge: Cambridge University Press, 1995), 520, 509.

13. A note from the editor of the Northwestern University Press indicates that the Northwestern-Newberry Library edition of Melville's works will publish his poetry in 2001. We do not know the extent or nature of the commentary which will be appended to the text.

Note on the Text

We reprint the 1866 edition of Melville's book, retaining the original page numbers in brackets. These bracketed pages are referred to in the introduction, in Melville's own notes to *Battle-Pieces*, and in the interpretive essays.

BATTLE-PIECES

and

ASPECTS of THE WAR.

BY

HERMAN MELVILLE.

NEW YORK
HARPER & BROTHERS, PUBLISHERS,
FRANKLIN SQUARE.
1866.

THE BATTLE-PIECES

IN THIS VOLUME ARE DEDICATED

TO THE MEMORY OF THE

THREE HUNDRED THOUSAND

WHO IN THE WAR

FOR THE MAINTENANCE OF THE UNION

FELL DEVOTEDLY

UNDER THE FLAG OF THEIR FATHERS.

[With few exceptions, the Pieces in this volume originated in an impulse imparted by the fall of Richmond. They were composed without reference to collective arrangement, but being brought together in review, naturally fall into the order assumed.

The events and incidents of the conflict—making up a whole, in varied amplitude, corresponding with the geographical area covered by the war—from these but a few themes have been taken, such as for any cause chanced to imprint themselves upon the mind.

The aspects which the strife as a memory assumes are as manifold as are the moods of involuntary meditation—moods variable, and at times widely at variance. Yielding instinctively, one after another, to feelings not inspired from any one source exclusively, and unmindful, without purposing to be, of consistency, I seem, in most of these verses, to have but placed a harp in a window, and noted the contrasted airs which wayward winds have played upon the strings.]

Contents. [vii]

VERSES INSCRIPTIVE AND MEMORIAL.

The Portent.

(1859.)

Hanging from the beam,
Slowly swaying (such the law),
Gaunt the shadow on your green,
Shenandoah!
The cut is on the crown
(Lo, John Brown),
And the stabs shall heal no more.

Hidden in the cap
Is the anguish none can draw;
So your future veils its face,
Shenandoah!
But the streaming beard is shown
(Weird John Brown),
The meteor of the war.

[12]

Misgivings. [13]

(1860.)

WHEN ocean-clouds over inland hills
        Sweep storming in late autumn brown,
And horror the sodden valley fills,
        And the spire falls crashing in the town,
I muse upon my country's ills—
The tempest bursting from the waste of Time
On the world's fairest hope linked with man's foulest crime.

Nature's dark side is heeded now—
        (Ah! optimist-cheer disheartened flown)—
A child may read the moody brow
        Of yon black mountain lone.
With shouts the torrents down the gorges go,
And storms are formed behind the storm we feel:
The hemlock shakes in the rafter, the oak in the driving keel.

[14] *The Conflict of Convictions.*[a]

(1860–1.)

ON starry heights
  A bugle wails the long recall;
Derision stirs the deep abyss,
  Heaven's ominous silence over all.
Return, return, O eager Hope,
  And face man's latter fall.
Events, they make the dreamers quail;
Satan's old age is strong and hale,
A disciplined captain, gray in skill,
And Raphael a white enthusiast still;
Dashed aims, at which Christ's martyrs pale,
Shall Mammon's slaves fulfill?

(Dismantle the fort,
Cut down the fleet—
Battle no more shall be!
While the fields for fight in æons to come
Congeal beneath the sea.)

[15] The terrors of truth and dart of death
  To faith alike are vain;
Though comets, gone a thousand years,
    Return again,
Patient she stands—she can no more—
And waits, nor heeds she waxes hoar.

(At a stony gate,
A statue of stone,
Weed overgrown—
Long 'twill wait!)

But God his former mind retains,
Confirms his old decree;
The generations are inured to pains,
And strong Necessity
Surges, and heaps Time's strand with wrecks.
The People spread like a weedy grass,
The thing they will they bring to pass,
And prosper to the apoplex.
The rout it herds around the heart,
The ghost is yielded in the gloom;
Kings wag their heads—Now save thyself
Who wouldst rebuild the world in bloom.

(Tide-mark [16]
And top of the ages' strike,
Verge where they called the world to come,
The last advance of life—
Ha ha, the rust on the Iron Dome!)

Nay, but revere the hid event;
In the cloud a sword is girded on,
I mark a twinkling in the tent
Of Michael the warrior one.
Senior wisdom suits not now,
The light is on the youthful brow.

(Ay, in caves the miner see:
His forehead bears a blinking light;
Darkness so he feebly braves—
A meagre wight!)

But He who rules is old—is old;
Ah! faith is warm, but heaven with age is cold.

(Ho ho, ho ho,
The cloistered doubt
Of olden times
Is blurted out!)

[17] The Ancient of Days forever is young,
Forever the scheme of Nature thrives;
I know a wind in purpose strong—
It spins *against* the way it drives.
What if the gulfs their slimed foundations bare?
So deep must the stones be hurled
Whereon the throes of ages rear
The final empire and the happier world.

(The poor old Past,
The Future's slave,
She drudged through pain and crime
To bring about the blissful Prime,
Then—perished. There's *a grave!)*

Power unanointed may come—
Dominion (unsought by the free)
And the Iron Dome,
Stronger for stress and strain,
Fling her huge shadow athwart the main;
But the Founders' dream shall flee.
Age after age shall be
As age after age has been,
(From man's changeless heart their way they win);
[18] And death be busy with all who strive—
Death, with silent negative.

YEA, AND NAY—
EACH HATH HIS SAY;
BUT GOD HE KEEPS THE MIDDLE WAY.
NONE WAS BY
WHEN HE SPREAD THE SKY;
WISDOM IS VAIN, AND PROPHESY.

Apathy and Enthusiasm. [19]

(1860–1.)

I.

O THE clammy cold November,
   And the winter white and dead,
And the terror dumb with stupor,
   And the sky a sheet of lead;
And events that came resounding
   With the cry that *All was lost*,
Like the thunder-cracks of massy ice
   In intensity of frost—
Bursting one upon another
   Through the horror of the calm.
   The paralysis of arm
In the anguish of the heart;
And the hollowness and dearth.
   The appealings of the mother
   To brother and to brother
Not in hatred so to part—
And the fissure in the hearth
      Growing momently more wide. [20]
Then the glances 'tween the Fates,
      And the doubt on every side,
And the patience under gloom
In the stoniness that waits
The finality of doom.

II.

So the winter died despairing,
And the weary weeks of Lent;
And the ice-bound rivers melted,
And the tomb of Faith was rent.
O, the rising of the People
Came with springing of the grass,
They rebounded from dejection
And Easter came to pass.
And the young were all elation
Hearing Sumter's cannon roar,
And they thought how tame the Nation
In the age that went before.
And Michael seemed gigantical,
The Arch-fiend but a dwarf;
And at the towers of Erebus
Our striplings flung the scoff.
But the elders with foreboding
Mourned the days forever o'er,
[21] And recalled the forest proverb,
The Iroquois' old saw:
Grief to every graybeard
When young Indians lead the war.

The March into Virginia, [22]

Ending in the First Manassas.

(July, 1861.)

DID all the lets and bars appear
To every just or larger end,
Whence should come the trust and cheer?
Youth must its ignorant impulse lend—
Age finds place in the rear.
All wars are boyish, and are fought by boys,
The champions and enthusiasts of the state:
Turbid ardors and vain joys
Not barrenly abate—
Stimulants to the power mature,
Preparatives of fate.

Who here forecasteth the event?
What heart but spurns at precedent
And warnings of the wise,
Contemned foreclosures of surprise?
The banners play, the bugles call, [23]
The air is blue and prodigal.
No berrying party, pleasure-wooed,
No picnic party in the May,
Ever went less loth than they
Into that leafy neighborhood.
In Bacchic glee they file toward Fate,
Moloch's uninitiate;
Expectancy, and glad surmise
Of battle's unknown mysteries.
All they feel is this: 'tis glory,
A rapture sharp, though transitory,
Yet lasting in belaureled story.

So they gayly go to fight,
Chatting left and laughing right.

But some who this blithe mood present,
As on in lightsome files they fare,
Shall die experienced ere three days are spent—
Perish, enlightened by the vollied glare;
Or shame survive, and, like to adamant,
The throe of Second Manassas share.

[24]

Lyon.

Battle of Springfield, Missouri.

(August, 1861.)

SOME hearts there are of deeper sort,
Prophetic, sad,
Which yet for cause are trebly clad;
Known death they fly on:
This wizard-heart and heart-of-oak had Lyon.

"They are more than twenty thousand strong,
We less than five,
Too few with such a host to strive."
"Such counsel, fie on!
'Tis battle, or 'tis shame;" and firm stood Lyon.

"For help at need in van we wait—
Retreat or fight:
Retreat the foe would take for flight,
And each proud scion
Feel more elate; the end must come," said Lyon.

[25] By candlelight he wrote the will,
And left his all
To Her for whom 'twas not enough to fall;
Loud neighed Orion
Without the tent; drums beat; we marched with Lyon.

The night-tramp done, we spied the Vale
With guard-fires lit;
Day broke, but trooping clouds made gloom of it:
"A field to die on,"
Presaged in his unfaltering heart, brave Lyon.

We fought on the grass, we bled in the corn—
        Fate seemed malign;
His horse the Leader led along the line—
        Star-browed Orion;
Bitterly fearless, he rallied us there, brave Lyon.

There came a sound like the slitting of air
        By a swift sharp sword—
A rush of the sound; and the sleek chest broad
        Of black Orion
Heaved, and was fixed; the dead mane waved toward Lyon.

[26] "General, you're hurt—this sleet of balls!"
        He seemed half spent;
With moody and bloody brow, he lowly bent:
        "The field to die on;
But not—not yet; the day is long," breathed Lyon.

For a time becharmed there fell a lull
        In the heart of the fight;
The tree-tops nod, the slain sleep light;
        Warm noon-winds sigh on,
And thoughts which he never spake had Lyon.

Texans and Indians trim for a charge:
        "Stand ready, men!
Let them come close, right up, and then
        After the lead, the iron;
Fire, and charge back!" So strength returned to Lyon.

The Iowa men who held the van,
        Half drilled, were new
To battle: "Some one lead us, then we'll do,"
        Said Corporal Tryon:
"Men! *I* will lead," and a light glared in Lyon.

On they came: they yelped, and fired; [27]
His spirit sped;
We leveled right in, and the half-breeds fled,
Nor stayed the iron,
Nor captured the crimson corse of Lyon.

This seer foresaw his soldier-doom,
Yet willed the fight.
He never turned; his only flight
Was up to Zion,
Where prophets now and armies greet brave Lyon.

[28] **Ball's Bluff.**

A Reverie.

(October, 1861.)

ONE noonday, at my window in the town,
I saw a sight—saddest that eyes can see—
Young soldiers marching lustily
Unto the wars,
With fifes, and flags in mottoed pageantry;
While all the porches, walks, and doors
Were rich with ladies cheering royally.

They moved like Juny morning on the wave,
Their hearts were fresh as clover in its prime
(It was the breezy summer time),
Life throbbed so strong,
How should they dream that Death in a rosy clime
Would come to thin their shining throng?
Youth feels immortal, like the gods sublime.

[29] Weeks passed; and at my window, leaving bed,
By night I mused, of easeful sleep bereft,
On those brave boys (Ah War! thy theft);
Some marching feet
Found pause at last by cliffs Potomac cleft;
Wakeful I mused, while in the street
Far footfalls died away till none were left.

Dupont's Round Fight. [30]

(November, 1861.)

IN time and measure perfect moves
    All Art whose aim is sure;
Evolving ryhme and stars divine
    Have rules, and they endure.

Nor less the Fleet that warred for Right,
    And, warring so, prevailed,
In geometric beauty curved,
    And in an orbit sailed.

The rebel at Port Royal felt
    The Unity overawe,
And rued the spell. A type was here,
    And victory of LAW.

[31] ## ***The Stone Fleet.***[b]

An Old Sailor's Lament.

(December, 1861.)

I HAVE a feeling for those ships,
Each worn and ancient one,
With great bluff bows, and broad in the beam:
Ay, it was unkindly done.
But so they serve the Obsolete—
Even so, Stone Fleet!

You'll say I'm doting; do but think
I scudded round the Horn in one—
The Tenedos, a glorious
Good old craft as ever run—
Sunk (how all unmeet!)
With the Old Stone Fleet.

An India ship of fame was she,
Spices and shawls and fans she bore;
[32] A whaler when her wrinkles came—
Turned off! till, spent and poor,
Her bones were sold (escheat)!
Ah! Stone Fleet.

Four were erst patrician keels
(Names attest what families be),
The Kensington, and Richmond too,
Leonidas, and Lee:
But now they have their seat
With the Old Stone Fleet.

To scuttle them—a pirate deed—
  Sack them, and dismast;
They sunk so slow, they died so hard,
  But gurgling dropped at last.
          Their ghosts in gales repeat
          Woe's us, Stone Fleet!

And all for naught. The waters pass—
  Currents will have their way;
Nature is nobody's ally; 'tis well;
  The harbor is bettered—will stay.
          A failure, and complete,
          Was your Old Stone Fleet.

[33] # *Donelson.*

(February, 1862.)

THE bitter cup
Of that hard countermand
Which gave the Envoys up,
Still was wormwood in the mouth,
And clouds involved the land,
When, pelted by sleet in the icy street,
About the bulletin-board a band
Of eager, anxious people met,
And every wakeful heart was set
On latest news from West or South.
"No seeing here," cries one—"don't crowd"—
"You tall man, pray you, read aloud."

IMPORTANT.
We learn that General Grant,
Marching from Henry overland,
And joined by a force up the Cumberland sent
(Some thirty thousand the command),
[34] *On Wednesday a good position won—*
Began the siege of Donelson.

This stronghold crowns a river-bluff,
A good broad mile of leveled top;
Inland the ground rolls off
Deep-gorged, and rocky, and broken up—
A wilderness of trees and brush.
The spaded summit shows the roods
Of fixed intrenchments in their hush;
Breast-works and rifle-pits in woods
Perplex the base.—

The welcome weather
Is clear and mild; 'tis much like May.
The ancient boughs that lace together
Along the stream, and hang far forth,
Strange with green mistletoe, betray
A dreamy contrast to the North.

Our troops are full of spirits—say
The siege won't prove a creeping one.
They purpose not the lingering stay
Of old beleaguerers; not that way;
But, full of vim *from Western prairies won,*
They'll make, ere long, a dash at Donelson.

Washed by the storm till the paper grew
Every shade of a streaky blue,
That bulletin stood. The next day brought
A second.

LATER FROM THE FORT.

Grant's investment is complete—
A semicircular one.
Both wings the Cumberland's margin meet,
Then, backward curving, clasp the rebel seat.
On Wednesday this good work was done;
But of the doers some lie prone.
Each wood, each hill, each glen was fought for;
The bold inclosing line we wrought for
Flamed with sharpshooters. Each cliff cost
A limb or life. But back we forced
Reserves and all; made good our hold;
And so we rest.

Events unfold.
On Thursday added ground was won,
A long bold steep: we near the Den.
Later the foe came shouting down

In sortie, which was quelled; and then
We stormed them on their left.
A chilly change in the afternoon;
[36] *The sky, late clear, is now bereft*
Of sun. Last night the ground froze hard—
Rings to the enemy as they run
Within their works. A ramrod bites
The lip it meets. The cold incites
To swinging of arms with brisk rebound.
Smart blows 'gainst lusty chests resound.

Along the outer line we ward
A crackle of skirmishing goes on.
Our lads creep round on hand and knee,
They fight from behind each trunk and stone;
And sometimes, flying for refuge, one
Finds 'tis an enemy shares the tree.
Some scores are maimed by boughs shot off
In the glades by the Fort's big gun.
We mourn the loss of Colonel Morrison,
Killed while cheering his regiment on.
Their far sharpshooters try our stuff;
And ours return them puff for puff:
'Tis diamond-cutting-diamond work.
Woe on the rebel cannoneer
Who shows his head. Our fellows lurk
Like Indians that waylay the deer
By the wild salt-spring.—The sky is dun,
Foredooming the fall of Donelson.
[37] *Stern weather is all unwonted here.*
The people of the country own
We brought it. Yea, the earnest North
Has elementally issued forth
To storm this Donelson.

FURTHER.

A yelling rout
Of ragamuffins broke profuse
To-day from out the Fort.
Sole uniform they wore, a sort
Of patch, or white badge (as you choose)
Upon the arm. But leading these,
Or mingling, were men of face
And bearing of patrician race,
Splendid in courage and gold lace—
The officers. Before the breeze
Made by their charge, down went our line;
But, rallying, charged back in force,
And broke the sally; yet with loss.
This on the left; upon the right
Meanwhile there was an answering fight;
Assailants and assailed reversed.
The charge too upward, and not down—
Up a steep ridge-side, toward its crown,
A strong redoubt. But they who first
Gained the fort's base, and marked the trees [38]
Felled, heaped in horned perplexities,
And shagged with brush; and swarming there
Fierce wasps whose sting was present death—
They faltered, drawing bated breath,
And felt it was in vain to dare;
Yet still, perforce, returned the ball,
Firing into the tangled wall
Till ordered to come down. They came;
But left some comrades in their fame,
Red on the ridge in icy wreath
And hanging gardens of cold Death.
But not quite unavenged these fell;
Our ranks once out of range, a blast
Of shrapnel and quick shell
Burst on the rebel horde, still massed,
Scattering them pell-mell.

(This fighting—judging what we read—
Both charge and countercharge,
Would seem but Thursday's told at large,
Before in brief reported.—Ed.)
Night closed in about the Den
Murky and lowering. Ere long, chill rains.
A night not soon to be forgot,
Reviving old rheumatic pains
And longings for a cot.
[39] *No blankets, overcoats, or tents.*
Coats thrown aside on the warm march here—
We looked not then for changeful cheer;
Tents, coats, and blankets too much care.
No fires; a fire a mark presents;
Near by, the trees show bullet-dents.
Rations were eaten cold and raw.
The men well soaked, came snow; and more—
A midnight sally. Small sleeping done—
But such is war;
No matter, we'll have Fort Donelson.

"Ugh! ugh!
'Twill drag along—drag along,"
Growled a cross patriot in the throng,
His battered umbrella like an ambulance-cover
Riddled with bullet-holes, spattered all over.
"Hurrah for Grant!" cried a stripling shrill;
Three urchins joined him with a will,
And some of taller stature cheered.
Meantime a Copperhead passed; he sneered.
"Win or lose," he pausing said,
"Caps fly the same; all boys, mere boys;
Any thing to make a noise.
Like to see the list of the dead;
[40] These '*craven Southerners*' hold out;
Ay, ay, they'll give you many a bout."
"We'll beat in the end, sir,"

Firmly said one in staid rebuke,
A solid merchant, square and stout.
  "And do you think it? that way tend, sir?"
Asked the lean Copperhead, with a look
Of splenetic pity. "Yes, I do."
His yellow death's head the croaker shook:
"The country's ruined, that I know."
A shower of broken ice and snow,
  In lieu of words, confuted him;
They saw him hustled round the corner go,
  And each by-stander said—Well suited him.

Next day another crowd was seen
In the dark weather's sleety spleen.
Bald-headed to the storm came out
A man, who, 'mid a joyous shout,
Silently posted this brief sheet:

GLORIOUS VICTORY OF THE FLEET!

FRIDAY'S GREAT EVENT!

THE ENEMY'S WATER-BATTERIES BEAT!

WE SILENCED EVERY GUN! [41]

THE OLD COMMODORE'S COMPLIMENTS SENT
PLUMP INTO DONELSON!

"Well, well, go on!" exclaimed the crowd
To him who thus much read aloud.
"That's all," he said. "What! nothing more?"
"Enough for a cheer, though—hip, hurrah!
"But here's old Baldy come again—
"More news!"—And now a different strain.

(Our own reporter a dispatch compiles,
As best he may, from varied sources.)

Large re-enforcements have arrived—
Munitions, men, and horses—
For Grant, and all debarked, with stores.

The enemy's field-works extend six miles—
The gate still hid; so well contrived.

Yesterday stung us; frozen shores
Snow-clad, and through the drear defiles
[42] *And over the desolate ridges blew*
A Lapland wind.
The main affair
Was a good two hours' steady fight
Between our gun-boats and the Fort.
The Louisville's wheel was smashed outright.
A hundred-and-twenty-eight-pound ball
Came planet-like through a starboard port,
Killing three men, and wounding all
The rest of that gun's crew,
(The captain of the gun was cut in two);
Then splintering and ripping went—
Nothing could be its continent.
In the narrow stream the Louisville,
Unhelmed, grew lawless; swung around,
And would have thumped and drifted, till
All the fleet was driven aground,
But for the timely order to retire.

Some damage from our fire, 'tis thought,
Was done the water-batteries of the Fort.

Little else took place that day,
Except the field artillery in line
Would now and then—for love, they say—

Exchange a valentine.
The old sharpshooting going on. [43]
Some plan afoot as yet unknown;
So Friday closed round Donelson.

LATER.

Great suffering through the night—
A stinging one. Our heedless boys
Were nipped like blossoms. Some dozen
Hapless wounded men were frozen.
During day being struck down out of sight,
And help-cries drowned in roaring noise,
They were left just where the skirmish shifted—
Left in dense underbrush snow-drifted.
Some, seeking to crawl in crippled plight,
So stiffened—perished.
Yet in spite
Of pangs for these, no heart is lost.
Hungry, and clothing stiff with frost,
Our men declare a nearing sun
Shall see the fall of Donelson.
And this they say, yet not disown
The dark redoubts round Donelson,
And ice-glazed corpses, each a stone—
A sacrifice to Donelson;
They swear it, and swerve not, gazing on
A flag, deemed black, flying from Donelson.
Some of the wounded in the wood [44]
Were cared for by the foe last night,
Though he could do them little needed good,
Himself being all in shivering plight.
The rebel is wrong, but human yet;
He's got a heart, and thrusts a bayonet.
He gives us battle with wondrous will—
This bluff's a perverted Bunker Hill.

The stillness stealing through the throng
The silent thought and dismal fear revealed;
They turned and went,
Musing on right and wrong
And mysteries dimly sealed—
Breasting the storm in daring discontent;
The storm, whose black flag showed in heaven,
As if to say no quarter there was given
To wounded men in wood,
Or true hearts yearning for the good—
All fatherless seemed the human soul.
But next day brought a bitterer bowl—
On the bulletin-board this stood:

Saturday morning at 3 A.M.
A stir within the Fort betrayed
That the rebels were getting under arms;
Some plot these early birds had laid.
[45] *But a lancing sleet cut him who stared*
Into the storm. After some vague alarms,
Which left our lads unscared,
Out sallied the enemy at dim of dawn,
With cavalry and artillery, and went
In fury at our environment.
Under cover of shot and shell
Three columns of infantry rolled on,
Vomited out of Donelson—
Rolled down the slopes like rivers of hell,
Surged at our line, and swelled and poured
Like breaking surf. But unsubmerged
Our men stood up, except where roared
The enemy through one gap. We urged
Our all of manhood to the stress,
But still showed shattered in our desperateness.
Back set the tide,
But soon afresh rolled in;
And so it swayed from side to side—

Far batteries joining in the din,
Though sharing in another fray—
Till all became an Indian fight,
Intricate, dusky, stretching far away,
Yet not without spontaneous plan
However tangled showed the plight:
Duels all over 'tween man and man,
Duels on cliff-side, and down in ravine, [46]
Duels at long range, and bone to bone;
Duels every where flitting and half unseen.
Only by courage good as their own,
And strength outlasting theirs,
Did our boys at last drive the rebels off.
Yet they went not back to their distant lairs
In strong-hold, but loud in scoff
Maintained themselves on conquered ground—
Uplands; built works, or stalked around.
Our right wing bore this onset. Noon
Brought calm to Donelson.

The reader ceased; the storm beat hard;
'Twas day, but the office-gas was lit;
Nature retained her sulking-fit,
In her hand the shard.
Flitting faces took the hue
Of that washed bulletin-board in view,
And seemed to bear the public grief
As private, and uncertain of relief;
Yea, many an earnest heart was won,
As broodingly he plodded on,
To find in himself some bitter thing,
Some hardness in his lot as harrowing
As Donelson.
That night the board stood barren there, [47]
Oft eyed by wistful people passing,
Who nothing saw but the rain-beads chasing
Each other down the wafered square,

As down some storm-beat grave-yard stone.
But next day showed—

MORE NEWS LAST NIGHT.

STORY OF SATURDAY AFTERNOON.

VICISSITUDES OF THE WAR.

The damaged gun-boats can't wage fight
For days; so says the Commodore.
Thus no diversion can be had.
Under a sunless sky of lead
Our grim-faced boys in blackened plight
Gaze toward the ground they held before,
And then on Grant. He marks their mood,
And hails it, and will turn the same to good.
Spite all that they have undergone,
Their desperate hearts are set upon
This winter fort, this stubborn fort,
This castle of the last resort,
This Donelson.

[48] *1 P.M.*
An order given
Requires withdrawal from the front
Of regiments that bore the brunt
Of morning's fray. Their ranks all riven
Are being replaced by fresh, strong men.
Great vigilance in the foeman's Den;
He snuffs the stormers. Need it is
That for that fell assault of his,
That rout inflicted, and self-scorn—
Immoderate in noble natures, torn
By sense of being through slackness overborne—
The rebel be given a quick return:
The kindest face looks now half stern.

Balked of their prey in airs that freeze,
Some fierce ones glare like savages.
And yet, and yet, strange moments are—
Well—blood, and tears, and anguished War!
The morning's battle-ground is seen
In lifted glades, like meadows rare;
The blood-drops on the snow-crust there
Like clover in the white-weed show—
Flushed fields of death, that call again—
Call to our men, and not in vain,
For that way must the stormers go.

3 P.M. [49]
The work begins.
Light drifts of men thrown forward, fade
In skirmish-line along the slope,
Where some dislodgments must be made
Ere the stormer with the strong-hold cope.

Lew Wallace, moving to retake
The heights late lost—
(Herewith a break.
Storms at the West derange the wires.
Doubtless, ere morning, we shall hear
The end; we look for news to cheer—
Let Hope fan all her fires.)

Next day in large bold hand was seen
The closing bulletin:

VICTORY!
Our troops have retrieved the day
By one grand surge along the line;
The spirit that urged them was divine.
The first works flooded, naught could stay
The stormers: on! still on!
Bayonets for Donelson!

[50] *Over the ground that morning lost*
Rolled the blue billows, tempest-tossed,
Following a hat on the point of a sword.
Spite shell and round-shot, grape and canister,
Up they climbed without rail or banister—
Up the steep hill-sides long and broad,
Driving the rebel deep within his works.
'Tis nightfall; not an enemy lurks
In sight. The chafing men
Fret for more fight:
"To-night, to-night let us take the Den!"
But night is treacherous, Grant is wary;
Of brave blood be a little chary.
Patience! the Fort is good as won;
To-morrow, and into Donelson.

LATER AND LAST.

THE FORT IS OURS.

A flag came out at early morn
Bringing surrender. From their towers
Floats out the banner late their scorn.
In Dover, hut and house are full
Of rebels dead or dying.
The National flag is flying
From the crammed court-house pinnacle.
[51] *Great boat-loads of our wounded go*
To-day to Nashville. The sleet-winds blow;
But all is right: the fight is won,
The winter-fight for Donelson.
Hurrah!
The spell of old defeat is broke,
The habit of victory begun;

Grant strikes the war's first sounding stroke
At Donelson.

For lists of killed and wounded, see
The morrow's dispatch: to-day 'tis victory.

The man who read this to the crowd
Shouted as the end he gained;
And though the unflagging tempest rained,
They answered him aloud.
And hand grasped hand, and glances met
In happy triumph; eyes grew wet.
O, to the punches brewed that night
Went little water. Windows bright
Beamed rosy on the sleet without,
And from the deep street came the frequent shout;
While some in prayer, as these in glee,
Blessed heaven for the winter-victory.
But others were who wakeful laid [52]
In midnight beds, and early rose,
And, feverish in the foggy snows,
Snatched the damp paper—wife and maid.
The death-list like a river flows
Down the pale sheet,
And there the whelming waters meet.

Ah God! may Time with happy haste
Bring wail and triumph to a waste,
And war be done;
The battle flag-staff fall athwart
The curs'd ravine, and wither; naught
Be left of trench or gun;
The bastion, let it ebb away,
Washed with the river bed; and Day
In vain seek Donelson.

[53] ## *The Cumberland.*

(March, 1862.)

SOME names there are of telling sound,
Whose voweled syllables free
Are pledge that they shall ever live renowned;
Such seem to be
A Frigate's name (by present glory spanned)—
The Cumberland.

Sounding name as ere was sung,
Flowing, rolling on the tongue—
Cumberland! Cumberland!

She warred and sunk. There's no denying
That she was ended—quelled;
And yet her flag above her fate is flying,
As when it swelled
Unswallowed by the swallowing sea: so grand—
The Cumberland.

[54] Goodly name as ere was sung,
Roundly rolling on the tongue—
Cumberland! Cumberland!

What need to tell how she was fought—
The sinking flaming gun—
The gunner leaping out the port—
Washed back, undone!
Her dead unconquerably manned
The Cumberland.

Noble name as ere was sung,
Slowly roll it on the tongue—
Cumberland! Cumberland!

Long as hearts shall share the flame
Which burned in that brave crew,
Her fame shall live—outlive the victor's name;
For this is due.
Your flag and flag-staff shall in story stand—
Cumberland!

Sounding name as ere was sung,
Long they'll roll it on the tongue—
Cumberland! Cumberland!

[55] **_In the Turret._**

(March, 1862.)

YOUR honest heart of duty, Worden,
So helped you that in fame you dwell;
You bore the first iron battle's burden
Sealed as in a diving-bell.
Alcides, groping into haunted hell
To bring forth King Admetus' bride,
Braved naught more vaguely direful and untried.
What poet shall uplift his charm,
Bold Sailor, to your height of daring,
And interblend therewith the calm,
And build a goodly style upon your bearing.

Escaped the gale of outer ocean—
Cribbed in a craft which like a log
Was washed by every billow's motion—
By night you heard of Og
The huge; nor felt your courage clog
[56] At tokens of his onset grim:
You marked the sunk ship's flag-staff slim,
Lit by her burning sister's heart;
You marked, and mused: "Day brings the trial:
Then be it proved if I have part
With men whose manhood never took denial."

A prayer went up—a champion's. Morning
Beheld you in the Turret walled
By adamant, where a spirit forewarning
And all-deriding called:
"Man, darest thou—desperate, unappalled—
Be first to lock thee in the armored tower?

I have thee now; and what the battle-hour
To me shall bring—heed well—thou'lt share;
This plot-work, planned to be the foeman's terror,
To thee may prove a goblin-snare;
Its very strength and cunning—monstrous error!"

"Stand up, my heart; be strong; what matter
If here thou seest thy welded tomb?
And let huge Og with thunders batter—
Duty be still my doom,
Though drowning come in liquid gloom;
First duty, duty next, and duty last; [57]
Ay, Turret, rivet me here to duty fast!"—
So nerved, you fought wisely and well;
And live, twice live in life and story;
But over your Monitor dirges swell,
In wind and wave that keep the rites of glory.

[58] **The Temeraire.**[c]

(Supposed to have been suggested to an Englishman of the old order by the fight of the Monitor and Merrimac.)

THE gloomy hulls, in armor grim,
Like clouds o'er moors have met,
And prove that oak, and iron, and man
Are tough in fibre yet.

But Splendors wane. The sea-fight yields
No front of old display;
The garniture, emblazonment,
And heraldry all decay.

Towering afar in parting light,
The fleets like Albion's forelands shine—
The full-sailed fleets, the shrouded show
Of Ships-of-the-Line.

[59] The fighting Temeraire,
Built of a thousand trees,
Lunging out her lightnings,
And beetling o'er the seas—
O Ship, how brave and fair,
That fought so oft and well,
On open decks you manned the gun
Armorial.[d]
What cheerings did you share,
Impulsive in the van,
When down upon leagued France and Spain

We English ran—
The freshet at your bowsprit
Like the foam upon the can.
Bickering, your colors
Licked up the Spanish air,
You flapped with flames of battle-flags—
Your challenge, Temeraire!
The rear ones of our fleet
They yearned to share your place,
Still vying with the Victory
Throughout that earnest race—
The Victory, whose Admiral,
With orders nobly won,
Shone in the globe of the battle glow—
The angel in that sun.

Parallel in story,
Lo, the stately pair,
As late in grapple ranging,
The foe between them there—
When four great hulls lay tiered,
And the fiery tempest cleared,
And your prizes twain appeared,
Temeraire!

But Trafalgar is over now,
The quarter-deck undone;
The carved and castled navies fire
Their evening-gun.
O, Titan Temeraire,
Your stern-lights fade away;
Your bulwarks to the years must yield,
And heart-of-oak decay.
A pigmy steam-tug tows you,
Gigantic, to the shore—
Dismantled of your guns and spars,
And sweeping wings of war.

The rivets clinch the iron-clads,
Men learn a deadlier lore;
But Fame has nailed your battle-flags—
Your ghost it sails before:
O, the navies old and oaken,
O, the Temeraire no more!

A Utilitarian View of the Monitor's Fight. [61]

PLAIN be the phrase, yet apt the verse,
More ponderous than nimble;
For since grimed War here laid aside
His Orient pomp, 'twould ill befit
Overmuch to ply
The rhyme's barbaric cymbal.

Hail to victory without the gaud
Of glory; zeal that needs no fans
Of banners; plain mechanic power
Plied cogently in War now placed—
Where War belongs—
Among the trades and artisans.

Yet this was battle, and intense—
Beyond the strife of fleets heroic;
Deadlier, closer, calm 'mid storm;
No passion; all went on by crank, [62]
Pivot, and screw,
And calculations of caloric.

Needless to dwell; the story's known.
The ringing of those plates on plates
Still ringeth round the world—
The clangor of that blacksmith's fray.
The anvil-din
Resounds this message from the Fates:

War shall yet be, and to the end;
But war-paint shows the streaks of weather;
War yet shall be, but warriors
Are now but operatives; War's made
Less grand than Peace,
And a singe runs through lace and feather.

[63]

Shiloh.

A Requiem.

(April, 1862.)

SKIMMING lightly, wheeling still,
The swallows fly low
Over the field in clouded days,
The forest-field of Shiloh—
Over the field where April rain
Solaced the parched ones stretched in pain
Through the pause of night
That followed the Sunday fight
Around the church of Shiloh—
The church so lone, the log-built one,
That echoed to many a parting groan
And natural prayer
Of dying foemen mingled there—
Foemen at morn, but friends at eve—
Fame or country least their care:
(What like a bullet can undeceive!)
But now they lie low,
While over them the swallows skim,
And all is hushed at Shiloh.

The Battle for the Mississippi. [64]

(April, 1862.)

WHEN Israel camped by Migdol hoar,
  Down at her feet her shawm she threw,
But Moses sung and timbrels rung
  For Pharaoh's stranded crew.
So God appears in apt events—
  The Lord is a man of war!
So the strong wing to the muse is given
      In victory's roar.

Deep be the ode that hymns the fleet—
  The fight by night—the fray
Which bore our Flag against the powerful stream,
  And led it up to day.
Dully through din of larger strife
  Shall bay that warring gun;
But none the less to us who live
  It peals—an echoing one.

The shock of ships, the jar of walls, [65]
  The rush through thick and thin—
The flaring fire-rafts, glare and gloom—
  Eddies, and shells that spin—
The boom-chain burst, the hulks dislodged,
  The jam of gun-boats driven,
Or fired, or sunk—made up a war
  Like Michael's waged with leven.

The manned Varuna stemmed and quelled
  The odds which hard beset;
The oaken flag-ship, half ablaze,

Passed on and thundered yet;
While foundering, gloomed in grimy flame,
The Ram Manassas—hark the yell!—
Plunged, and was gone; in joy or fright,
The River gave a startled swell.

They fought through lurid dark till dawn;
The war-smoke rolled away
With clouds of night, and showed the fleet
In scarred yet firm array,
Above the forts, above the drift
Of wrecks which strife had made;
[66] And Farragut sailed up to the town
And anchored—sheathed the blade.

The moody broadsides, brooding deep,
Hold the lewd mob at bay,
While o'er the armed decks' solemn aisles
The meek church-pennons play;
By shotted guns the sailors stand,
With foreheads bound or bare;
The captains and the conquering crews
Humble their pride in prayer.

They pray; and after victory, prayer
Is meet for men who mourn their slain;
The living shall unmoor and sail,
But Death's dark anchor secret deeps detain.
Yet Glory slants her shaft of rays
Far through the undisturbed abyss;
There must be other, nobler worlds for them
Who nobly yield their lives in this.

Malvern Hill. [67]

(July, 1862.)

YE elms that wave on Malvern Hill
In prime of morn and May,
Recall ye how McClellan's men
Here stood at bay?
While deep within yon forest dim
Our rigid comrades lay—
Some with the cartridge in their mouth,
Others with fixed arms lifted South—
Invoking so
The cypress glades? Ah wilds of woe!

The spires of Richmond, late beheld
Through rifts in musket-haze,
Were closed from view in clouds of dust
On leaf-walled ways,
Where streamed our wagons in caravan;
And the Seven Nights and Days
Of march and fast, retreat and fight, [68]
Pinched our grimed faces to ghastly plight—
Does the elm wood
Recall the haggard beards of blood?

The battle-smoked flag, with stars eclipsed,
We followed (it never fell!)—
In silence husbanded our strength—
Received their yell;
Till on this slope we patient turned
With cannon ordered well;
Reverse we proved was not defeat;
But ah, the sod what thousands meet!—

Does Malvern Wood
Bethink itself, and muse and brood?

We elms of Malvern Hill
Remember every thing;
But sap the twig will fill:
Wag the world how it will,
Leaves must be green in Spring.

The Victor of Antietam.[e] [69]

(1862.)

WHEN tempest winnowed grain from bran;
And men were looking for a man,
Authority called you to the van,
McClellan:
Along the line the plaudit ran,
As later when Antietam's cheers began.

Through storm-cloud and eclipse must move
Each Cause and Man, dear to the stars and Jove;
Nor always can the wisest tell
Deferred fulfillment from the hopeless knell—
The struggler from the floundering ne'er-do-well.
A pall-cloth on the Seven Days fell,
McClellan—
Unprosperously heroical!
Who could Antietam's wreath foretell?

Authority called you; then, in mist [70]
And loom of jeopardy—dismissed.
But staring peril soon appalled;
You, the Discarded, she recalled—
Recalled you, nor endured delay;
And forth you rode upon a blasted way,
Arrayed Pope's rout, and routed Lee's array,
McClellan:
Your tent was choked with captured flags that day,
McClellan.
Antietam was a telling fray.

Recalled you; and she heard your drum
Advancing through the ghastly gloom.
You manned the wall, you propped the Dome,
You stormed the powerful stormer home,
McClellan:
Antietam's cannon long shall boom.

At Alexandria, left alone,
McClellan—
Your veterans sent from you, and thrown
To fields and fortunes all unknown—
What thoughts were yours, revealed to none,
[71] While faithful still you labored on—
Hearing the far Manassas gun!
McClellan,
Only Antietam could atone.

You fought in the front (an evil day,
McClellan)—
The fore-front of the first assay;
The Cause went sounding, groped its way;
The leadsmen quarrelled in the bay;
Quills thwarted swords; divided sway;
The rebel flushed in his lusty May:
You did your best, as in you lay,
McClellan.
Antietam's sun-burst sheds a ray.

Your medalled soldiers love you well,
McClellan:
Name your name, their true hearts swell;
With you they shook dread Stonewall's spell,[f]
With you they braved the blended yell
Of rebel and maligner fell;

With you in shame or fame they dwell,
McClellan:
Antietam-braves a brave can tell.

And when your comrades (now so few, [72]
McClellan—
Such ravage in deep files they rue)
Meet round the board, and sadly view
The empty places; tribute due
They render to the dead—and you!
Absent and silent o'er the blue;
The one-armed lift the wine to *you*,
McClellan,
And great Antietam's cheers renew.

[73] *Battle of Stone River, Tennessee.*

A View from Oxford Cloisters.

(January, 1863.)

WITH Tewksbury and Barnet heath
In days to come the field shall blend,
The story dim and date obscure;
In legend all shall end.
Even now, involved in forest shade
A Druid-dream the strife appears,
The fray of yesterday assumes
The haziness of years.
In North and South still beats the vein
Of Yorkist and Lancastrian.

Our rival Roses warred for Sway—
For Sway, but named the name of Right;
And Passion, scorning pain and death,
Lent sacred fervor to the fight.
Each lifted up a broidered cross,
While crossing blades profaned the sign;
[74] Monks blessed the fratricidal lance,
And sisters scarfs could twine.
Do North and South the sin retain
Of Yorkist and Lancastrian?

But Rosecrans in the cedarn glade,
And, deep in denser cypress gloom,
Dark Breckinridge, shall fade away
Or thinly loom.
The pale throngs who in forest cowed
Before the spell of battle's pause,
Forefelt the stillness that shall dwell

On them and on their wars.
North and South shall join the train
Of Yorkist and Lancastrian.

But where the sword has plunged so deep,
And then been turned within the wound
By deadly Hate; where Climes contend
On vasty ground—
No warning Alps or seas between,
And small the curb of creed or law,
And blood is quick, and quick the brain;
Shall North and South their rage deplore,
And reunited thrive amain
Like Yorkist and Lancastrian?

[75] **Running the Batteries,**

As observed from the Anchorage above Vicksburgh.

(April, 1863.)

A MOONLESS night—a friendly one;
   A haze dimmed the shadowy shore
As the first lampless boat slid silent on;
   Hist! and we spake no more;
We but pointed, and stilly, to what we saw.

We felt the dew, and seemed to feel
   The secret like a burden laid.
The first boat melts; and a second keel
   Is blent with the foliaged shade—
Their midnight rounds have the rebel officers made?

Unspied as yet. A third—a fourth—
   Gun-boat and transport in Indian file
Upon the war-path, smooth from the North;
   But the watch may they hope to beguile?
The manned river-batteries stretch for mile on mile.

[76] A flame leaps out; they are seen;
   Another and another gun roars;
We tell the course of the boats through the screen
   By each further fort that pours,
And we guess how they jump from their beds on those
         Shrouded shores.

Converging fires. We speak, though low:
   "That blastful furnace can they thread?"
"Why, Shadrach, Meshach, and Abed-nego
   Came out all right, we read;
The Lord, be sure, he helps his people, Ned."

How we strain our gaze. On bluffs they shun
A golden growing flame appears—
Confirms to a silvery steadfast one:
"The town is afire!" crows Hugh: "three cheers!"
Lot stops his mouth: "Nay, lad, better three tears."

A purposed light; it shows our fleet;
Yet a little late in its searching ray,
So far and strong, that in phantom cheat
Lank on the deck our shadows lay;
The shining flag-ship stings their guns to furious play.

How dread to mark her near the glare [77]
And glade of death the beacon throws
Athwart the racing waters there;
One by one each plainer grows,
Then speeds a blazoned target to our gladdened foes.

The impartial cresset lights as well
The fixed forts to the boats that run;
And, plunged from the ports, their answers swell
Back to each fortress dun:
Ponderous words speaks every monster gun.

Fearless they flash through gates of flame,
The salamanders hard to hit,
Though vivid shows each bulky frame;
And never the batteries intermit,
Nor the boats huge guns; they fire and flit.

Anon a lull. The beacon dies:
"Are they out of that strait accurst?"
But other flames now dawning rise,
Not mellowly brilliant like the first,
But rolled in smoke, whose whitish volumes burst.

[78] A baleful brand, a hurrying torch
Whereby anew the boats are seen—
A burning transport all alurch!
Breathless we gaze; yet still we glean
Glimpses of beauty as we eager lean.

The effulgence takes an amber glow
Which bathes the hill-side villas far;
Affrighted ladies mark the show
Painting the pale magnolia—
The fair, false, Circe light of cruel War.

The barge drifts doomed, a plague-struck one.
Shoreward in yawls the sailors fly.
But the gauntlet now is nearly run,
The spleenful forts by fits reply,
And the burning boat dies down in morning's sky.

All out of range. Adieu, Messieurs!
Jeers, as it speeds, our parting gun.
So burst we through their barriers
And menaces every one:
So Porter proves himself a brave man's son.[g]

Stonewall Jackson. [79]

Mortally wounded at Chancellorsville.

(May, 1863.)

THE Man who fiercest charged in fight,
Whose sword and prayer were long—
Stonewall!
Even him who stoutly stood for Wrong,
How can we praise? Yet coming days
Shall not forget him with this song.

Dead is the Man whose Cause is dead,
Vainly he died and set his seal—
Stonewall!
Earnest in error, as we feel;
True to the thing he deemed was due,
True as John Brown or steel.

Relentlessly he routed us; [80]
But *we* relent, for he is low—
Stonewall!
Justly his fame we outlaw; so
We drop a tear on the bold Virginian's bier,
Because no wreath we owe.

[81] ## *Stonewall Jackson.*
(Ascribed to a Virginian.)

ONE man we claim of wrought renown
Which not the North shall care to slur;
A Modern lived who sleeps in death,
Calm as the marble Ancients are:
'Tis he whose life, though a vapor's wreath,
Was charged with the lightning's burning breath—
Stonewall, stormer of the war.

But who shall hymn the Roman heart?
A stoic he, but even more:
The iron will and lion thew
Were strong to inflict as to endure:
Who like him could stand, or pursue?
His fate the fatalist followed through;
In all his great soul found to do
Stonewall followed his star.

[82] He followed his star on the Romney march
Through the sleet to the wintry war;
And he followed it on when he bowed the grain—
The Wind of the Shenandoah;
At Gaines's Mill in the giants' strain—
On the fierce forced stride to Manassas-plain,
Where his sword with thunder was clothed again,
Stonewall followed his star.

His star he followed athwart the flood
To Potomac's Northern shore,
When midway wading, his host of braves
"My *Maryland!*" loud did roar—
To red Antietam's field of graves,

Through mountain-passes, woods and waves,
They followed their pagod with hymns and glaives,
For Stonewall followed a star.

Back it led him to Marye's slope,
Where the shock and the fame he bore;
And to green Moss-Neck it guided him—
Brief respite from throes of war:
To the laurel glade by the Wilderness grim,
Through climaxed victory naught shall dim,
Even unto death it piloted him—
Stonewall followed his star.

Its lead he followed in gentle ways [83]
Which never the valiant mar;
A cap we sent him, bestarred, to replace
The sun-scorched helm of war:
A fillet he made of the shining lace
Childhood's laughing brow to grace—
Not his was a goldsmith's star.

O, much of doubt in after days
Shall cling, as now, to the war;
Of the right and the wrong they'll still debate,
Puzzled by Stonewall's star:
"Fortune went with the North elate,"
"Ay, but the South had Stonewall's weight,
And he fell in the South's vain war."

[84]

Gettysburg.

The Check.

(July, 1863.)

O PRIDE of the days in prime of the months
Now trebled in great renown,
When before the ark of our holy cause
Fell Dagon down—
Dagon foredoomed, who, armed and targed,
Never his impious heart enlarged
Beyond that hour; God walled his power,
And there the last invader charged.

He charged, and in that charge condensed
His all of hate and all of fire;
He sought to blast us in his scorn,
And wither us in his ire.
Before him went the shriek of shells—
Aerial screamings, taunts and yells;
Then the three waves in flashed advance
[85] Surged, but were met, and back they set:
Pride was repelled by sterner pride,
And Right is a strong-hold yet.

Before our lines it seemed a beach
Which wild September gales have strown
With havoc on wreck, and dashed therewith
Pale crews unknown—
Men, arms, and steeds. The evening sun
Died on the face of each lifeless one,
And died along the winding marge of fight
And searching-parties lone.

Sloped on the hill the mounds were green,
  Our centre held that place of graves,
And some still hold it in their swoon,
  And over these a glory waves.
The warrior-monument, crashed in fight,[h]
Shall soar transfigured in loftier light,
    A meaning ampler bear;
Soldier and priest with hymn and prayer
Have laid the stone, and every bone
    Shall rest in honor there.

[86] **The House-top.**

A Night Piece.

(July, 1863.)

NO sleep. The sultriness pervades the air
And binds the brain—a dense oppression, such
As tawny tigers feel in matted shades,
Vexing their blood and making apt for ravage.
Beneath the stars the roofy desert spreads
Vacant as Libya. All is hushed near by.
Yet fitfully from far breaks a mixed surf
Of muffled sound, the Atheist roar of riot.
Yonder, where parching Sirius set in drought,
Balefully glares red Arson—there—and there.
The Town is taken by its rats—ship-rats
And rats of the wharves. All civil charms
And priestly spells which late held hearts in awe—
Fear-bound, subjected to a better sway
Than sway of self; these like a dream dissolve,
And man rebounds whole æons back in nature.[i]
[87] Hail to the low dull rumble, dull and dead,
And ponderous drag that shakes the wall.
Wise Draco comes, deep in the midnight roll
Of black artillery; he comes, though late;
In code corroborating Calvin's creed
And cynic tyrannies of honest kings;
He comes, nor parlies; and the Town, redeemed,
Give thanks devout; nor, being thankful, heeds
The grimy slur on the Republic's faith implied,
Which holds that Man is naturally good,
And—more—is Nature's Roman, never to be scourged.

Look-out Mountain. [88]

The Night Fight.

(November, 1863.)

WHO inhabiteth the Mountain
   That it shines in lurid light,
And is rolled about with thunders,
   And terrors, and a blight,
Like Kaf the peak of Eblis—
   Kaf, the evil height?
Who has gone up with a shouting
   And a trumpet in the night?

There is battle in the Mountain—
   Might assaulteth Might;
'Tis the fastness of the Anarch,
   Torrent-torn, an ancient height;
The crags resound the clangor
   Of the war of Wrong and Right;
And the armies in the valley
   Watch and pray for dawning light.

Joy, joy, the day is breaking, [89]
   And the cloud is rolled from sight;
There is triumph in the Morning
   For the Anarch's plunging flight;
God has glorified the Mountain
   Where a Banner burneth bright,
And the armies in the valley
   They are fortified in right.

[90] # *Chattanooga.*

(November, 1863.)

A KINDLING impulse seized the host
Inspired by heaven's elastic air;[j]
Their hearts outran their General's plan,
Though Grant commanded there—
Grant, who without reserve can dare;
And, "Well, go on and do your will,"
He said, and measured the mountain then:
So master-riders fling the rein—
But you must know your men.

On yester-morn in grayish mist,
Armies like ghosts on hills had fought,
And rolled from the cloud their thunders loud
The Cumberlands far had caught:
To-day the sunlit steeps are sought.
Grant stood on cliffs whence all was plain,
And smoked as one who feels no cares;
But mastered nervousness intense
Alone such calmness wears.

[91] The summit-cannon plunge their flame
Sheer down the primal wall,
But up and up each linking troop
In stretching festoons crawl—
Nor fire a shot. Such men appall
The foe, though brave. He, from the brink,
Looks far along the breadth of slope,
And sees two miles of dark dots creep,
And knows they mean the cope.

He sees them creep. Yet here and there
Half hid 'mid leafless groves they go;
As men who ply through traceries high
Of turreted marbles show—
So dwindle these to eyes below.
But fronting shot and flanking shell
Sliver and rive the inwoven ways;
High tops of oaks and high hearts fall,
But never the climbing stays.

From right to left, from left to right
They roll the rallying cheer—
Vie with each other, brother with brother,
Who shall the first appear—
What color-bearer with colors clear
In sharp relief, like sky-drawn Grant,
Whose cigar must now be near the stump— [92]
While in solicitude his back
Heaps slowly to a hump.

Near and more near; till now the flags
Run like a catching flame;
And one flares highest, to peril nighest—
He means to make a name:
Salvos! they give him his fame.
The staff is caught, and next the rush,
And then the leap where death has led;
Flag answered flag along the crest,
And swarms of rebels fled.

But some who gained the envied Alp,
And—eager, ardent, earnest there—
Dropped into Death's wide-open arms,
Quelled on the wing like eagles struck in air—
Forever they slumber young and fair,

The smile upon them as they died;
Their end attained, that end a height:
Life was to these a dream fulfilled,
And death a starry night.

The Armies of the Wilderness. [93]

(1863–4.)

I.

LIKE snows the camps on Southern hills
 Lay all the winter long,
Our levies there in patience stood—
 They stood in patience strong.
On fronting slopes gleamed other camps
 Where faith as firmly clung:
Ah, froward kin! so brave amiss—
 The zealots of the Wrong.

In this strife of brothers
 (God, hear their country call),
However it be, whatever betide,
 Let not the just one fall.

Through the pointed glass our soldiers saw
 The base-ball bounding sent;
They could have joined them in their sport [94]
 But for the vale's deep rent.
And others turned the reddish soil,
 Like diggers of graves they bent:
The reddish soil and trenching toil
  Begat presentiment.

Did the Fathers feel mistrust?
 Can no final good be wrought?
Over and over, again and again
 Must the fight for the Right be fought?

They lead a Gray-back to the crag:
"Your earth-works yonder—tell us, man!"
"A prisoner—no deserter, I,
Nor one of the tell-tale clan."
His rags they mark: "True-blue like you
Should wear the color—your Country's, man!"
He grinds his teeth: "However that be,
Yon earth-works have their plan."

Such brave ones, foully snared
By Belial's wily plea,
Were faithful unto the evil end—
Feudal fidelity.

[95] "Well, then, your camps—come, tell the names!"
Freely he leveled his finger then:
"Yonder—see—are our Georgians; on the crest,
The Carolinians; lower, past the glen,
Virginians—Alabamians—Mississippians—Kentuckians
(Follow my finger)—Tennesseeans; and the ten
Camps *there*—ask your grave-pits; they'll tell.
Halloa! I see the picket-hut, the den
Where I last night lay." "Where's Lee?"
"In the hearts and bayonets of all yon men!"

The tribes swarm up to war
As in ages long ago,
Ere the palm of promise leaved
And the lily of Christ did blow.

Their mounted pickets for miles are spied
Dotting the lowland plain,
The nearer ones in their veteran-rags—
Loutish they loll in lazy disdain.
But ours in perilous places bide
With rifles ready and eyes that strain
Deep through the dim suspected wood
Where the Rapidan rolls amain.

The Indian has passed away, [96]
But creeping comes another—
Deadlier far. Picket,
Take heed—take heed of thy brother!

From a wood-hung height, an outpost lone,
Crowned with a woodman's fort,
The sentinel looks on a land of dole,
Like Paran, all amort.
Black chimneys, gigantic in moor-like wastes,
The scowl of the clouded sky retort;
The hearth is a houseless stone again—
Ah! where shall the people be sought?

Since the venom such blastment deals,
The South should have paused, and thrice,
Ere with heat of her hate she hatched
The egg with the cockatrice.

A path down the mountain winds to the glade
Where the dead of the Moonlight Fight lie low;
A hand reaches out of the thin-laid mould
As begging help which none can bestow.
But the field-mouse small and busy ant [97]
Heap their hillocks, to hide if they may the woe:
By the bubbling spring lies the rusted canteen,
And the drum which the drummer-boy dying let go.

Dust to dust, and blood for blood—
Passion and pangs! Has Time
Gone back? or is this the Age
Of the world's great Prime?

The wagon mired and cannon dragged
Have trenched their scar; the plain
Tramped like the cindery beach of the damned—
A site for the city of Cain.

And stumps of forests for dreary leagues
  Like a massacre show. The armies have lain
By fires where gums and balms did burn,
  And the seeds of Summer's reign.

Where are the birds and boys?
  Who shall go chestnutting when
October returns? The nuts—
  O, long ere they grow again.

[98] They snug their huts with the chapel-pews,
  In court-houses stable their steeds—
Kindle their fires with indentures and bonds,
  And old Lord Fairfax's parchment deeds;
And Virginian gentlemen's libraries old—
  Books which only the scholar heeds—
Are flung to his kennel. It is ravage and range,
  And gardens are left to weeds.

Turned adrift into war
  Man runs wild on the plain,
Like the jennets let loose
  On the Pampas—zebras again.

Like the Pleiads dim, see the tents through the storm—
  Aloft by the hill-side hamlet's graves,
On a head-stone used for a hearth-stone there
  The water is bubbling for punch for our braves.
What if the night be drear, and the blast
  Ghostly shrieks? their rollicking staves
Make frolic the heart; beating time with their swords,
  What care they if Winter raves?

Is life but a dream? and so,
  In the dream do men laugh aloud?
[99] *So strange seems mirth in a camp,*
  So like a white tent to a shroud.

II.

The May-weed springs; and comes a Man
And mounts our Signal Hill;
A quiet Man, and plain in garb—
Briefly he looks his fill,
Then drops his gray eye on the ground,
Like a loaded mortar he is still:
Meekness and grimness meet in him—
The silent General.

Were men but strong and wise,
Honest as Grant, and calm,
War would be left to the red and black ants,
And the happy world disarm.

That eve a stir was in the camps,
Forerunning quiet soon to come
Among the streets of beechen huts
No more to know the drum.
The weed shall choke the lowly door,
And foxes peer within the gloom,
Till scared perchance by Mosby's prowling men,
Who ride in the rear of doom.

Far West, and farther South,
Wherever the sword has been,
Deserted camps are met,
And desert graves are seen.

The livelong night they ford the flood;
With guns held high they silent press,
Till shimmers the grass in their bayonets' sheen—
On Morning's banks their ranks they dress;
Then by the forests lightly wind,
Whose waving boughs the pennons seem to bless,
Borne by the cavalry scouting on—
Sounding the Wilderness.

Like shoals of fish in spring
That visit Crusoe's isle,
The host in the lonesome place—
The hundred thousand file.

The foe that held his guarded hills
Must speed to woods afar;
[101] For the scheme that was nursed by the Culpepper hearth
With the slowly-smoked cigar—
The scheme that smouldered through winter long
Now bursts into act—into war—
The resolute scheme of a heart as calm
As the Cyclone's core.

The fight for the city is fought
In Nature's old domain;
Man goes out to the wilds,
And Orpheus' charm is vain.

In glades they meet skull after skull
Where pine-cones lay—the rusted gun,
Green shoes full of bones, the mouldering coat
And cuddled-up skeleton;
And scores of such. Some start as in dreams,
And comrades lost bemoan:
By the edge of those wilds Stonewall had charged—
But the Year and the Man were gone.

At the height of their madness
The night winds pause,
Recollecting themselves;
But no lull in these wars.

[102] A gleam!—a volley! And who shall go
Storming the swarmers in jungles dread?
No cannon-ball answers, no proxies are sent—
They rush in the shrapnel's stead.

Plume and sash are vanities now—
Let them deck the pall of the dead;
They go where the shade is, perhaps into Hades,
Where the brave of all times have led.

There's a dust of hurrying feet,
Bitten lips and bated breath,
And drums that challenge to the grave,
And faces fixed, forefeeling death.

What husky huzzahs in the hazy groves—
What flying encounters fell;
Pursuer and pursued like ghosts disappear
In gloomed shade—their end who shall tell?
The crippled, a ragged-barked stick for a crutch,
Limp to some elfin dell—
Hobble from the sight of dead faces—white
As pebbles in a well.

Few burial rites shall be;
No priest with book and band
Shall come to the secret place [103]
Of the corpse in the foeman's land.

Watch and fast, march and fight—clutch your gun!
Day-fights and night-fights; sore is the stress;
Look, through the pines what line comes on?
Longstreet slants through the hauntedness!
'Tis charge for charge, and shout for yell:
Such battles on battles oppress—
But Heaven lent strength, the Right strove well,
And emerged from the Wilderness.

Emerged, for the way was won;
But the Pillar of Smoke that led
Was brand-like with ghosts that went up
Ashy and red.

None can narrate that strife in the pines,
  A seal is on it—Sabæan lore!
Obscure as the wood, the entangled rhyme
  But hints at the maze of war—
Vivid glimpses or livid through peopled gloom,
  And fires which creep and char—
A riddle of death, of which the slain
    Sole solvers are.

[104] *Long they withhold the roll*
  Of the shroudless dead. It is right;
Not yet can we bear the flare
    Of the funeral light.

On the Photograph of a Corps Commander. [105]

AY, man is manly. Here you see
  The warrior-carriage of the head,
And brave dilation of the frame;
  And lighting all, the soul that led
In Spottsylvania's charge to victory,
  Which justifies his fame.

A cheering picture. It is good
  To look upon a Chief like this,
In whom the spirit moulds the form.
  Here favoring Nature, oft remiss,
With eagle mien expressive has endued
  A man to kindle strains that warm.

Trace back his lineage, and his sires,
  Yeoman or noble, you shall find
Enrolled with men of Agincourt,
  Heroes who shared great Harry's mind.
Down to us come the knightly Norman fires, [106]
  And front the Templars bore.

Nothing can lift the heart of man
  Like manhood in a fellow-man.
The thought of heaven's great King afar
  But humbles us—too weak to scan;
But manly greatness men can span,
  And feel the bonds that draw.

[107] **The Swamp Angel.**[k]

THERE is a coal-black Angel
   With a thick Afric lip,
And he dwells (like the hunted and harried)
   In a swamp where the green frogs dip.
But his face is against a City
   Which is over a bay of the sea,
And he breathes with a breath that is blastment,
   And dooms by a far decree.

By night there is fear in the City,
   Through the darkness a star soareth on;
There's a scream that screams up to the zenith,
   Then the poise of a meteor lone—
Lighting far the pale fright of the faces,
   And downward the coming is seen;
Then the rush, and the burst, and the havoc,
   And wails and shrieks between.

[108] It comes like the thief in the gloaming;
   It comes, and none may foretell
The place of the coming—the glaring;
   They live in a sleepless spell
That wizens, and withers, and whitens;
   It ages the young, and the bloom
Of the maiden is ashes of roses—
   The Swamp Angel broods in his gloom.

Swift is his messengers' going,
   But slowly he saps their halls,
As if by delay deluding.
   They move from their crumbling walls
Farther and farther away;

But the Angel sends after and after,
By night with the flame of his ray—
By night with the voice of his screaming—
Sends after them, stone by stone,
And farther walls fall, farther portals,
And weed follows weed through the Town.

Is this the proud City? the scorner
Which never would yield the ground?
Which mocked at the coal-black Angel?
The cup of despair goes round.
Vainly she calls upon Michael [109]
(The white man's seraph was he),
For Michael has fled from his tower
To the Angel over the sea.

Who weeps for the woeful City
Let him weep for our guilty kind;
Who joys at her wild despairing—
Christ, the Forgiver, convert his mind.

[110] **The Battle for the Bay.**

(August, 1864.)

O MYSTERY of noble hearts,
To whom mysterious seas have been
In midnight watches, lonely calm and storm,
A stern, sad discipline,
And rooted out the false and vain,
And chastened them to aptness for
Devotion and the deeds of war,
And death which smiles and cheers in spite of pain.

Beyond the bar the land-wind dies,
The prows becharmed at anchor swim:
A summer night; the stars withdrawn look down—
Fair eve of battle grim.
The sentries pace, bonetas glide;
Below, the sleeping sailors swing,
And in their dreams to quarters spring,
Or cheer their flag, or breast a stormy tide.

[111] But drums are beat: *Up anchor all!*
The triple lines steam slowly on;
Day breaks, and through the sweep of decks each man
Stands coldly by his gun—
As cold as it. But he shall warm—
Warm with the solemn metal there,
And all its ordered fury share,
In attitude a gladiatorial form.

The Admiral—yielding to the love
Which held his life and ship so dear—
Sailed second in the long fleet's midmost line;

Yet thwarted all their care:
He lashed himself aloft, and shone
Star of the fight, with influence sent
Throughout the dusk embattlement;
And so they neared the strait and walls of stone.

No sprightly fife as in the field,
The decks were hushed like fanes in prayer;
Behind each man a holy angel stood—
He stood, though none was 'ware.
Out spake the forts on either hand,
Back speak the ships when spoken to,
And set their flags in concert true, [112]
And *On and in!* is Farragut's command.

But what delays? 'mid wounds above
Dim buoys give hint of death below—
Sea-ambuscades, where evil art had aped
Hecla that hides in snow.
The centre-van, entangled, trips;
The starboard leader holds straight on:
A cheer for the Tecumseh!—nay,
Before their eyes the turreted ship goes down!

The fire redoubles. While the fleet
Hangs dubious—ere the horror ran—
The Admiral rushes to his rightful place—
Well met! apt hour and man!—
Closes with peril, takes the lead,
His action is a stirring call;
He strikes his great heart through them all,
And is the genius of their daring deed.

The forts are daunted, slack their fire,
Confounded by the deadlier aim
And rapid broadsides of the speeding fleet, [113]
And fierce denouncing flame.

Yet shots from four dark hulls embayed
Come raking through the loyal crews,
Whom now each dying mate endues
With his last look, anguished yet undismayed.

A flowering time to guilt is given,
And traitors have their glorying hour;
O late, but sure, the righteous Paramount comes—
Palsy is on their power!
So proved it with the rebel keels,
The strong-holds past: assailed, they run;
The Selma strikes, and the work is done:
The dropping anchor the achievement seals.

But no, she turns—the Tennessee!
The solid Ram of iron and oak,
Strong as Evil, and bold as Wrong, though lone—
A pestilence in her smoke.
The flag-ship is her singled mark,
The wooden Hartford. Let her come;
She challenges the planet of Doom,
And naught shall save her—not her iron bark.

[114] *Slip anchor, all! and at her, all!*
Bear down with rushing beaks—and now!
First the Monongahela struck—and reeled;
The Lackawana's prow
Next crashed—crashed, but not crashing; then
The Admiral rammed, and rasping nigh
Sloped in a broadside, which glanced by:
The Monitors battered at her adamant den.

The Chickasaw plunged beneath the stern
And pounded there; a huge wrought orb
From the Manhattan pierced one wall, but dropped;
Others the seas absorb.
Yet stormed on all sides, narrowed in,

Hampered and cramped, the bad one fought—
Spat ribald curses from the port
Who shutters, jammed, locked up this Man-of-Sin.

No pause or stay. They made a din
Like hammers round a boiler forged;
Now straining strength tangled itself with strength,
Till Hate her will disgorged.
The white flag showed, the fight was won—
Mad shouts went up that shook the Bay;
But pale on the scarred fleet's decks there lay
A silent man for every silenced gun.

And quiet far below the wave,
Where never cheers shall move their sleep,
Some who did boldly, nobly earn them, lie—
Charmed children of the deep.
But decks that now are in the seed,
And cannon yet within the mine,
Shall thrill the deeper, gun and pine,
Because of the Tecumseh's glorious deed.

[116] **_Sheridan at Cedar Creek._**

(October, 1864.)

SHOE the steed with silver
That bore him to the fray,
When he heard the guns at dawning—
Miles away;
When he heard them calling, calling—
Mount! nor stay:
Quick, or all is lost;
They've surprised and stormed the post,
They push your routed host—
Gallop! retrieve the day.

House the horse in ermine—
For the foam-flake blew
White through the red October;
He thundered into view;
They cheered him in the looming,
Horseman and horse they knew.
[117] The turn of the tide began,
The rally of bugles ran,
He swung his hat in the van;
The electric hoof-spark flew.

Wreathe the steed and lead him—
For the charge he led
Touched and turned the cypress
Into amaranths for the head
Of Philip, king of riders,
Who raised them from the dead.
The camp (at dawning lost),
By eve, recovered—forced,

Rang with laughter of the host
At belated Early fled.

Shroud the horse in sable—
For the mounds they heap!
There is firing in the Valley,
And yet no strife they keep;
It is the parting volley,
It is the pathos deep.
There is glory for the brave
Who lead, and nobly save,
But no knowledge in the grave
Where the nameless followers sleep.

[118] **In the Prison Pen.**

(1864.)

LISTLESS he eyes the palisades
    And sentries in the glare;
'Tis barren as a pelican-beach—
    But his world is ended there.

Nothing to do; and vacant hands
    Bring on the idiot-pain;
He tries to think—to recollect,
    But the blur is on his brain.

Around him swarm the plaining ghosts
    Like those on Virgil's shore—
A wilderness of faces dim,
    And pale ones gashed and hoar.

A smiting sun. No shed, no tree;
    He totters to his lair—
A den that sick hands dug in earth
    Ere famine wasted there,
[119] Or, dropping in his place, he swoons,
    Walled in by throngs that press,
Till forth from the throngs they bear him dead—
    Dead in his meagreness.

The College Colonel. [120]

HE rides at their head;
   A crutch by his saddle just slants in view,
One slung arm is in splints, you see,
   Yet he guides his strong steed—how coldly too.

He brings his regiment home—
   Not as they filed two years before,
But a remnant half-tattered, and battered, and worn,
Like castaway sailors, who—stunned
      By the surf's loud roar,
   Their mates dragged back and seen no more—
Again and again breast the surge,
   And at last crawl, spent, to shore.

A still rigidity and pale—
   An Indian aloofness lones his brow;
He has lived a thousand years
Compressed in battle's pains and prayers,
   Marches and watches slow.
There are welcoming shouts, and flags; [121]
   Old men off hat to the Boy,
Wreaths from gay balconies fall at his feet,
   But to *him*—there comes alloy.

It is not that a leg is lost,
   It is not that an arm is maimed.
It is not that the fever has racked—
   Self he has long disclaimed.

But all through the Seven Days' Fight,
   And deep in the Wilderness grim,
And in the field-hospital tent,
   And Petersburg crater, and dim
Lean brooding in Libby, there came—
   Ah heaven!—what *truth* to him.

[122] ## *The Eagle of the Blue.*[1]

ALOFT he guards the starry folds
  Who is the brother of the star;
The bird whose joy is in the wind
  Exulteth in the war.

No painted plume—a sober hue,
  His beauty is his power;
That eager calm of gaze intent
  Foresees the Sibyl's hour.

Austere, he crowns the swaying perch,
  Flapped by the angry flag;
The hurricane from the battery sings,
  But his claw has known the crag.

Amid the scream of shells, his scream
  Runs shrilling; and the glare
Of eyes that brave the blinding sun
  The vollied flame can bear.

[123] The pride of quenchless strength is his—
  Strength which, though chained, avails;
The very rebel looks and thrills—
  The anchored Emblem hails.

Though scarred in many a furious fray,
  No deadly hurt he knew;
Well may we think his years are charmed—
  The Eagle of the Blue.

A *Dirge for* McPherson,[m] [124]

Killed in front of Atlanta.

(July, 1864.)

ARMS reversed and banners craped—
Muffled drums;
Snowy horses sable-draped—
McPherson comes.

But, tell us, shall we know him more,
Lost-Mountain and lone Kenesaw?

Brave the sword upon the pall—
A gleam in gloom;
So a bright name lighteth all
McPherson's doom.

Bear him through the chapel-door—
Let priest in stole
Pace before the warrior
Who led. Bell—toll!

Lay him down within the nave, [125]
The Lesson read—
Man is noble, man is brave,
But man's—a weed.

Take him up again and wend
Graveward, nor weep:
There's a trumpet that shall rend
This Soldier's sleep.

Pass the ropes the coffin round,
And let descend;
Prayer and volley—let it sound
McPherson's end.

True fame is his, for life is o'er—
Sarpedon of the mighty war.

At the Cannon's Mouth. [126]

Destruction of the Ram Albermarle
by the Torpedo-launch.

(October, 1864.)

PALELY intent, he urged his keel
Full on the guns, and touched the spring;
Himself involved in the bolt he drove
Timed with the armed hull's shot that stove
His shallop—die or do!
Into the flood his life he threw,
Yet lives—unscathed—a breathing thing
To marvel at.

He has his fame;
But that mad dash at death, how name?

Had Earth no charm to stay the Boy
From the martyr-passion? Could he dare
Disdain the Paradise of opening joy
Which beckons the fresh heart every where?
Life has more lures than any girl
For youth and strength; puts forth a share
Of beauty, hinting of yet rarer store; [127]
And ever with unfathomable eyes,
Which baffingly entice,
Still strangely does Adonis draw.
And life once over, who shall tell the rest?
Life is, of all we know, God's best.
What imps these eagles then, that they
Fling disrespect on life by that proud way
In which they soar above our lower clay.

Pretense of wonderment and doubt unblest:
   In Cushing's eager deed was shown
   A spirit which brave poets own—
That scorn of life which earns life's crown;
   Earns, but not always wins; but *he*—
   The star ascended in his nativity.

The March to the Sea. [128]

(December, 1864.)

NOT Kenesaw high-arching,
Nor Allatoona's glen—
Though there the graves lie parching—
Stayed Sherman's miles of men;
From charred Atlanta marching
They launched the sword again.
The columns streamed like rivers
Which in their course agree,
And they streamed until their flashing
Met the flashing of the sea:
It was glorious glad marching,
That marching to the sea.

They brushed the foe before them
(Shall gnats impede the bull?);
Their own good bridges bore them
Over swamps or torrents full,
And the grand pines waving o'er them [129]
Bowed to axes keen and cool.
The columns grooved their channels.
Enforced their own decree,
And their power met nothing larger
Until it met the sea:
It was glorious glad marching,
A marching glad and free.

Kilpatrick's snare of riders
In zigzags mazed the land,
Perplexed the pale Southsiders
With feints on every hand;

Vague menace awed the hiders
In forts beyond command.
To Sherman's shifting problem
No foeman knew the key;
But onward went the marching
Unpausing to the sea :
It was glorious glad marching,
The swinging step was free.

The flankers ranged like pigeons
In clouds through field or wood;
The flocks of all those regions,
The herds and horses good,
Poured in and swelled the legions,
For they caught the marching mood.
A volley ahead! They hear it;
And they hear the repartee:
Fighting was but frolic
In that marching to the sea:
It was glorious glad marching,
A marching bold and free.

All nature felt their coming,
The birds like couriers flew,
And the banners brightly blooming
The slaves by thousands drew,
And they marched beside the drumming,
And they joined the armies blue.
The cocks crowed from the cannon
(Pets named from Grant and Lee),
Plumed fighters and campaigners
In that marching to the sea:
It was glorious glad marching,
For every man was free.

The foragers through calm lands [131]
Swept in tempest gay,
And they breathed the air of balm-lands
Where rolled savannas lay,
And they helped themselves from farm-lands—
As who should say them nay?
The regiments uproarious
Laughed in Plenty's glee;
And they marched till their broad laughter
Met the laughter of the sea:
It was glorious glad marching,
That marching to the sea.

The grain of endless acres
Was threshed (as in the East)
By the trampling of the Takers,
Strong march of man and beast;
The flails of those earth-shakers
Left a famine where they ceased.
The arsenals were yielded;
The sword (that was to be),
Arrested in the forging,
Rued that marching to the sea:
It was glorious glad marching,
But ah, the stern decree!

For behind they left a wailing, [132]
A terror and a ban,
And blazing cinders sailing,
And houseless households wan,
Wide zones of counties paling,
And towns where maniacs ran.
Was it Treason's retribution—
Necessity the plea?
They will long remember Sherman
And his streaming columns free—
They will long remember Sherman
Marching to the sea.

[133] **The Frenzy in the Wake.**[n]

Sherman's advance through the Carolinas.

(February, 1865.)

SO strong to suffer, shall we be
Weak to contend, and break
The sinews of the Oppressor's knee
That grinds upon the neck?
O, the garments rolled in blood
Scorch in cities wrapped in flame,
And the African—the imp!
He gibbers, imputing shame.

Shall Time, avenging every woe,
To us that joy allot
Which Israel thrilled when Sisera's brow
Showed gaunt and showed the clot?
Curse on their foreheads, cheeks, and eyes—
The Northern faces—true
To the flag we hate, the flag whose stars
Like planets strike us through.

[134] From frozen Maine they come,
Far Minnesota too;
They come to a sun whose rays disown—
May it wither them as the dew!
The ghosts of our slain appeal:
"Vain shall our victories be?"
But back from its ebb the flood recoils—
Back in a whelming sea.

With burning woods our skies are brass,
  The pillars of dust are seen;
The live-long day their cavalry pass—
  No crossing the road between.
    We were sore deceived—an awful host!
      They move like a roaring wind.
    Have we gamed and lost? but even despair
      Shall never our hate rescind.

[135] **The Fall of Richmond.**

The tidings received in the Northern Metropolis.

(April, 1865.)

WHAT mean these peals from every tower,
   And crowds like seas that sway?
The cannon reply; they speak the heart
   Of the People impassioned, and say—
A city in flags for a city in flames,
   Richmond goes Babylon's way—
         Sing and pray.

O weary years and woeful wars,
   And armies in the grave;
But hearts unquelled at last deter
The helmed dilated Lucifer—
   Honor to Grant the brave,
Whose three stars now like Orion's rise
When wreck is on the wave—
         Bless his glaive.

[136] Well that the faith we firmly kept,
   And never our aim forswore
For the Terrors that trooped from each recess
When fainting we fought in the Wilderness,
   And Hell made loud hurrah;
But God is in Heaven, and Grant in the Town,
   And Right through might is Law—
         God's way adore.

The Surrender at Appomattox. [137]

(April, 1865.)

AS billows upon billows roll,
   On victory victory breaks;
Ere yet seven days from Richmond's fall
   And crowning triumph wakes
The loud joy-gun, whose thunders run
   By sea-shore, streams, and lakes.
         The hope and great event agree
         In the sword that Grant received from Lee.

The warring eagles fold the wing,
   But not in Cæsar's sway;
Not Rome o'ercome by Roman arms we sing,
   As on Pharsalia's day,
But Treason thrown, though a giant grown,
   And Freedom's larger play.
         All human tribes glad token see
         In the close of the wars of Grant and Lee.

[138] ## A Canticle:

Significant of the national exaltation of enthusiasm at the close of the War.

O THE precipice Titanic
Of the congregated Fall,
And the angle oceanic
Where the deepening thunders call—
And the Gorge so grim,
And the firmamental rim!
Multitudinously thronging
The waters all converge,
Then they sweep adown in sloping
Solidity of surge.

The Nation, in her impulse
Mysterious as the Tide,
In emotion like an ocean
Moves in power, not in pride;
And is deep in her devotion
As Humanity is wide.
[139] Thou Lord of hosts victorious,
The confluence Thou hast twined;
By a wondrous way and glorious
A passage Thou dost find—
A passage Thou dost find:
Hosanna to the Lord of hosts,
The hosts of human kind.

Stable in its baselessness
When calm is in the air,
The Iris half in tracelessness
Hovers faintly fair.
Fitfully assailing it

A wind from heaven blows,
Shivering and paling it
To blankness of the snows;
While, incessant in renewal,
The Arch rekindled grows,
Till again the gem and jewel
Whirl in blinding overthrows—
Till, prevailing and transcending,
Lo, the Glory perfect there,
And the contest finds an ending,
For repose is in the air.

But the foamy Deep unsounded,
And the dim and dizzy ledge,
And the booming roar rebounded,
And the gull that skims the edge!
The Giant of the Pool
Heaves his forehead white as wool—
Toward the Iris ever climbing
From the Cataracts that call—
Irremovable vast arras
Draping all the Wall.

The Generations pouring
From times of endless date,
In their going, in their flowing
Ever form the steadfast State;
And Humanity is growing
Toward the fullness of her fate.

Thou Lord of hosts victorious,
Fulfill the end designed;
By a wondrous way and glorious
A passage Thou dost find—
A passage Thou dost find:
Hosanna to the Lord of hosts,
The hosts of human kind.

[141] ## ***The Martyr.***

Indicative of the passion of the people
on the 15th of April, 1865.

GOOD Friday was the day
Of the prodigy and crime,
When they killed him in his pity,
When they killed him in his prime
Of clemency and calm—
When with yearning he was filled
To redeem the evil-willed,
And, though conqueror, be kind;
But they killed him in his kindness,
In their madness and their blindness,
And they killed him from behind.

There is sobbing of the strong,
And a pall upon the land;
But the People in their weeping
Bare the iron hand:
Beware the People weeping
When they bare the iron hand.

[142] He lieth in his blood—
The father in his face;
They have killed him, the Forgiver—
The Avenger takes his place,°
The Avenger wisely stern,
Who in righteousness shall do
What the heavens call him to,
And the parricides remand;
For they killed him in his kindness,
In their madness and their blindness,
And his blood is on their hand.

There is sobbing of the strong,
  And a pall upon the land;
But the People in their weeping
      Bare the iron hand:
Beware the People weeping
  When they bare the iron hand.

[143]

"The Coming Storm:"

A Picture by S. R. Gifford, and owned by E. B.
Included in the N. A. Exhibition, April, 1865.

ALL feeling hearts must feel for him
  Who felt this picture. Presage dim—
Dim inklings from the shadowy sphere
  Fixed him and fascinated here.

A demon-cloud like the mountain one
  Burst on a spirit as mild
As this urned lake, the home of shades.
  But Shakspeare's pensive child

Never the lines had lightly scanned,
  Steeped in fable, steeped in fate;
The Hamlet in his heart was 'ware,
  Such hearts can antedate.

No utter surprise can come to him
  Who reaches Shakspeare's core;
That which we seek and shun is there—
    Man's final lore.

Rebel Color-bearers at Shiloh:[p] [144]

A plea against the vindictive cry raised by civilians shortly after the surrender at Appomattox.

THE color-bearers facing death
White in the whirling sulphurous wreath,
  Stand boldly out before the line;
Right and left their glances go,
Proud of each other, glorying in their show;
Their battle-flags about them blow,
  And fold them as in flame divine:
Such living robes are only seen
Round martyrs burning on the green—
And martyrs for the Wrong have been.

Perish their Cause! but mark the men—
Mark the planted statues, then
Draw trigger on them if you can.

The leader of a patriot-band
Even so could view rebels who so could stand;
  And this when peril pressed him sore, [145]
Left aidless in the shivered front of war—
  Skulkers behind, defiant foes before,.
And fighting with a broken brand.
The challenge in that courage rare—
Courage defenseless, proudly bare—
Never could tempt him; he could dare
Strike up the leveled rifle there.

Sunday at Shiloh, and the day
When Stonewall charged—McClellan's crimson May,
And Chickamauga's wave of death,

And of the Wilderness the cypress wreath—
        All these have passed away.
The life in the veins of Treason lags,
Her daring color-bearers drop their flags,
    And yield. *Now* shall we fire?
        Can poor spite be?
    Shall nobleness in victory less aspire
    Than in reverse? Spare Spleen her ire,
        And think how Grant met Lee.

The Muster:[q] [146]

Suggested by the Two Days' Review at Washington.

(May, 1865.)

THE Abrahamic river—
  Patriarch of floods,
Calls the roll of all his streams
  And watery multitudes:
    Torrent cries to torrent,
      The rapids hail the fall;
    With shouts the inland freshets
      Gather to the call.

The quotas of the Nation,
  Like the water-shed of waves,
Muster into union—
  Eastern warriors, Western braves.

Martial strains are mingling, [147]
  Though distant far the bands,
And the wheeling of the squadrons
  Is like surf upon the sands.

The bladed guns are gleaming—
  Drift in lengthened trim,
Files on files for hazy miles—
    Nebulously dim.

O Milky Way of armies—
  Star rising after star,
New banners of the Commonwealths,
  And eagles of the War.

The Abrahamic river
    To sea-wide fullness fed,
Pouring from the thaw-lands
    By the God of floods is led:
                His deep enforcing current
                    The streams of ocean own,
                And Europe's marge is evened
                    By rills from Kansas lone.

Aurora-Borealis. [148]
Commemorative of the
Dissolution of Armies at the Peace.

(May, 1865.)

WHAT power disbands the Northern Lights
   After their steely play?
The lonely watcher feels an awe
   Of Nature's sway,
      As when appearing,
      He marked their flashed uprearing
In the cold gloom—
   Retreatings and advancings,
(Like dallyings of doom),
   Transitions and enhancings,
      And bloody ray.

The phantom-host has faded quite,
   Splendor and Terror gone—
Portent or promise—and gives way
   To pale, meek Dawn;
      The coming, going, [149]
      Alike in wonder showing—
Alike the God,
   Decreeing and commanding
The million blades that glowed,
   The muster and disbanding—
      Midnight and Morn.

[150] # *The Released Rebel Prisoner.*[r]

(June, 1865.)

ARMIES he's seen—the herds of war,
  But never such swarms of men
As now in the Nineveh of the North—
  How mad the Rebellion then!

And yet but dimly he divines
  The depth of that deceit,
And superstition of vast pride
  Humbled to such defeat.

Seductive shone the Chiefs in arms—
  His steel the nearest magnet drew;
Wreathed with its kind, the Gulf-weed drives—
  'Tis Nature's wrong they rue.

His face is hidden in his beard,
  But his heart peers out at eye—
[151] And such a heart! like a mountain-pool
  Where no man passes by.

He thinks of Hill—a brave soul gone;
  And Ashby dead in pale disdain;
And Stuart with the Rupert-plume,
  Whose blue eye never shall laugh again.

He hears the drum; he sees our boys
  From his wasted fields return;
Ladies feast them on strawberries,
  And even to kiss them yearn.

He marks them bronzed, in soldier-trim,
  The rifle proudly borne;
They bear it for an heir-loom home,
  And he—disarmed—jail-worn.

Home, home—his heart is full of it;
  But home he never shall see,
Even should he stand upon the spot:
  'Tis gone!—where his brothers be.

The cypress-moss from tree to tree [152]
  Hangs in his Southern land;
As weird, from thought to thought of his
  Run memories hand in hand.

And so he lingers—lingers on
  In the City of the Foe—
His cousins and his countrymen
  Who see him listless go.

[153] *A Grave near Petersburg, Virginia.*[s]

HEAD-BOARD and foot-board duly placed—
  Grassed is the mound between;
Daniel Drouth is the slumberer's name—
  Long may his grave be green!

Quick was his way—a flash and a blow,
  Full of his fire was he—
A fire of hell—'tis burnt out now—
  Green may his grave long be!

May his grave be green, though he
  Was a rebel of iron mould;
Many a true heart—true to the Cause,
  Through the blaze of his wrath lies cold.

May his grave be green—still green
  While happy years shall run;
May none come nigh to disinter
  The—*Buried Gun.*

"Formerly a Slave." [154]

An idealized Portrait, by E. Vedder, in the Spring Exhibition of the National Academy, 1865.

THE sufferance of her race is shown,
  And retrospect of life,
Which now too late deliverance dawns upon;
  Yet is she not at strife.

Her children's children they shall know
  The good withheld from her;
And so her reverie takes prophetic cheer—
  In spirit she sees the stir

Far down the depth of thousand years,
  And marks the revel shine;
Her dusky face is lit with sober light,
  Sibylline, yet benign.

[155] **The Apparition.**

(A Retrospect.)

CONVULSIONS came; and, where the field
  Long slept in pastoral green,
A goblin-mountain was upheaved
(Sure the scared sense was all deceived),
  Marl-glen and slag-ravine.

The unreserve of Ill was there,
  The clinkers in her last retreat;
But, ere the eye could take it in,
Or mind could comprehension win,
  It sunk!—and at our feet.

So, then, Solidity's a crust—
  The core of fire below;
All may go well for many a year,
But who can think without a fear
  Of horrors that happen so?

Magnanimity Baffled. [156]

"SHARP words we had before the fight;
    But—now the fight is done—
Look, here's my hand," said the Victor bold,
    "Take it—an honest one!
What, holding back? I mean you well;
  Though worsted, you strove stoutly, man;
The odds were great; I honor you;
      Man honors man.

"Still silent, friend? can grudges be?
    Yet am I held a foe?—
Turned to the wall, on his cot he lies—
    Never I'll leave him so!
Brave one! I here implore your hand;
  Dumb still? all fellowship fled?
Nay, then, I'll have this stubborn hand!"
  He snatched it—it was dead.

[157] **On the Slain Collegians.**[t]

YOUTH is the time when hearts are large,
And stirring wars
Appeal to the spirit which appeals in turn
To the blade it draws.
If woman incite, and duty show
(Though made the mask of Cain),
Or whether it be Truth's sacred cause,
Who can aloof remain
That shares youth's ardor, uncooled by the snow
Of wisdom or sordid gain?

The liberal arts and nurture sweet
Which give his gentleness to man—
Train him to honor, lend him grace
Through bright examples meet—
That culture which makes never wan
With underminings deep, but holds
The surface still, its fitting place,
And so gives sunniness to the face
[158] And bravery to the heart; what troops
Of generous boys in happiness thus bred—
Saturnians through life's Tempe led,
Went from the North and came from the South,
With golden mottoes in the mouth,
To lie down midway on a bloody bed.

Woe for the homes of the North,
And woe for the seats of the South;
All who felt life's spring in prime,
And were swept by the wind of their place and time—
All lavish hearts, on whichever side,
Of birth urbane or courage high,

Armed them for the stirring wars—
Armed them—some to die.
Apollo-like in pride,
Each would slay his Python—caught
The maxims in his temple taught—
Aflame with sympathies whose blaze
Perforce enwrapped him—social laws,
Friendship and kin, and by-gone days—
Vows, kisses—every heart unmoors,
And launches into the seas of wars.
What could they else—North or South?
Each went forth with blessings given
By priests and mothers in the name of Heaven; [159]
And honor in both was chief.
Warred one for Right, and one for Wrong?
So be it; but they both were young—
Each grape to his cluster clung,
All their elegies are sung.

The anguish of maternal hearts
Must search for balm divine;
But well the striplings bore their fated parts
(The heavens all parts assign)—
Never felt life's care or cloy.
Each bloomed and died an unabated Boy;
Nor dreamed what death was—thought it mere
Sliding into some vernal sphere.
They knew the joy, but leaped the grief,
Like plants that flower ere comes the leaf—
Which storms lay low in kindly doom,
And kill them in their flush of bloom.

[160] ## America.

I.

WHERE the wings of a sunny Dome expand
I saw a Banner in gladsome air—
Starry, like Berenice's Hair—
Afloat in broadened bravery there;
With undulating long-drawn flow,
As rolled Brazilian billows go
Voluminously o'er the Line.
The Land reposed in peace below;
  The children in their glee
Were folded to the exulting heart
  Of young Maternity.

II.

Later, and it streamed in fight
  When tempest mingled with the fray,
And over the spear-point of the shaft
  I saw the ambiguous lightning play.
Valor with Valor strove, and died:
Fierce was Despair, and cruel was Pride;
[161] And the lorn Mother speechless stood,
Pale at the fury of her brood.

III.

Yet later, and the silk did wind
    Her fair cold form;
Little availed the shining shroud,
  Though ruddy in hue, to cheer or warm.

A watcher looked upon her low, and said—
She sleeps, but sleeps, she is not dead.
But in that sleep contortion showed
The terror of the vision there—
A silent vision unavowed,
Revealing earth's foundation bare,
And Gorgon in her hidden place.
It was a thing of fear to see
So foul a dream upon so fair a face,
And the dreamer lying in that starry shroud.

IV.

But from the trance she sudden broke—
The trance, or death into promoted life;
At her feet a shivered yoke,
And in her aspect turned to heaven
No trace of passion or of strife—
A clear calm look. It spake of pain, [162]
But such as purifies from stain—
Sharp pangs that never come again—
And triumph repressed by knowledge meet,
Power dedicate, and hope grown wise,
And youth matured for age's seat—
Law on her brow and empire in her eyes.
So she, with graver air and lifted flag;
While the shadow, chased by light,
Fled along the far-drawn height,
And left her on the crag.

VERSES

INSCRIPTIVE AND MEMORIAL

On the Home Guards [165]

who perished in the Defense of Lexington, Missouri.

THE men who here in harness died
   Fell not in vain, though in defeat.
They by their end well fortified
   The Cause, and built retreat
(With memory of their valor tried)
For emulous hearts in many an after fray—
Hearts sore beset, which died at bay.

[166] Inscription

for Graves at Pea Ridge, Arkansas.

LET none misgive we died amiss
   When here we strove in furious fight:
Furious it was; nathless was this
   Better than tranquil plight,
And tame surrender of the Cause
Hallowed by hearts and by the laws.
   We here who warred for Man and Right,
The choice of warring never laid with us.
   There we were ruled by the traitor's choice.
   Nor long we stood to trim and poise,
But marched, and fell—victorious!

The Fortitude of the North [167]

Under the Disaster of the Second Manassas.

THEY take no shame for dark defeat
While prizing yet each victory won,
Who fight for the Right through all retreat,
Nor pause until their work is done.
The Cape-of-Storms is proof to every throe;
Vainly against that foreland beat
Wild winds aloft and wilder waves below:
The black cliffs gleam through rents in sleet
When the livid Antarctic storm-clouds glow.

[168]

On the Men of Maine

killed in the Victory of Baton Rouge, Louisiana.

AFAR they fell. It was the zone
   Of fig and orange, cane and lime
(A land how all unlike their own,
With the cold pine-grove overgrown),
   But still their Country's clime.
And there in youth they died for her—
            The Volunteers,
For her went up their dying prayers:
   So vast the Nation, yet so strong the tie.
What doubt shall come, then, to deter
   The Republic's earnest faith and courage high.

An Epitaph.

WHEN Sunday tidings from the front
  Made pale the priest and people,
And heavily the blessing went,
  And bells were dumb in the steeple;
The Soldier's widow (summering sweetly here,
  In shade by waving beeches lent)
  Felt deep at heart her faith content,
And priest and people borrowed of her cheer.

[170]

Inscription
for Marye's Heights, Fredericksburg.

TO them who crossed the flood
And climbed the hill, with eyes
   Upon the heavenly flag intent,
   And through the deathful tumult went
Even unto death: to them this Stone—
Erect, where they were overthrown—
   Of more than victory the monument.

The Mound by the Lake. [171]

THE grass shall never forget this grave.
When homeward footing it in the sun
  After the weary ride by rail,
The stripling soldiers passed her door,
  Wounded perchance, or wan and pale,
She left her household work undone—
Duly the wayside table spread,
  With evergreens shaded, to regale
Each travel-spent and grateful one.
So warm her heart—childless—unwed,
Who like a mother comforted.

On the Slain at Chickamauga.

HAPPY are they and charmed in life
   Who through long wars arrive unscarred
At peace. To such the wreath be given,
If they unfalteringly have striven—
   In honor, as in limb, unmarred.
Let cheerful praise be rife,
   And let them live their years at ease,
Musing on brothers who victorious died—
   Loved mates whose memory shall ever please.

And yet mischance is honorable too—
   Seeming defeat in conflict justified
Whose end to closing eyes is hid from view.
The will, that never can relent—
The aim, survivor of the bafflement,
         Make this memorial due.

An uninscribed Monument [173]
on one of the Battle-fields of the Wilderness.

SILENCE and Solitude may hint
(Whose home is in yon piny wood)
What I, though tableted, could never tell—
The din which here befell,
And striving of the multitude.
The iron cones and spheres of death
Set round me in their rust,
These, too, if just,
Shall speak with more than animated breath.
Thou who beholdest, if thy thought,
Not narrowed down to personal cheer,
Take in the import of the quiet here—
The after-quiet—the calm full fraught;
Thou too wilt silent stand—
Silent as I, and lonesome as the land.

[174] **On Sherman's Men**

Who fell in the Assault of Kenesaw Mountain, Georgia.

THEY said that Fame her clarion dropped
Because great deeds were done no more—
That even Duty knew no shining ends,
And Glory—'twas a fallen star!
But battle can heroes and bards restore.
Nay, look at Kenesaw:
Perils the mailed ones never knew
Are lightly braved by the ragged coats of blue,
And gentler hearts are bared to deadlier war.

On the Grave [175]

of a young Cavalry Officer killed in the Valley of Virginia.

BEAUTY and youth, with manners sweet, and friends—
    Gold, yet a mind not unenriched had he
Whom here low violets veil from eyes.
    But all these gifts transcended be:
His happier fortune in this mound you see.

[176]

A Requiem

for Soldiers lost in Ocean Transports.

WHEN, after storms that woodlands rue,
To valleys comes atoning dawn,
The robins blithe their orchard-sports renew;
And meadow-larks, no more withdrawn,
Caroling fly in the languid blue;
The while, from many a hid recess,
Alert to partake the blessedness,
The pouring mites their airy dance pursue.
So, after ocean's ghastly gales,
When laughing light of hoyden morning breaks,
Every finny hider wakes—
From vaults profound swims up with glittering scales;
Through the delightsome sea he sails,
With shoals of shining tiny things
Frolic on every wave that flings
Against the prow its showery spray;
All creatures joying in the morn,
Save them forever from joyance torn,
Whose bark was lost where now the dolphins play;
[177] Save them that by the fabled shore,
Down the pale stream are washed away,
Far to the reef of bones are borne;
And never revisits them the light,
Nor sight of long-sought land and pilot more;
Nor heed they now the lone bird's flight
Round the lone spar where mid-sea surges pour.

On a natural Monument [178]
in a field of Georgia.[u]

NO trophy this—a Stone unhewn,
And stands where here the field immures
The nameless brave whose palms are won.
Outcast they sleep; yet fame is nigh—
Pure fame of deeds, not doers;
Nor deeds of men who bleeding die
In cheer of hymns that round them float:
In happy dreams such close the eye.
But withering famine slowly wore,
And slowly fell disease did gloat.
Even Nature's self did aid deny;
They choked in horror the pensive sigh.
Yea, off from home sad Memory bore
(Though anguished Yearning heaved that way),
Lest wreck of reason might befall.
As men in gales shun the lee shore,
Though there the homestead be, and call,
And thitherward winds and waters sway—
As such lorn mariners, so fared they.
But naught shall now their peace molest. [179]
The fame is this: they did endure—
Endure, when fortitude was vain
To kindle any approving strain
Which they might hear. To these who rest,
This healing sleep alone was sure.

[180] *Commemorative of a Naval Victory.*

SAILORS there are of gentlest breed,
Yet strong, like every goodly thing;
The discipline of arms refines,
And the wave gives tempering.
The damasked blade its beam can fling;
It lends the last grave grace:
The hawk, the hound, and sworded nobleman
In Titian's picture for a king,
Are of hunter or warrior race.

In social halls a favored guest
In years that follow victory won,
How sweet to feel your festal fame
In woman's glance instinctive thrown:
Repose is yours—your deed is known,
It musks the amber wine;
It lives, and sheds a light from storied days
Rich as October sunsets brown,
Which make the barren place to shine.

[181] But seldom the laurel wreath is seen
Unmixed with pensive pansies dark;
There's a light and a shadow on every man
Who at last attains his lifted mark—
Nursing through night the ethereal spark.
Elate he never can be;
He feels that spirits which glad had hailed his worth,
Sleep in oblivion.—The shark
Glides white through the prosphorus sea.

Presentation to the Authorities, [182]
by Privates, of Colors captured in Battles ending in the Surrender of Lee.

THESE flags of armies overthrown—
Flags fallen beneath the sovereign one
In end foredoomed which closes war;
We here, the captors, lay before
   The altar which of right claims all—
Our Country. And as freely we,
   Revering ever her sacred call,
Could lay our lives down—though life be
Thrice loved and precious to the sense
Of such as reap the recompense
   Of life imperiled for just cause—
Imperiled, and yet preserved;
While comrades, whom Duty as strongly nerved,
Whose wives were all as dear, lie low.
But these flags given, glad we go
   To waiting homes with vindicated laws.

[183] *The Returned Volunteer to his Rifle.*

OVER this hearth—my father's seat—
  Repose, to patriot-memory dear,
Thou tried companion, whom at last I greet
  By steepy banks of Hudson here.
How oft I told thee of this scene—
The Highlands blue—the river's narrowing sheen.
Little at Gettysburg we thought
To find such haven; but God kept it green.
Long rest! with belt, and bayonet, and canteen.

[184, blank]

THE SCOUT TOWARD ALDIE. [185]

The Scout toward Aldie. [187]

THE cavalry-camp lies on the slope
  Of what was late a vernal hill,
But now like a pavement bare—
An outpost in the perilous wilds
  Which ever are lone and still;
    But Mosby's men are there—
    Of Mosby best beware.

Great trees the troopers felled, and leaned
  In antlered walls about their tents;
Strict watch they kept; 'twas *Hark!* and *Mark!*
Unarmed none cared to stir abroad
  For berries beyond their forest-fence:
    As glides in seas the shark,
    Rides Mosby through green dark.

All spake of him, but few had seen [188]
  Except the maimed ones or the low;
Yet rumor made him every thing—
A farmer—woodman—refugee—
  The man who crossed the field but now;
    A spell about his life did cling—
    Who to the ground shall Mosby bring?

The morning-bugles lonely play,
  Lonely the evening-bugle calls—
Unanswered voices in the wild;
The settled hush of birds in nest
  Becharms, and all the wood enthralls:
    Memory's self is so beguiled
    That Mosby seems a satyr's child.

They lived as in the Eerie Land—
The fire-flies showed with fairy gleam;
And yet from pine-tops one might ken
The Capitol dome—hazy—sublime—
A vision breaking on a dream:
So strange it was that Mosby's men
Should dare to prowl where the Dome was seen.

[189] A scout toward Aldie broke the spell.—
The Leader lies before his tent
Gazing at heaven's all-cheering lamp
Through blandness of a morning rare;
His thoughts on bitter-sweets are bent:
His sunny bride is in the camp—
But Mosby—graves are beds of damp!

The trumpet calls; he goes within;
But none the prayer and sob may know:
Her hero he, but bridegroom too.
Ah, love in a tent is a queenly thing,
And fame, be sure, refines the vow;
But fame fond wives have lived to rue,
And Mosby's men fell deeds can do.

Tan-tara! tan-tara! tan-tara!
Mounted and armed he sits a king;
For pride she smiles if now she peep—
Elate he rides at the head of his men;
He is young, and command is a boyish thing:
They file out into the forest deep—
Do Mosby and his rangers sleep?

[190] The sun is gold, and the world is green,
Opal the vapors of morning roll;
The champing horses lightly prance—
Full of caprice, and the riders too
Curving in many a caricole.

But marshaled soon, by fours advance—
Mosby had checked that airy dance.

By the hospital-tent the cripples stand—
Bandage, and crutch, and cane, and sling,
And palely eye the brave array;
The froth of the cup is gone for them
(Caw! caw! the crows through the blueness wing):
Yet these were late as bold, as gay;
But Mosby—a clip, and grass is hay.

How strong they feel on their horses free,
Tingles the tendoned thigh with life;
Their cavalry-jackets make boys of all—
With golden breasts like the oriole;
The chat, the jest, and laugh are rife.
But word is passed from the front—a call
For order; the wood is Mosby's hall.

To which behest one rider sly [191]
(Spurred, but unarmed) gave little heed—
Of dexterous fun not slow or spare,
He teased his neighbors of touchy mood,
Into plungings he pricked his steed:
A black-eyed man on a coal-black mare,
Alive as Mosby in mountain air.

His limbs were long, and large and round;
He whispered, winked—did all but shout:
A healthy man for the sick to view;
The taste in his mouth was sweet at morn;
Little of care he cared about.
And yet of pains and pangs he knew—
In others, maimed by Mosby's crew.

The Hospital Steward—even he
(Sacred in person as a priest),

And on his coat-sleeve broidered nice
Wore the caduceus, black and green.
No wonder he sat so light on his beast;
This cheery man in suit of price
Not even Mosby dared to slice.

[192] They pass the picket by the pine
And hollow log—a lonesome place;
His horse adroop, and pistol clean;
'Tis cocked—kept leveled toward the wood;
Strained vigilance ages his childish face.
Since midnight has that stripling been
Peering for Mosby through the green.

Splashing they cross the freshet-flood,
And up the muddy bank they strain;
A horse at the spectral white-ash shies—
One of the span of the ambulance,
Black as a hearse. They give the rein:
Silent speed on a scout were wise,
Could cunning baffle Mosby's spies.

Rumor had come that a band was lodged
In green retreats of hills that peer
By Aldie (famed for the swordless charge[v]).
Much store they'd heaped of captured arms
And, peradventure, pilfered cheer;
For Mosby's lads oft hearts enlarge
In revelry by some gorge's marge.

[193] "Don't let your sabres rattle and ring;
To his oat-bag let each man give heed—
There now, that fellow's bag's untied,
Sowing the road with the precious grain.
Your carbines swing at hand—you need!
Look to yourselves, and your nags beside,
Men who after Mosby ride."

Picked lads and keen went sharp before—
A guard, though scarce against surprise;
And rearmost rode an answering troop,
But flankers none to right or left.
No bugle peals, no pennon flies:
Silent they sweep, and fain would swoop
On Mosby with an Indian whoop.

On, right on through the forest land,
Nor man, nor maid, nor child was seen—
Not even a dog. The air was still;
The blackened hut they turned to see,
And spied charred benches on the green;
A squirrel sprang from the rotting mill
Whence Mosby sallied late, brave blood to spill.

By worn-out fields they cantered on— [194]
Drear fields amid the woodlands wide;
By cross-roads of some olden time,
In which grew groves; by gate-stones down—
Grassed ruins of secluded pride:
A strange lone land, long past the prime,
Fit land for Mosby or for crime.

The brook in the dell they pass. One peers
Between the leaves: "Ay, there's the place—
There, on the oozy ledge—'twas there
We found the body (Blake's you know);
Such whirlings, gurglings round the face—
Shot drinking! Well, in war all's fair—
So Mosby says. The bough—take care!"

Hard by, a chapel. Flower-pot mould
Danked and decayed the shaded roof;
The porch was punk; the clapboards spanned
With ruffled lichens gray or green;
Red coral-moss was not aloof;

And mid dry leaves green dead-man's-hand
Groped toward that chapel in Mosby-land.

[195] They leave the road and take the wood,
And mark the trace of ridges there—
A wood where once had slept the farm—
A wood where once tobacco grew
Drowsily in the hazy air,
And wrought in all kind things a calm—
Such influence, Mosby! bids disarm.

To ease even yet the place did woo—
To ease which pines unstirring share,
For ease the weary horses sighed:
Halting, and slackening girths, they feed,
Their pipes they light, they loiter there;
Then up, and urging still the Guide,
On, and after Mosby ride.

This Guide in frowzy coat of brown,
And beard of ancient growth and mould,
Bestrode a bony steed and strong,
As suited well with bulk he bore—
A wheezy man with depth of hold
Who jouncing went. A staff he swung—
A wight whom Mosby's wasp had stung.

[196] Burnt out and homeless—hunted long!
That wheeze he caught in autumn-wood
Crouching (a fat man) for his life,
And spied his lean son 'mong the crew
That probed the covert. Ah! black blood
Was his 'gainst even child and wife—
Fast friends to Mosby. Such the strife.

A lad, unhorsed by sliding girths,
Strains hard to readjust his seat

Ere the main body show the gap
'Twixt them and the rear-guard; scrub-oaks near
He sidelong eyes, while hands move fleet;
Then mounts and spurs. One drops his cap—
"Let Mosby find!" nor heeds mishap.

A gable time-stained peeps through trees:
"You mind the fight in the haunted house?
That's it; we clenched them in the room—
An ambuscade of ghosts, we thought,
But proved sly rebels on a bouse!
Luke lies in the yard." The chimneys loom:
Some muse on Mosby—some on doom.

Less nimbly now through brakes they wind, [197]
And ford wild creeks where men have drowned;
They skirt the pool, avoid the fen,
And so till night, when down they lie,
They steeds still saddled, in wooded ground:
Rein in hand they slumber then,
Dreaming of Mosby's cedarn den.

But Colonel and Major friendly sat
Where boughs deformed low made a seat.
The Young Man talked (all sworded and spurred)
Of the partisan's blade he longed to win,
And frays in which he meant to beat.
The grizzled Major smoked, and heard:
"But what's that—Mosby?" "No, a bird."

A contrast here like sire and son,
Hope and Experience sage did meet;
The Youth was brave, the Senior too;
But through the Seven Days one had served,
And gasped with the rear-guard in retreat:
So he smoked and smoked, and the wreath he blew—
"Any *sure* news of Mosby's crew?"

He smoked and smoked, eying the while [198]
A huge tree hydra-like in growth—
Moon-tinged—with crook'd boughs rent or lopped—
Itself a haggard forest. "Come!"
The Colonel cried, "to talk you're loath;
D'ye hear? I say he must be stopped,
This Mosby—caged, and hair close cropped."

"Of course; but what's that dangling there?"
"Where?" "From the tree—that gallows-bough;"
"A bit of frayed bark, is it not?"
"Ay—or a rope; did *we* hang last?—
Don't like my neckerchief any how;"
He loosened it: "O ay, we'll stop
This Mosby—but that vile jerk and drop!"[w]

By peep of light they feed and ride,
Gaining a grove's green edge at morn,
And mark the Aldie hills uprear
And five gigantic horsemen carved
Clear-cut against the sky withdrawn;
Are more behind? an open snare?
Or Mosby's men but watchmen there?

[199] The ravaged land was miles behind,
And Loudon spread her landscape rare;
Orchards in pleasant lowlands stood,
Cows were feeding, a cock loud crew,
But not a friend at need was there;
The valley-folk were only good
To Mosby and his wandering brood.

What best to do? what mean yon men?
Colonel and Guide their minds compare;
Be sure some looked their Leader through;
Dismounted, on his sword he leaned
As one who feigns an easy air;

And yet perplexed he was they knew—
Perplexed by Mosby's mountain-crew.

The Major hemmed as he would speak,
But checked himself, and left the ring
Of cavalrymen about their Chief—
Young courtiers mute who paid their court
By looking with confidence on their king;
They knew him brave, foresaw no grief—
But Mosby—the time to think is brief.

The Surgeon (sashed in sacred green) [200]
Was glad 'twas not for *him* to say
What next should be; if a trooper bleeds,
Why he will do his best, as wont,
And his partner in black will aid and pray;
But judgment bides with him who leads,
And Mosby many a problem breeds.

The Surgeon was the kindliest man
That ever a callous trade professed;
He felt for him, that Leader young,
And offered medicine from his flask:
The Colonel took it with marvelous zest.
For such fine medicine good and strong,
Oft Mosby and his foresters long.

A charm of proof. "Ho, Major, come—
Pounce on yon men! Take half your troop,
Through the thickets wind—pray speedy be—
And gain their rear. And, Captain Morn,
Picket these roads—all travelers stop;
The rest to the edge of this crest with me,
That Mosby and his scouts may see."

Commanded and done. Ere the sun stood steep, [201]
Back came the Blues, with a troop of Grays,

Ten riding double—luckless ten!—
Five horses gone, and looped hats lost,
And love-locks dancing in a maze—
Certes, but sophomores from the glen
Of Mosby—not his veteran men.

"Colonel," said the Major, touching his cap,
"We've had our ride, and here they are."
"Well done! how many found you there?"
"As many as I bring you here."
"And no one hurt?" "There'll be no scar—
One fool was battered." "Find their lair?"
"Why, Mosby's brood camp every where."

He sighed, and slid down from his horse,
And limping went to a spring-head nigh.
"Why, bless me, Major, not hurt, I hope?"
"Battered my knee against a bar
When the rush was made; all right by-and-by.—
Halloa! they gave you too much rope—
Go back to Mosby, eh? elope?"

[202] Just by the low-hanging skirt of wood
The guard, remiss, had given a chance
For a sudden sally into the cover—
But foiled the intent, nor fired a shot,
Though the issue was a deadly trance;
For, hurled 'gainst an oak that humped low over,
Mosby's man fell, pale as a lover.

They pulled some grass his head to ease
(Lined with blue shreds a ground-nest stirred).
The Surgeon came—"Here's a to-do!"
"Ah!" cried the Major, darting a glance,
"This fellow's the one that fired and spurred
Down hill, but met reserves below—
My boys, not Mosby's—so we go!"

The Surgeon—bluff, red, goodly man—
Kneeled by the hurt one; like a bee
He toiled. The pale young Chaplain too—
(Who went to the wars for cure of souls,
And his own student-ailments)—he
Bent over likewise; spite the two,
Mosby's poor man more pallid grew.

Meanwhile the mounted captives near [203]
Jested; and yet they anxious showed;
Virginians; some of family-pride,
And young, and full of fire, and fine
In open feature and cheek that glowed;
And here thralled vagabonds now they ride—
But list! one speaks for Mosby's side.

"Why, three to one—your horses strong—
Revolvers, rifles, and a surprise—
Surrender we account no shame!
We live, are gay, and life is hope;
We'll fight again when fight is wise.
There are plenty more from where we came;
But go find Mosby—start the game!"

Yet one there was who looked but glum;
In middle-age, a father he,
And this his first experience too:
"They shot at my heart when my hands were up—
This fighting's crazy work, I see!"
But noon is high; what next to do?
The woods are mute, and Mosby is the foe.

"Save what we've got," the Major said; [204]
"Bad plan to make a scout too long;
The tide may turn, and drag them back,
And more beside. These rides I've been,
And every time a mine was sprung.

To rescue, mind, they won't be slack—
Look out for Mosby's rifle-crack."

"We'll welcome it! give crack for crack!
Peril, old lad, is what I seek."
"O then, there's plenty to be had—
By all means on, and have our fill!"
With that, grotesque, he writhed his neck,
Showing a scar by buck-shot made—
Kind Mosby's Christmas gift, he said.

"But, Colonel, my prisoners—let a guard
Make sure of them, and lead to camp.
That done, we're free for a dark-room fight
If so you say." The other laughed;
"Trust me, Major, nor throw a damp.
But first to try a little sleight—
Sure news of Mosby would suit me quite."

[205] Herewith he turned—"Reb, have a dram?"
Holding the Surgeon's flask with a smile
To a young scapegrace from the glen.
"O yes!" he eagerly replied,
"And thank you, Colonel, but—any guile?
For if you think we'll blab—why, then
You don't know Mosby or his men."

The Leader's genial air relaxed.
"Best give it up," a whisperer said.
"By heaven, I'll range their rebel den!"
"They'll treat you well," the captive cried;
"They're all like us—handsome—well bred:
In wood or town, with sword or pen,
Polite is Mosby, bland his men."

"Where were you, lads, last night?—come, tell!"
"We?—at a wedding in the Vale—

The bridegroom our comrade; by his side
Belisent, my cousin—O, so proud
Of her young love with old wounds pale—
A Virginian girl! God bless her pride—
Of a crippled Mosby-man the bride!"

"Four wall shall mend that saucy mood, [206]
And moping prisons tame him down,"
Said Captain Cloud. "God help that day,"
Cried Captain Morn, "and he so young.
But hark, he sings—a madcap one!"
"O we multiply merrily in the May,
The birds and Mosby's men, they say!"

While echoes ran, a wagon old,
Under stout guard of Corporal Chew
Came up; a lame horse, dingy white,
With clouted harness; ropes in hand,
Cringed the humped driver, black in hue;
By him (for Mosby's band a sight)
A sister-rebel sat, her veil held tight.

"I picked them up," the Corporal said,
"Crunching their way over stick and root,
Through yonder wood. The man here—Cuff—
Says they are going to Leesburg town."
The Colonel's eye took in the group;
The veiled one's hand he spied—enough!
Not Mosby's. Spite the gown's poor stuff,

Off went his hat: "Lady, fear not; [207]
We soldiers do what we deplore—
I must detain you till we march,"
The stranger nodded. Nettled now,
He grew politer than before:—
"'Tis Mosby's fault, this halt and search:"
The lady stiffened in her starch.

"My duty, madam, bids me now
Ask what may seem a little rude.
Pardon—that veil—withdraw it, please
(Corporal! make every man fall back);
Pray, now, I do but what I should;
Bethink you, 'tis in masks like these
That Mosby haunts the villages."

Slowly the stranger drew her veil,
And looked the Soldier in the eye—
A glance of mingled foul and fair;
Sad patience in a proud disdain,
And more than quietude. A sigh
She heaved, as if all unaware,
And far seemed Mosby from her care.

[208] She came from Yewton Place, her home,
So ravaged by the war's wild play—
Campings, and foragings, and fires—
That now she sought an aunt's abode.
Her kinsmen? In Lee's army, they.
The black? A servant, late her sire's.
And Mosby? Vainly he inquires.

He gazed, and sad she met his eye;
"In the wood yonder were you lost?"
No; at the forks they left the road
Because of hoof-prints (thick they were—
Thick as the words in notes thrice crossed),
And fearful, made that episode.
In fear of Mosby? None she showed.

Her poor attire again he scanned:
"Lady, once more; I grieve to jar
On all sweet usage, but must plead
To have what peeps there from your dress;
That letter—'tis justly prize of war."

She started—gave it—she must need.
"'Tis not from Mosby? May I read?"

And straight such matter he perused [209]
That with the Guide he went apart.
The Hospital Steward's turn began:
"Must squeeze this darkey; every tap
Of knowledge we are bound to start."
"Garry," she said, "tell all you can
Of Colonel Mosby—that brave man."

"Dun know much, sare; and missis here
Know less dan me. But dis I know—"
"Well, what?" "I dun know what I know."
"A knowing answer!" The hump-back coughed,
Rubbing his yellowish wool like tow.
"Come—Mosby—tell!" "O dun look so!
My gal nursed missis—let we go."

"Go where?" demanded Captain Cloud;
"Back into bondage? Man, you're free!"
"Well, *let* we free!" The Captain's brow
Lowered; the Colonel came—had heard:
"Pooh! pooh! his simple heart I see—
A faithful servant.—Lady" (a bow),
"Mosby's abroad—with us you'll go.

"Guard! look to your prisoners; back to camp! [210]
The man in the grass—can he mount and away?
Why, how he groans!" "Bad inward bruise—
Might lug him along in the ambulance."
"Coals to Newcastle! let him stay.
Boots and saddles!—our pains we lose,
Nor care I if Mosby hear the news!"

But word was sent to a house at hand,
And a flask was left by the hurt one's side.

They seized in that same house a man,
Neutral by day, by night a foe—
So charged his neighbor late, the Guide.
A grudge? Hate will do what it can;
Along he went for a Mosby-man.

No secrets now; the bugle calls;
The open road they take, nor shun
The hill; retrace the weary way.
But one there was who whispered low,
"This is a feint—we'll back anon;
Young Hair-Brains don't retreat, they say;
A brush with Mosby is the play!"

[211] They rode till eve. Then on a farm
That lay along a hill-side green,
Bivouacked. Fires were made, and then
Coffee was boiled; a cow was coaxed
And killed, and savory roasts were seen;
And under the lee of a cattle-pen
The guard supped freely with Mosby's men.

The ball was bandied to and fro;
Hits were given and hits were met:
"Chickamauga, Feds—take off your hat!"
"But the Fight in the Clouds repaid you, Rebs!"
"Forgotten about Manassas yet?"
Chatting and chaffing, and tit for tat,
Mosby's clan with the troopers sat.

"Here comes the moon!" a captive cried;
"A song! what say? Archy, my lad!"
Hailing the still one of the clan
(A boyish face with girlish hair),
"Give us that thing poor Pansy made
Last year." He brightened, and began;
And this was the song of Mosby's man:

Spring is come; she shows her pass— [212]
Wild violets cool!
South of woods a small close grass—
A vernal wool!
Leaves are a'bud on the sassafras—
They'll soon be full:
Blessings on the friendly screen—
I'm for the South! says the leafage green.

Robins! fly, and take your fill
Of out-of-doors—
Garden, orchard, meadow, hill,
Barns and bowers;
Take your fill, and have your will—
Virginia's yours!
But, bluebirds! keep away, and fear
The ambuscade in bushes here.

"A green song that," a seargeant said;
"But where's poor Pansy? gone, I fear."
"Ay, mustered out at Ashby's Gap."
"I see; now for a live man's song;
Ditty for ditty—prepare to cheer.
My bluebirds, you can fling a cap!
You barehead Mosby-boys—why—clap!"

Nine Blue-coats went a-nutting [213]
Slyly in Tennessee—
Not for chestnuts—better than that—
Hush, you bumble-bee!
Nutting, nutting—
All through the year there's nutting!

A tree they spied so yellow,
Rustling in motion queer;
In they fired, and down they dropped—
Butternuts, my dear!

Nutting, nutting—
Who'll 'list to go a-nutting?

Ah! why should good fellows foemen be?
And who would dream that foes they were—
Larking and singing so friendly then—
A family likeness in every face.
But Captain Cloud made sour demur:
"Guard! keep your prisoners *in* the pen,
And let none talk with Mosby's men."

[214] That captain was a valorous one
(No irony, but honest truth),
Yet down from his brain cold drops distilled,
Making stalactites in his heart—
A conscientious soul, forsooth;
And with a formal hate was filled
Of Mosby's band; and some he'd killed.

Meantime the lady rueful sat,
Watching the flicker of a fire
Where the Colonel played the outdoor host
In brave old hall of ancient Night.
But ever the dame grew shyer and shyer,
Seeming with private grief engrossed—
Grief far from Mosby, housed or lost.

The ruddy embers showed her pale.
The Soldier did his best devoir:
"Some coffee?—no?—a cracker?—one?"
Cared for her servant—sought to cheer:
"I know, I know—a cruel war!
But wait—even Mosby'll eat his bun;
The Old Hearth—back to it anon!"

[215] But cordial words no balm could bring;
She sighed, and kept her inward chafe,

And seemed to hate the voice of glee—
Joyless and tearless. Soon he called
An escort: "See this lady safe
In yonder house.—Madam, you're free.
And now for Mosby.—Guide! with me."

("A night-ride, eh?") "Tighten your girths!
But, buglers! not a note from you.
Fling more rails on the fires—a blaze!"
("Sergeant, a feint—I told you so—
Toward Aldie again. Bivouac, adieu!")
After the cheery flames they gaze,
Then back for Mosby through the maze.

The moon looked through the trees, and tipped
The scabbards with her elfin beam;
The Leader backward cast his glance,
Proud of the cavalcade that came—
A hundred horses, bay and cream:
"Major! look how the lads advance—
Mosby we'll have in the ambulance!"

"No doubt, no doubt:—was that a hare?— [216]
First catch, then cook; and cook him brown."
"Trust me to catch," the other cried—
"The lady's letter!—a dance, man, dance
This night is given in Leesburg town!"
"He'll be there too!" wheezed out the Guide;
"That Mosby loves a dance and ride!"

"The lady, ah!—the lady's letter—
A *lady*, then, is in the case,"
Muttered the Major. "Ay, her aunt
Writes her to come by Friday eve
(To-night), for people of the place,
At Mosby's last fight jubilant,
A party give, though table-cheer be scant."

The Major hemmed. "Then this night-ride
 We owe to her?—One lighted house
In a town else dark.—The moths, begar!
Are not quite yet all dead!" "How? how?"
 "A mute, meek, mournful little mouse!—
  Mosby has wiles which subtle are—
  But woman's wiles in wiles of war!"

[217] "Tut, Major! by what craft or guile—"
 "Can't tell! but he'll be found in wait.
Softly we enter, say, the town—
Good! pickets post, and all so sure—
 When—crack! the rifles from every gate,
  The Gray-backs fire—dash up and down—
  Each alley unto Mosby known!"

"Now, Major, now—you take dark views
 Of a moonlight night." "Well, well, we'll see,"
And smoked as if each whiff were gain.
The other mused; then sudden asked,
 "What would you do in grand decree?"
  "I'd beat, if I could, Lee's armies—then
  Send constables after Mosby's men."

"Ay! ay!—you're odd." The moon sailed up;
 On through the shadowy land they went.
"Names must be made and printed be!"
Hummed the blithe Colonel. "Doc, your flask!
 Major, I drink to your good content.
  My pipe is out—enough for me!
  One's buttons shine—does Mosby see?

[218] "But what comes here?" A man from the front
 Reported a tree athwart the road.
"Go round it, then; no time to bide;
All right—go on! Were one to stay
 For each distrust of a nervous mood,

Long miles we'd make in this our ride
Through Mosby-land.—On! with the Guide!"

Then sportful to the Surgeon turned:
"Green sashes hardly serve by night!"
"Nor bullets nor bottles," the Major sighed,
"Against these moccasin-snakes—such foes
As seldom come to solid fight:
They kill and vanish; through grass they glide;
Devil take Mosby!"—his horse here shied.

"Hold! look—the tree, like a dragged balloon;
A globe of leaves—some trickery here;
My nag is right—best now be shy."
A movement was made, a hubbub and snarl;
Little was plain—they blindly steer.
The Pleiads, as from ambush sly,
Peep out—Mosby's men in the sky!

As restive they turn, how sore they feel, [219]
And cross, and sleepy, and full of spleen,
And curse the war. "Fools, North and South!"
Said one right out. "O for a bed!
O now to drop in this woodland green!"
He drops as the syllables leave his mouth—
Mosby speaks from the undergrowth—

Speaks in a volley! out jets the flame!
Men fall from their saddles like plums from trees;
Horses take fright, reins tangle and bind;
"Steady—dismount—form—and into the wood!"
They go, but find what scarce can please:
Their steeds have been tied in the field behind,
And Mosby's men are off like the wind.

Sound the recall! vain to pursue—
The enemy scatters in wilds he knows,

To reunite in his own good time;
And, to follow, they need divide—
To come lone and lost on crouching foes:
Maple and hemlock, beech and lime,
Are Mosby's confederates, share the crime.

[220] "Major," burst in a bugler small,
"The fellow we left in Loudon grass—
Sir Slyboots with the inward bruise,
His voice I heard—the very same—
Some watchword in the ambush pass;
Ay, sir, we had him in his shoes—
We caught him—Mosby—but to lose!"

"Go, go!—these saddle-dreamers! Well,
And here's another.—Cool, sir, cool!"
"Major, I saw them mount and sweep,
And one was humped, or I mistake,
And in the skurry dropped his wool."
"A wig! go fetch it:—the lads need sleep;
They'll next see Mosby in a sheep!

"Come, come, fall back! reform your ranks—
All's jackstraws here! Where's Captain Morn?—
We've parted like boats in a raging tide!
But stay—the Colonel—did he charge?
And comes he there? 'Tis streak of dawn;
Mosby is off, the woods are wide—
Hist! there's a groan—this crazy ride!"

[221] As they searched for the fallen, the dawn grew chill;
They lay in the dew: "Ah! hurt much, Mink?
And—yes—the Colonel!" Dead! but so calm
That death seemed nothing—even death,
The thing we deem every thing heart can think;
Amid wilding roses that shed their balm,
Careless of Mosby he lay—in a charm!

The Major took him by the hand—
Into the friendly clasp it bled
(A ball through heart and hand he rued):
"Good-by" and gazed with humid glance;
Then in a hollow revery said
"The weakest thing is lustihood;
But Mosby"—and he checked his mood.

"Where's the advance?—cut off, by heaven!
Come, Surgeon, how with your wounded there?"
"The ambulance will carry all."
"Well, get them in; we go to camp.
Seven prisoners gone? for the rest have care."
Then to himself, "This grief is gall;
That Mosby!—I'll cast a silver ball!"

"Ho!" turning—"Captain Cloud, you mind [222]
The place where the escort went—so shady?
Go search every closet low and high,
And barn, and bin, and hidden bower—
Every covert—find that lady!
And yet I may misjudge her—ay,
Women (like Mosby) mystify.

"We'll see. Ay, Captain, go—with speed!
Surround and search; each living thing
Secure; that done, await us where
We last turned off. Stay! fire the cage
If the birds be flown." By the cross-road spring
The bands rejoined; no words; the glare
Told all. Had Mosby plotted there?

The weary troop that wended now—
Hardly it seemed the same that pricked
Forth to the forest from the camp:
Foot-sore horses, jaded men;
Every backbone felt as nicked,

Each eye dim as a sick-room lamp,
All faces stamped with Mosby's stamp.

[223] In order due the Major rode—
Chaplain and Surgeon on either hand;
A riderless horse a negro led;
In a wagon the blanketed sleeper went;
Then the ambulance with the bleeding band;
And, an emptied oat-bag on each head,
Went Mosby's men, and marked the dead.

What gloomed them? what so cast them down,
And changed the cheer that late they took,
As double-guarded now they rode
Between the files of moody men?
Some sudden consciousness they brook,
Or dread the sequel. That night's blood
Disturbed even Mosby's brotherhood.

The flagging horses stumbled at roots,
Floundered in mires, or clinked the stones;
No rider spake except aside;
But the wounded cramped in the ambulance,
It was horror to hear their groans—
Jerked along in the woodland ride,
While Mosby's clan their revery hide.

[224] The Hospital Steward—even he—
Who on the sleeper kept his glance,
Was changed; late bright-black beard and eye
Looked now hearse-black; his heavy heart,
Like his fagged mare, no more could dance;
His grape was now a raisin dry:
'Tis Mosby's homily—*Man must die.*

The amber sunset flushed the camp
As on the hill their eyes they fed;

The pickets dumb looks at the wagon dart;
A handkerchief waves from the bannered tent—
As white, alas! the face of the dead:
Who shall the withering news impart?
The bullet of Mosby goes through heart to heart!

They buried him where the lone ones lie
(Lone sentries shot on midnight post)—
A green-wood grave-yard hid from ken,
Where sweet-fern flings an odor nigh—
Yet held in fear for the gleaming ghost!
Though the bride should see threescore and ten,
She will dream of Mosby and his men.

Now halt the verse, and turn aside— [225]
The cypress falls athwart the way;
No joy remains for bard to sing;
And heaviest dole of all is this,
That other hearts shall be as gay
As hers that now no more shall spring:
To Mosby-land the dirges cling.

LEE IN THE CAPITOL. [227]

Lee in the Capitol.[x] [229]

(April, 1866.)

HARD pressed by numbers in his strait,
Rebellion's soldier-chief no more contends—
Feels that the hour is come of Fate,
Lays down one sword, and widened warfare ends.
The captain who fierce armies led
Becomes a quiet seminary's head—
Poor as his privates, earns his bread.
In studious cares and aims engrossed,
Strives to forget Stuart and Stonewall dead—
Comrades and cause, station and riches lost,
And all the ills that flock when fortune's fled.
No word he breathes of vain lament,
Mute to reproach, nor hears applause—
His doom accepts, perforce content,
And acquiesces in asserted laws;
Secluded now would pass his life,
And leave to time the sequel of the strife.
But missives from the Senators ran; [230]
Not that they now would gaze upon a swordless foe,
And power made powerless and brought low:
Reasons of state, 'tis claimed, require the man.
Demurring not, promptly he comes
By ways which show the blackened homes,
And—last—the seat no more his own,
But Honor's; patriot grave-yards fill
The forfeit slopes of that patrician hill,
And fling a shroud on Arlington.
The oaks ancestral all are low;
No more from the porch his glance shall go
Ranging the varied landscape o'er,

Far as the looming Dome—no more.
One look he gives, then turns aside,
Solace he summons from his pride:
"So be it! They await me now
Who wrought this stinging overthrow;
They wait me; not as on the day
Of Pope's impelled retreat in disarray—
By me impelled—when toward yon Dome
The clouds of war came rolling home."
The burst, the bitterness was spent,
The heart-burst bitterly turbulent,
And on he fared.

[231] In nearness now
He marks the Capitol—a show
Lifted in amplitude, and set
With standards flushed with a glow of Richmond yet;
Trees and green terraces sleep below.
Through the clear air, in sunny light,
The marble dazes—a temple white.

Intrepid soldier! had his blade been drawn
For yon starred flag, never as now
Bid to the Senate-house had he gone,
But freely, and in pageant borne,
As when brave numbers without number, massed,
Plumed the broad way, and pouring passed—
Bannered, beflowered—between the shores
Of faces, and the dinn'd huzzas,
And balconies kindling at the sabre-flash,
'Mid roar of drums and guns, and cymbal-crash,
While Grant and Sherman shone in blue—
Close of the war and victory's long review.

Yet pride at hand still aidful swelled,
And up the hard ascent he held.
The meeting follows. In his mien

The victor and the vanquished both are seen—
All that he is, and what he late had been.
Awhile, with curious eyes they scan [232]
The Chief who led invasion's van—
Allied by family to one,
Founder of the Arch the Invader warred upon:
Who looks at Lee must think of Washington;
In pain must think, and hide the thought,
So deep with grievous meaning it is fraught.

Secession in her soldier shows
Silent and patient; and they feel
(Developed even in just success)
Dim inklings of a hazy future steal;
Their thoughts their questions well express:
"Does the sad South still cherish hate?
Freely will Southern men with Northern mate?
The blacks—should we our arm withdraw,
Would that betray them? some distrust your law.
And how if foreign fleets should come—
Would the South then drive her wedges home?"
And more hereof. The Virginian sees—
Replies to such anxieties.
Discreet his answers run—appear
Briefly straightforward, coldly clear.

"If now," the Senators, closing, say,
"Aught else remain, speak out, we pray."
Hereat he paused; his better heart [233]
Strove strongly then; prompted a worthier part
Than coldly to endure his doom.
Speak out? Ay, speak, and for the brave,
Who else no voice or proxy have;
Frankly their spokesman here become,
And the flushed North from her own victory save.
That inspiration overrode—
Hardly it quelled the galling load

Of personal ill. The inner feud
He, self-contained, a while withstood;
They waiting. In his troubled eye
Shadows from clouds unseen they spy;
They could not mark within his breast
The pang which pleading thought oppressed:
He spoke, nor felt the bitterness die.

"My word is given—it ties my sword;
Even were banners still abroad,
Never could I strive in arms again
While you, as fit, that pledge retain.
Our cause I followed, stood in field and gate—
All's over now, and now I follow Fate.
But this is naught. A People call—
A desolated land, and all
[234] The brood of ills that press so sore,
The natural offspring of this civil war,
Which ending not in fame, such as might rear
Fitly its sculptured trophy here,
Yields harvest large of doubt and dread
To all who have the heart and head
To feel and know. How shall I speak?
Thoughts knot with thoughts, and utterance check.
Before my eyes there swims a haze,
Through mists departed comrades gaze—
First to encourage, last that shall upbraid!
How shall I speak? The South would fain
Feel peace, have quiet law again—
Replant the trees for homestead-shade.
    You ask if she recants: she yields.
Nay, and would more; would blend anew,
As the bones of the slain in her forests do,
Bewailed alike by us and you.
    A voice comes out from these charnel-fields,
A plaintive yet unheeded one:
'Died all in vain? both sides undone?'

Push not your triumph; do not urge
Submissiveness beyond the verge.
Intestine rancor would you bide,
Nursing eleven sliding daggers in your side?
Far from my thought to school or threat; [235]
I speak the things which hard beset.
Where various hazards meet the eyes,
To elect in magnanimity is wise.
Reap victory's fruit while sound the core;
What sounder fruit than re-established law?
I know your partial thoughts do press
Solely on us for war's unhappy stress;
But weigh—consider—look at all,
And broad anathema you'll recall.
The censor's charge I'll not repeat,
The meddlers kindled the war's white heat—
Vain intermeddlers and malign,
Both of the palm and of the pine;
I waive the thought—which never can be rife—
Common's the crime in every civil strife:
But this I feel, that North and South were driven
By Fate to arms. For *our* unshriven,
What thousands, truest souls, were tried—
  As never may any be again—
All those who stemmed Secession's pride,
But at last were swept by the urgent tide
  Into the chasm. I know their pain.
A story here may be applied:
'In Moorish lands there lived a maid
  Brought to confess by vow the creed
  Of Christians. Fain would priests persuade [236]
That now she must approve by deed
  The faith she kept. "What deed?" she asked.
"Your old sire leave, nor deem it sin,
  And come with us." Still more they tasked
The sad one: "If heaven you'd win—
  Far from the burning pit withdraw,

Then must you learn to hate your kin,
Yea, side against them—such the law,
For Moor and Christian are at war."
"Then will I never quit my sire,
But here with him through every trial go,
Nor leave him though in flames below—
God help me in his fire!" '
So in the South; vain every plea
'Gainst Nature's strong fidelity;
True to the home and to the heart,
Throngs cast their lot with kith and kin,
Foreboding, cleaved to the natural part—
Was this the unforgivable sin?
These noble spirits are yet yours to win.
Shall the great North go Sylla's way?
Proscribe? prolong the evil day?
Confirm the curse? infix the hate?
In Union's name forever alienate?
From reason who can urge the plea— [237]
Freemen conquerors of the free?
When blood returns to the shrunken vein,
Shall the wound of the Nation bleed again?
Well may the wars wan thought supply,
And kill the kindling of the hopeful eye,
Unless you do what even kings have done
In leniency—unless you shun
To copy Europe in her worst estate—
Avoid the tyranny you reprobate."

He ceased. His earnestness unforeseen
Moved, but not swayed their former mien;
And they dismissed him. Forth he went
Through vaulted walks in lengthened line
Like porches erst upon the Palatine:
Historic reveries their lesson lent,
The Past her shadow through the Future sent.

But no. Brave though the Soldier, grave his plea—
    Catching the light in the future's skies,
Instinct disowns each darkening prophecy:
    Faith in America never dies;
Heaven shall the end ordained fulfill,
We march with Providence cheery still.

A *MEDITATION:* [239]

ATTRIBUTED TO A NORTHERNER AFTER ATTENDING THE LAST OF TWO FUNERALS FROM THE SAME HOMESTEAD— THOSE OF A NATIONAL AND A CONFEDERATE OFFICER (BROTHERS), HIS KINSMEN, WHO HAD DIED FROM THE EFFECTS OF WOUNDS RECEIVED IN THE CLOSING BATTLES.

A Meditation. [241]

How often in the years that close,
When truce had stilled the sieging gun,
The soldiers, mounting on their works,
With mutual curious glance have run
From face to face along the fronting show,
And kinsman spied, or friend—even in a foe.

What thoughts conflicting then were shared,
While sacred tenderness perforce
Welled from the heart and wet the eye;
And something of a strange remorse
Rebelled against the sanctioned sin of blood,
And Christian wars of natural brotherhood.

Then stirred the god within the breast—
The witness that is man's at birth;
A deep misgiving undermined
Each plea and subterfuge of earth;
They felt in that rapt pause, with warning rife,
Horror and anguish for the civil strife.

Of North or South they recked not then, [242]
Warm passion cursed the cause of war:
Can Africa pay back this blood
Spilt on Potomac's shore?
Yet doubts, as pangs, were vain the strife to stay,
And hands that fain had clasped again could slay.

How frequent in the camp was seen
The herald from the hostile one,
A guest and frank companion there
When the proud formal talk was done;
The pipe of peace was smoked even 'mid the war,
And fields in Mexico again fought o'er.

In Western battle long they lay
    So near opposed in trench or pit,
That foeman unto foeman called
As men who screened in tavern sit:
"You bravely fight" each to the other said—
"Toss us a biscuit!" o'er the wall it sped.

And pale on those same slopes, a boy—
    A stormer, bled in noon-day glare;
No aid the Blue-coats then could bring,
    He cried to them who nearest were,
And out there came 'mid howling shot and shell
A daring foe who him befriended well.

[243] Mark the great Captains on both sides,
    The soldiers with the broad renown—
They all were messmates on the Hudson's marge,
    Beneath one roof they laid them down;
And, free from hate in many an after pass,
Strove as in school-boy rivalry of the class.

A darker side there is; but doubt
    In Nature's charity hovers there:
If men for new agreement yearn,
    Then old upbraiding best forbear:
"*The South's the sinner!*" Well, so let it be;
But shall the North sin worse, and stand the Pharisee?

O, now that brave men yield the sword,
    Mine be the manful soldier-view;
By how much more they boldly warred,
    By so much more is mercy due:
When Vicksburg fell, and the moody files marched out,
Silent the victors stood, scorning to raise a shout.

[244 blank]

NOTES

NOTES.

NOTE [a], *page* 14.

The gloomy lull of the early part of the winter of 1860–1, seeming big with final disaster to our institutions, affected some minds that believed them to constitute one of the great hopes of mankind, much as the eclipse which came over the promise of the first French Revolution affected kindred natures, throwing them for the time into doubt and misgivings universal.

NOTE [b], *page* 31.

"The terrible Stone Fleet, on a mission as pitiless as the granite that freights it, sailed this morning from Port Royal, and before two days are past will have made Charleston an inland city. The ships are all old whalers, and cost the government from $2500 to $5000 each. Some of them were once famous ships." —(From Newspaper Correspondence of the day.)

Sixteen vessels were accordingly sunk on the bar at the river entrance. Their names were as follows:

Amazon,	Leonidas,
America,	Maria Theresa,
American,	Potomac,
Archer,	Rebecca Simms,
Courier,	L. C. Richmond,
Fortune,	Robin Hood,
Herald,	Tenedos,
Kensington,	William Lee.

All accounts seem to agree that the object proposed was not accomplished. The channel is even said to have become ultimately benefited by the means employed to obstruct it.

[248] NOTE [c], *page* 58.

The *Temeraire*, that storied ship of the old English fleet, and the subject of the well-known painting by Turner, commends itself to the mind seeking for some one craft to stand for the poetic ideal of those great historic wooden warships, whose gradual displacement is lamented by none more than by regularly educated navy officers, and of all nations.

NOTE [d], *page* 59.

Some of the cannon of old times, especially the brass ones, unlike the more effective ordnance of the present day, were cast in shapes which Cellini might have designed, were gracefully enchased, generally with the arms of the country. A few of them—field-pieces—captured in our earlier wars, are preserved in arsenals and navy-yards.

NOTE [e], *page* 69.

Whatever just military criticism, favorable or otherwise, has at any time been made upon General McClellan's campaigns, will stand. But if, during the excitement of the conflict, aught was spread abroad tending to unmerited disparagement of the man, it must necessarily die out, though not perhaps without leaving some traces, which may or may not prove enduring. Some there are whose votes aided in the re-election of Abraham Lincoln, who yet believed, and retain the belief, that General McClellan, to say the least, always proved himself a patriotic and honorable soldier. The feeling which surviving comrades entertain for their late commander is one which, from its passion, is susceptible of versified representation, and such it receives.

NOTE [f], *page* 71.

At Antietam Stonewall Jackson led one wing of Lee's army, consequently sharing that day in whatever may be deemed to have been the fortunes of his superior.

NOTE [g], *page* 78. [249]

Admiral Porter is a son of the late Commodore Porter, commander of the frigate Essex on that Pacific cruise which ended in the desparate fight off Valparaiso with the English frigates Cherub and Phœbe, in the year 1814.

NOTE [h], *page* 85.

Among numerous head-stones or monuments on Cemetery Hill, marred or destroyed by the enemy's concentrated fire, was one, somewhat conspicuous, of a Federal officer killed before Richmond in 1862.

On the 4th of July, 1865, the Gettysburg National Cemetery, on the same height with the original burial-ground, was consecrated, and the corner-stone laid of a commemorative pile.

NOTE [i], *page* 86.

"I dare not write the horrible and inconceivable atrocities committed," says Froissart, in alluding to the remarkable sedition in France during his time. The like may be hinted of some proceedings of the draft-rioters.

NOTE [j], *page* 90.

Although the month was November, the day was in character an October one—cool, clear, bright, intoxicatingly invigorating; one of those days peculiar to the ripest hours of our American autumn. This weather must have had much to do with the spontaneous enthusiasm which seized the troops—an enthusiasm aided, doubtless, by glad thoughts of the victory of Look-out Mountain won the day previous, and also by the elation attending the capture, after a fierce struggle, of the long ranges of rifle-pits at the mountain's base, where orders for the time should have stopped the advance. But there and then it was that the army took the bit between its teeth, and ran away with the generals to the victory commemorated. General Grant, at Culpepper, a few weeks prior to crossing the Rapidan for the Wilderness, expressed to a visitor his impression of the impulse and the spectacle: Said he, "I never saw any thing like it:" [250] language which seems curiously undertoned, considering its application; but from the taciturn Commander it was equivalent to a superlative or hyperbole from the talkative.

The height of the Ridge, according to the account at hand, varies along its length from six to seven hundred feet above the plain; it slopes at an angle of about forty-five degrees.

NOTE [k], *page* 107.

The great Parrott gun, planted in the marshes of James Island, and employed in the prolonged, though at times intermitted bombardment of Charleston, was known among our soldiers as the Swamp Angel.

St. Michael's, characterized by its venerable tower, was the historic and aristocratic church of the town.

NOTE [l], *page* 122.

Among the Northwestern regiments there would seem to have been more than one which carried a living eagle as an added ensign. The bird commemorated here was, according to the account, borne aloft on a perch beside the standard; went through successive battles and campaigns; was more than once under the surgeon's hands; and at the close of the contest found honorable repose in the capital of Wisconsin, from which state he had gone to the wars.

NOTE [m], *page* 124.

The late Major General McPherson, commanding the Army of the Tennessee, a native of Ohio and a West Pointer, was one of the foremost spirits of the war. Young, though a veteran; hardy, intrepid, sensitive in honor, full of engaging qualities, with manly beauty; possessed of genius, a favorite with the army, and with Grant and Sherman. Both Generals have generously acknowledged their professional obligations to the able engineer and admirable soldier, their subordinate and junior.

In an informal account written by the Achilles to this Sarpedon, he says: [251] "On that day we avenged his death. Near twenty-two hundred of the enemy's dead remained on the ground when night closed upon the scene of action."

It is significant of the scale on which the war was waged, that the engagement thus written of goes solely (so far as can be learned) under the vague designation of one of the battles before Atlanta.

NOTE [n], *page* 133.

This piece was written while yet the reports were coming North of Sherman's homeward advance from Savannah. It is needless to point out its purely dramatic character.

Though the sentiment ascribed in the beginning of the second stanza must, in the present reading, suggest the historic tragedy of the 14th of April, nevertheless, as intimated, it was written prior to that event, and without any distinct application in the writer's mind. After consideration, it is allowed to remain.

Few need be reminded that, by the less intelligent classes of the South, Abraham Lincoln, by nature the most kindly of men, was regarded as a monster wantonly warring upon liberty. He stood for the personification of tyrannic power. Each Union soldier was called a Lincolnite.

Undoubtedly Sherman, in the desolation he inflicted after leaving Atlanta, acted not in contravention of orders; and all, in a military point of view, is by military judges deemed to have been expedient, and nothing can abate General Sherman's shining renown; his claims to it rest on no single campaign. Still, there are those who can not but contrast some of the scenes enacted in Georgia and the Carolinas, and also in the Shenandoah, with a circumstance in a great Civil War of heathen antiquity. Plutarch relates that in a military council held by Pompey and the chiefs of that party which stood for the Commonwealth, it was decided that under no plea should any city be sacked that was subject to the people of Rome. There was this difference, however, between the Roman civil conflict and the American one. The war of Pompey and Cæsar divided the Roman people promiscuously; that of the North and South ran a frontier line between what for the time were distinct communities or nations. In this circumstance, possibly, and some others, may be found both the cause and the justification of some of the sweeping measures adopted.

[252] NOTE [o], *page* 142.

At this period of excitement the thought was by some passionately welcomed that the Presidential successor had been raised up by heaven to wreak vengeance on the South. The idea originated in the remembrance that Andrew Johnson by birth belonged to that class of Southern whites who never cherished love for the dominant one: that he was a citizen of Tennessee, where the contest at times and in places had been close and bitter as a Middle-Age feud; that himself and family had been hardly treated by the Secessionists.

But the expectations built hereon (if, indeed, ever soberly entertained), happily for the country, have not been verified.

Likely the feeling which would have held the entire South chargeable with the crime of one exceptional assassin, this too has died away with the natural excitement of the hour.

NOTE [p], *page* 144.

The incident on which this piece is based is narrated in a newspaper account of the battle to be found in the "Rebellion Record." During the disaster to the national forces on the first day, a brigade on the extreme left found itself isolated. The perils it encountered are given in detail. Among others, the following sentences occur:

"Under cover of the fire from the bluffs, the rebels rushed down, crossed the ford, and in a moment were seen forming this side the creek in open fields, and within close musket-range. Their color-bearers stepped defiantly to the front as the engagement opened furiously; the rebels pouring in sharp, quick volleys of musketry, and their batteries above continuing to support them with a destructive fire. Our sharpshooters wanted to pick off the audacious rebel color-bearers, but Colonel Stuart interposed: 'No, no, they're too brave fellows to be killed.' "

NOTE [q], *page* 146.

According to a report of the Secretary of War, there were on the first day of March, 1865, 965,000 men on the army pay-rolls. Of these, some 200,000—[253] artillery, cavalry, and infantry—made up from the larger portion of the veterans of Grant and Sherman, marched by the President. The total number of Union troops enlisted during the war was 2,668,000.

NOTE [r], *page* 150.

For a month or two after the completion of peace, some thousands of released captives from the military prisons of the North, natives of all parts of the South, passed through the city of New York, sometimes waiting farther transportation for days, during which interval they wandered penniless about the streets, or lay in their worn and patched gray uniforms under the trees of the Battery, near the barracks where they were lodged and fed. They were transported and provided for at the charge of government.

NOTE [s], *page* 153.

Shortly prior to the evacuation of Petersburg, the enemy, with a view to ultimate repossession, interred some of his heavy guns in the same field with his dead, and with every circumstance calculated to deceive. Subsequently the negroes exposed the stratagem.

NOTE [t], *page* 157.

The records of Northern colleges attest what numbers of our noblest youth went from them to the battle-field. Southern members of the same classes arrayed themselves on the side of Secession; while Southern seminaries contributed large quotas. Of all these, what numbers marched who never returned except on the shield.

NOTE [u], *page* 178.

Written prior to the founding of the National Cemetery at Andersonville, where 15,000 of the reinterred captives now sleep, each beneath his personal head-board, inscribed from records found in the prison-hospital. Some hundreds rest apart and without name. A glance at the published pamphlet containing [254] the list of the buried at Andersonville conveys a feeling mournfully impressive. Seventy-four large double-columned pages in fine print. Looking through them is like getting lost among the old turbaned head-stones and cypresses in the interminable Black Forest of Scutari, over against Constantinople.

NOTE [v], *page* 192.

In one of Kilpatrick's earlier cavalry fights near Aldie, a Colonel who, being under arrest, had been temporarily deprived of his sword, nevertheless, unarmed, insisted upon charging at the head of his men, which he did, and the onset proved victorious.

NOTE [w], *page* 198.

Certain of Mosby's followers, on the charge of being unlicensed foragers or fighters, being hung by order of a Union cavalry commander, the Partisan promptly retaliated in the woods. In turn, this also was retaliated, it is said. To what extent such deplorable proceedings were carried, it is not easy to learn.

South of the Potomac in Virginia, and within a gallop of the Long Bridge at Washington, is the confine of a country, in some places wild, which throughout the war it was unsafe for a Union man to traverse except with an armed escort. This was the chase of Mosby, the scene of many of his exploits or those of his men. In the heart of this region at least one fortified camp was maintained by our cavalry, and from time to time expeditions were made therefrom. Owing to the nature of the country and the embittered feeling of its inhabitants, many of these expeditions ended disastrously. Such results were helped by the exceeding cunning of the enemy, born of his wood-craft, and, in some instances, by undue confidence on the part of our men. A body of cavalry, starting from camp with the view of breaking up a nest of rangers, and absent say three days, would return with a number of their own forces killed and wounded (ambushed), without being able to retaliate farther than by foraging on the country, destroying a house or two reported to be haunts of the guerrillas, or capturing non-combatants accused of being secretly active in their behalf.

[255] In the verse the name of Mosby is invested with some of those associations with which the popular mind is familiar. But facts do not warrant the belief that every clandestine attack of men who passed for Mosby's was made under his eye, or even by his knowledge.

In partisan warfare he proved himself shrewd, able, and enterprising, and always a wary fighter. He stood well in the confidence of his superior officers, and was employed by them at times in furtherance of important movements. To our wounded on more than one occasion he showed considerate kindness. Officers and civilians captured by forces under his immediate command were, so long as remaining under his orders, treated with civility. These things are well known to those personally familiar with the irregular fighting in Virginia.

NOTE [x], *page* 229.

Among those summoned during the spring just passed to appear before the Reconstruction Committee of Congress was Robert E. Lee. His testimony is deeply interesting, both in itself and as coming from him. After various questions had been put and briefly answered, these words were addressed to him:

"If there be any other matter about which you wish to speak on this occasion, do so freely." Waiving this invitation, he responded by a short personal explanation of some point in a previous answer, and, after a few more brief questions and replies, the interview closed.

In the verse a poetical liberty has been ventured. Lee is not only represented as responding to the invitation, but also as at last renouncing his cold reserve, doubtless the cloak to feelings more or less poignant. If for such freedom warrant be necessary, the speeches in ancient histories, not to speak of those in Shakespeare's historic plays, may not unfitly perhaps be cited.

The character of the original measures proposed about time in the National Legislature for the treatment of the (as yet) Congressionally excluded South, and the spirit in which those measures were advocated—these are circumstances which it is fairly supposable would have deeply influenced the thoughts, whether spoken or withheld, of a Southerner placed in the position of Lee before the Reconstruction Committee.

SUPPLEMENT.

[259]

WERE I fastidiously anxious for the symmetry of this book, it would close with the notes. But the times are such that patriotism—not free from solicitude—urges a claim overriding all literary scruples.

It is more than a year since the memorable surrender, but events have not yet rounded themselves into completion. Not justly can we complain of this. There has been an upheaval affecting the basis of things; to altered circumstances complicated adaptations are to be made; there are difficulties great and novel. But is Reason still waiting for Passion to spend itself? We have sung of the soldiers and sailors, but who shall hymn the politicians?

In view of the infinite desirableness of Re-establishment, and considering that, so far as feeling is concerned, it depends not mainly on the temper in which the South regards the North, but rather conversely; one who never was a blind adherent feels constrained to submit some thoughts, counting on the indulgence of his countrymen.

And, first, it may be said that, if among the feelings and opinions growing immediately out of a great civil [260] convulsion, there are any which time shall modify or do away, they are presumably those of a less temperate and charitable cast.

There seems no reason why patriotism and narrowness should go together, or why intellectual impartiality should be confounded with political trimming, or why serviceable truth should keep cloistered because not partisan. Yet the work of Reconstruction, if admitted to be feasible at all, demands little but common sense and Christian charity. Little but these? These are much.

Some of us are concerned because as yet the South shows no penitence. But what exactly do we mean by this? Since down to the close of the war she never confessed any for braving it, the only penitence now left her is that which springs solely from the sense of discomfiture; and since this evidently would be a contrition hypocritical, it would be unworthy in us to demand it. Certain it is that penitence, in the sense of voluntary humiliation, will never be displayed. Nor does this afford just ground for unreserved condemnation. It is enough, for all practical purposes, if the South have been taught by the terrors of civil war to feel that Secession, like Slavery, is against Destiny; that both now lie buried in one grave; that her fate is linked with ours; and that together we comprise the Nation.

The clouds of heroes who battled for the Union it is [261] needless to eulogize here. But how of the soldiers on the other side? And when of a free community we name the soldiers, we thereby name the people. It was in subserviency to the slave-interest that Secession was plotted; but it was under the plea, plausibly urged, that certain inestimable rights guaranteed by the Constitution were directly menaced, that the people of the South were cajoled into revolution. Through the arts of the conspirators and the perversity of fortune, the most sensitive love of liberty was entrapped into the support of a war whose implied end was the erecting in our advanced century of an Anglo-American empire based upon the systematic degradation of man.

Spite this clinging reproach, however, signal military virtues and achievements have conferred upon the Confederate arms historic fame, and upon certain of the commanders a renown extending beyond the sea—a renown which we of the North could not suppress, even if we would. In personal character, also, not a few of the military leaders of the South enforce forbearance; the memory of others the North refrains from disparaging; and some, with more or less of reluctance, she can respect. Posterity, sympathizing with our convictions, but removed from our passions, may perhaps go farther here. If George IV. could, out of the graceful instinct of a gentleman, raise an honorable monument in [262] the great fane of Christendom over the remains of the enemy of his dynasty, Charles Edward, the invader of England and victor in the rout at Preston Pans—upon whose head the king's ancestor but one reign removed has set a price—is it probable that the grandchildren of General Grant will pursue with rancor, or slur by sour neglect, the memory of Stonewall Jackson?

But the South herself is not wanting in recent histories and biographies which record the deeds of her chieftains—writings freely published at the North by loyal houses, widely read here, and with a deep though saddened interest. By students of the war such works are hailed as welcome accessories, and tending to the completeness of the record.

Supposing a happy issue out of present perplexities, then, in the generation next to come, Southerners there will be yielding allegiance to the Union, feeling all their interests bound up in it, and yet cherishing unrebuked that kind of feeling for the memory of the soldiers of the fallen Confederacy that Burns, Scott, and the Ettrick Shepherd felt for the memory of the gallant clansmen ruined through their fidelity to the Stuarts—a feeling whose passion was tempered by the poetry imbuing it, and which in no wise affected their loyalty to the Georges, and which, it may be added, indirectly contributed excellent things to literature. But, setting [263] this view aside, dishonorable would it be in the South were she willing to abandon to shame the memory of brave men who with signal personal disinterestedness warred in her behalf, though from motives, as we believe, so deplorably astray.

Patriotism is not baseness, neither is it inhumanity. The mourners who this summer bear flowers to the mounds of the Virginian and Georgian dead are, in their domestic bereavement and proud affection, as sacred in the eye of Heaven as are those who go with similar offerings of tender grief and love into the cemeteries of our Northern martyrs. And yet, in one aspect, how needless to point the contrast.

Cherishing such sentiments, it will hardly occasion surprise that, in looking over the battle-pieces in the foregoing collection, I have been tempted to withdraw or modify some of them, fearful lest in presenting, though but dramatically and by way of a poetic record, the passions and epithets of civil war, I might be contributing to a bitterness which every sensible American must wish at an end. So, too, with the emotion of victory as reproduced on some pages, and particularly toward the close. It should not be construed into an exultation misapplied—an exultation as ungenerous as unwise, and made to minister, however indirectly, to that kind of censoriousness too apt to be produced in certain natures [264] by success after trying reverses. Zeal is not of necessity religion, neither is it always of the same essence with poetry or patriotism.

There were excesses which marked the conflict, most of which are perhaps inseparable from a civil strife so intense and prolonged, and involving warfare in some border countries new and imperfectly civilized. Barbarities also there were, for which the Southern people collectively can hardly be held responsible, though perpetrated by ruffians in their name. But surely other qualities—exalted ones—courage and fortitude matchless, were likewise displayed, and largely; and justly may these be held the characteristic traits, and not the former.

In this view, what Northern writer, however patriotic, but must revolt from acting on paper a part any way akin to that of the live dog to the dead lion; and yet it is right to rejoice for our triumph, so far as it may justly imply an advance for our whole country and for humanity.

Let it be held no reproach to any one that he pleads for reasonable consideration for our late enemies, now stricken down and unavoidably debarred, for the time, from speaking through authorized agencies for themselves. Nothing has been urged here in the foolish hope of conciliating those men—few in number, we trust—who have resolved never to be reconciled to the [265] Union. On such hearts every thing is thrown away except it be religious commiseration, and the sincerest. Yet let them call to mind that unhappy Secessionist, not a military man, who with impious alacrity fired the first shot of the Civil War at Sumter, and a little more than four years afterward fired the last one into his own heart at Richmond.

Noble was the gesture into which patriotic passion surprised the people in a utilitarian time and country; yet the glory of the war falls short of its pathos—a pathos which now at last ought to disarm all animosity.

How many and earnest thoughts still rise, and how hard to repress them. We feel what past years have been, and years, unretarded years, shall come. May we all have moderation; may we all show candor. Though, perhaps, nothing could ultimately have averted the strife, and though to treat of human actions is to deal wholly with second causes, nevertheless, let us not cover up or try to extenuate what, humanly speaking, is the truth—namely, that those unfraternal denunciations, continued through years, and which at last inflamed to deeds that ended in bloodshed, were reciprocal; and that, had the preponderating strength and the prospect of its unlimited increase lain on the other side, on ours might have lain those actions which now in our late opponents we stigmatize under the name of Rebellion. As frankly [266] let us own—what it would be unbecoming to parade were foreigners concerned—that our triumph was won not more by skill and bravery than by superior resources and crushing numbers; that it was a triumph, too, over a people for years politically misled by designing men, and also by some honestly-erring men, who from their position could not have been otherwise than broadly influential; a people who, though, indeed, they sought to perpetuate the curse of slavery, and even extend it, were not the authors of it, but (less fortunate, not less righteous than we) were the fated inheritors; a people who, having a like origin with ourselves, share essentially in whatever worthy qualities we may possess. No one can add to the lasting reproach which hopeless defeat has now cast upon Secession by withholding the recognition of these verities.

Surely we ought to take it to heart that that kind of pacification, based upon principles operating equally all over the land, which lovers of their country yearn for, and which our arms, though signally triumphant, did not bring about, and which law-making, however anxious, or energetic, or repressive, never by itself can achieve, may yet be largely aided by generosity of sentiment public and private. Some revisionary legislation and adaptive is indispensable; but with this should harmoniously work another kind of prudence, not unallied [267] with entire magnanimity. Benevolence and policy—Christianity and Machiavelli—dissuade from penal severities toward the subdued. Abstinence here is as obligatory as considerate care for our unfortunate fellow-men late in bonds, and, if observed, would equally prove to be wise forecast. The great qualities of the South, those attested in the War, we can perilously alienate, or we may make them nationally available at need.

The blacks, in their infant pupilage to freedom, appeal to the sympathies of every humane mind. The paternal guardianship which for the interval government exercises over them was prompted equally by duty and benevolence. Yet such kindliness should not be allowed to exclude kindliness to communities who stand nearer to us in nature. For the future of the freed slaves we may well be concerned; but the future of the whole country, involving the future of the blacks, urges a paramount claim upon our anxiety. Effective benignity, like the Nile, is not narrow in its bounty, and true policy is always broad. To be sure, it is vain to seek to glide, with moulded words, over the difficulties of the situation. And for them who are neither partisans, nor enthusiasts, nor theorists, nor cynics, there are some doubts not readily to be solved. And there are fears. Why is not the cessation of war now at length attended with the settled calm of peace? [268] Wherefore in a clear sky do we still turn our eyes toward the South, as the Neapolitan, months after the eruption, turns his toward Vesuvius? Do we dread lest the repose may be deceptive? In the recent convulsion has the crater but shifted? Let us revere that sacred uncertainty which forever impends over men and nations. Those of us who always abhorred slavery as an atheistical iniquity, gladly we join in the exulting chorus of humanity over its downfall. But we should remember that emancipation was accomplished not by deliberate legislation; only through agonized violence could so mighty a result be effected. In our natural solicitude to confirm the benefit of liberty to the blacks, let us forbear from measures of dubious constitutional rightfulness toward our white countrymen—measures of a nature to provoke, among other of the last evils, exterminating hatred of race toward race. In imagination let us place ourselves in the unprecedented position of the Southerners—their position as regards the millions of ignorant manumitted slaves in their midst, for whom some of us now claim the suffrage. Let us be Christians toward our fellow-whites, as well as philanthropists toward the blacks, our fellow-men. In all things, and toward all, we are enjoined to do as we would be done by. Nor should we forget that benevolent desires, after passing a certain point, can not un[269]dertake their own fulfillment without incurring the risk of evils beyond those sought to be remedied. Something may well be left to the graduated care of future legislation, and to heaven. In one point of view the co-existence of the two races in the South—whether the negro be bond or free—seems (even as it did to Abraham Lincoln) a grave evil. Emancipation has ridded the country of the reproach, but not wholly of the calamity. Especially in the present transition period for both races in the South, more or less of trouble may not unreasonably be anticipated; but let us not hereafter be too swift to charge the blame exclusively in any one quarter. With certain evils men must be more or less patient. Our institutions have a potent digestion, and may in time convert and assimilate to good all elements thrown in, however originally alien.

But, so far as immediate measures looking toward permanent Re-establishment are concerned, no consideration should tempt us to pervert the national victory into oppression for the vanquished. Should plausible promise of eventual good, or a deceptive or spurious sense of duty, lead us to essay this, count we must on serious consequences, not the least of which would be divisions among the Northern adherents of the Union. Assuredly, if any honest Catos there be who thus far have gone with us, no longer will they do so, but oppose us, and [270] as resolutely as hitherto they have supported. But this path of thought leads toward those waters of bitterness from which one can only turn aside and be silent.

But supposing Re-establishment so far advanced that the Southern seats in Congress are occupied, and by men qualified in accordance with those cardinal principles of representative government which hitherto have prevailed in the land—what then? Why the Congressman elected by the people of the South will—represent the people of the South. This may seem a flat conclusion; but, in view of the last five years, may there not be latent significance in it? What will be the temper of those Southern members? and, confronted by them, what will be the mood of our own representatives? In private life true reconciliation seldom follows a violent quarrel; but, if subsequent intercourse be unavoidable, nice observances and mutual are indispensable to the prevention of a new rupture. Amity itelf can only be maintained by reciprocal respect, and true friends are punctilious equals. On the floor of Congress North and South, are to come together after a passionate duel, in which the South, though proving her valor, has been made to bite the dust. Upon differences in debate shall acrimonious recriminations be exchanged? shall censorious superiority assumed by one section provoke defiant self-assertion on the other? shall [271] Manassas and Chickamauga be retorted for Chattanooga and Richmond? Under the supposition that the full Congress will be composed of gentlemen, all this is impossible. Yet, if otherwise, it needs no prophet of Israel to foretell the end. The maintenance of Congressional decency in the future will rest mainly with the North. Rightly will more forbearance be required from the North than the South, for the North is victor.

But some there are who may deem these latter thoughts inapplicable, and for this reason: Since the test-oath operatively excludes from Congress all who in any way participated in Secession, therefore none but Southerners wholly in harmony with the North are eligible to seats. This is true for the time being. But the oath is alterable; and in the wonted fluctuations of parties not improbably it will undergo alteration, assuming such a form, perhaps, as not to bar the admission into the National Legislature of men who represent the populations lately in revolt. Such a result would involve no violation of the principles of democratic government. Not readily can one perceive how the political existence of the millions of late Secessionists can permanently be ignored by this Republic. The years of the war tried our devotion to the Union; the time of peace may test the sincerity of our faith in democracy.

In no spirit of opposition, not by way of challenge, [272] is any thing here thrown out. These thoughts are sincere ones; they seem natural—inevitable. Here and there they must have suggested themselves to many thoughtful patriots. And, if they be just thoughts, ere long they must have that weight with the public which already they have had with individuals.

For that heroic band—those children of the furnace who, in regions like Texas and Tennessee, maintained their fidelity through terrible trials—we of the North felt for them, and profoundly we honor them. Yet passionate sympathy, with resentments so close as to be almost domestic in their bitterness, would hardly in the present juncture tend to discreet legislation. Were the Unionists and Secessionists but as Guelphs and Ghibellines? If not, then far be it from a great nation now to act in the spirit that animated a triumphant town-faction in the Middle Ages. But crowding thoughts must at last be checked; and, in times like the present, one who desires to be impartially just in the expression of his views, moves as among sword-points presented on every side.

Let us pray that the terrible historic tragedy of our time may not have been enacted without instructing our whole beloved country through terror and pity; and may fulfillment verify in the end those expectations which kindle the bards of Progress and Humanity.

THE END

Interpretive Essays

Melville and the Lyric of History

Helen Vendler

To literary history, Herman Melville (1819–1891) is above all the author of *Moby-Dick* and other novels. His arresting and wholly original poetry, written between 1850 and 1890, is visibly a product of the same mind that produced the greatest American novel, but it remains unknown to most readers. The chief monuments of that poetry are the volumes *Battle-Pieces and Aspects of the War* (1866) and *Clarel* (privately published in 1876, but begun much earlier, after Melville's 1856 tour of the Holy Land). The central event behind both books is the American Civil War.

To understand what the carnage of the Civil War meant to Melville—a definitive break with the ethical promise of the United States—one must know something of his life preceding it. He was born into a family of New York state that had long been connected to American history: his ancestors had been in America since the seventeenth century, and both his grandfathers fought in the Revolution. His grandfather on his mother's side, General Peter Gansevoort, defended Fort Stanwix in the Revolutionary

From the *Southern Review* 35, no. 3 (summer 1999): 579–94. Reprinted with permission of the author and publisher.

War, and was tendered official thanks by Congress for his actions. Many of Melville's relatives were involved in the Civil War, some as civilians, some as politicians, some as soldiers: his cousin Henry Gansevoort, to whom he was close, served as a militiaman, as a regular army officer, and as a volunteer in Virginia. Yet for the United States to become disunited, for brother to kill brother, for the Constitution to be impugned—this was to Melville a destruction of all that his family had fought to accomplish.

Melville's formal education ended at fifteen, when his father declared bankruptcy. That the learned, philosophical, and considered poetry of Melville's maturity was produced by a writer with no university education is astonishing. The poet made up for his lack of formal training by two means: his wide and deep reading in his father's library, and his travels as a seaman ("The whaling ship," he later said, "was my Yale College and my Harvard"). Melville went to sea at seventeen and became a cabin-boy on the *Highlander*, which took him to Liverpool. Though he then returned to New York, he shipped out again in 1841 on the whaler *Acushnet*, and the subsequent year-and-a-half voyage to the South Seas (before he jumped ship) gave Melville the foundation for *Moby-Dick*. He lived in the Marquesas and Tahiti before returning as an ordinary seaman to the United States in 1844. The years between 1837 and 1844 yielded fodder for several novels, of which the first two (the adventure stories *Typee* in 1846 and *Omoo* in 1847) made him famous as "the man who had lived among the cannibals." Melville, who had taken on family responsibilities by his 1847 marriage to Elizabeth Shaw, could have had a successful career as a novelist of exotic travel, but he had deeper motives governing his work, among them an adventurous and strenuous sense of the formal possibilities of the novel.

Disappointed by the uncomprehending reception of *Moby-Dick* (1851) and the total failure of *Pierre; or, The Ambiguities* (1852), he stopped writing and fell into a depression so severe that his family feared for his sanity. They persuaded him to go abroad, to the Holy Land. He consented, and the journal he kept on that 1856 journey formed the basis for his long-sustained writing of *Clarel*, a poem twice as long as *Paradise Lost*. (A few copies were printed privately, for family consumption, in 1876.)

When civil war broke out in 1861, Melville was a man in his early forties who had seen his genius unrecognized and misunderstood, and his ability to make money severely compromised. The shamefulness of his breakdown, and of his financial dependence on his own family and that of his wife, brought on a melancholy he could never wholly shake off. He was also disheartened by the inexplicable failure of his friendship with Nathaniel Hawthorne, which had reached such a high point during the composition of *Moby-Dick* that Melville dedicated the novel to him. Though in 1866 Melville was to receive an appointment as a customs inspector, during the war he was still applying, without success, for a government consulship like Hawthorne's (he was even introduced to Lincoln in Washington, but nothing came of it).

The Civil War arrived, then, as the external equivalent of Melville's inner crisis. Just as the America that his family had served had no use for him as its epic recorder, it had debased its own ideals in permitting the practice of slavery. Even before the Civil War, in the 1850s, Melville had written his own dark parable of a slave uprising in the story "Benito Cereno." The country had now fallen into a "conflict of convictions" (as one title in *Battle-Pieces* puts it) that could not be resolved except in the outburst of war. This fact confirmed all that Melville had suspected concerning the irrationality of human nature and the chaos at the center of all political systems. Had *Moby-Dick* and *Pierre* not been such commercial and critical failures, Melville might have written a great novel of the War Between the States. Instead, he turned to poetry, condensing whole episodes of the conflict into the lyrics of *Battle-Pieces and Aspects of the War*. These lyrics were for the most part composed after the hostilities ceased. They were not favorably received: even his family criticized them. His cousin

Henry said that his writing in these pieces "never will really touch the common heart," and his sister Kate remarked, "I must say I cannot get interested in his style—of Poetry. It is too deep for my comprehension." Many public reviews were no kinder: "His poetry runs into the epileptic. His rhymes are fearful," said one critic, and William Dean Howells found the poems filled with "phantasms" rather than real events, showing "tortured humanity shedding, not words and blood, but words alone."

Two late volumes of Melville's verse were privately published for friends during his lifetime: *John Marr and Other Sailors* (1888) and *Timoleon* (1891). Neither of these has the sustained passion of *Battle-Pieces* or the philosophical depth of *Clarel*, but each contains unforgettable poems. Though Melville did return to prose, writing *Billy Budd* in the last year of his life, he never ceased to compose poetry. In his final years, he avoided society and passed into obscurity; when he died, his works were almost forgotten. It was not until the Melville revival in the twentieth century that *Billy Budd* and *Clarel* were published. Now, of course, Melville's canonical status as a novelist is secure, but as a poet he is still relatively ignored.

What sort of a poet is Melville? Why has he not achieved a popularity comparable to that of Whitman or Dickinson? These are both questions with complicated answers, but—to address the latter one first—it is enough to point out how profoundly Melville's grim view of history, war, politics, and religion differs from the Emersonian optimism that American readers have tended to prefer. Melville's gaze is not upward, like Dickinson's, nor directed in a democratic horizontal, like Whitman's; it is pitched downward, to the drowned under the sea, or to the fiery hell at the core of the earth. In "Pebbles," the unappeasable sea speaks: "Implacable I, the old implacable Sea:/ Implacable most when most I smile serene—/ Pleased, not appeased, by myriad wrecks in me." Or the poet, walking on the placid grass of the New World but aware of imminent civil volcanoes, speaks:

So, then, Solidity's a crust—
    The core of fire below;
All may go well for many a year,
But who can think without a fear
    Of horrors that happen so?
("The Apparition: A Retrospect")

Like Keats in the epistle "To Reynolds," Melville had "seen too far into the core/ Of an eternal fierce destruction." It made him the messenger of bad news, not only metaphysical or cosmic, but also personal and political:

Found a family, build a state,
The pledged event is still the same:
Matter in end will never abate
His ancient brutal claim.

Worse yet, even good actions tend to increase the sum of evil in the universe:

Indolence is heaven's ally here,
And energy the child of hell:
The Good Man pouring from his pitcher clear,
But brims the poisoned well.
("Fragments of a Lost Gnostic Poem of the 12th Century")

And there is nothing to be hoped from new political arrangements, not even from the U.S. Constitution, as the epigram "A Reasonable Constitution" asserts:

What though Reason forged your scheme?
'Twas Reason dreamed the Utopia's dream:
'Tis dream to think that Reason can
Govern the reasoning creature, man.

Melville refuses to praise a utopian America over a degenerate Europe: he sees original corruption everywhere. And though this belief is not incompatible with Calvinism, nineteenth-century America tended to forget the darker side of its own Protestantism. In its triumphant mercantile and industrial success, it lacked the long historical perspective that informs Melville's work. His poetry, even at its most political and social, is written from a conviction of the loneliness of thought in human life, and his consequent rhetorical aloofness estranges many readers.

Quite aside from Melville's philosophic gloom, his political attitudes did not render him popular with his contemporaries. He wrote with clear sympathy for the Indians, for instance, saying that they had been "all but exterminated in their recent and final war with regular white troops, a war waged by the Red Men for their native soil and natural rights." In 1860—a time when by no means all northerners were abolitionists—he called slavery "man's foulest crime" and saw with foreboding that it had been linked to democracy, "the world's fairest hope." In "Lee in the Capitol," he imagines Robert E. Lee, after the war, as having the long foresight gained by one who has studied the history of Empire, and knowing what Reconstruction will mean to the South:

> Forth he went
> Through vaulted walks in lengthened line
> Like porches erst upon the Palatine:
> Historic reveries their lesson lent,
> The Past her shadow through the Future sent.

In his poetry, Melville makes the divisive shadow of the Civil War reach through to the nation's future. The closing poem in *Battle-Pieces* is true to his conviction that the American conscience was profoundly violated by a governmentally "sanctioned" war pitting brother against brother. To Melville, all one could feel in the presence of such evil was "horror and anguish for the civil strife."

His views were not shared by his fellow northerners, who were eager to blame the South. In "A Meditation" he writes, quoting and then answering them: " '*The South's the sinner!*' Well, so let it be;/ But shall the North sin worse, and stand the Pharisee?"

Precisely because of his exposure of the moral ambiguities in American history, the poet Melville has not been incorporated into American culture in the way that Whitman and Dickinson have. Whitman is more conventionally patriotic, more anecdotal, more colloquial, more genial, and more personal; Dickinson is briefer, less forbidding, less historical. Both are in their outer reaches as heretical as Melville, but the schoolbooks and anthologies for the general reader never look to their outer reaches. Almost anything by Melville, on the other hand, is subversive enough to raise hackles. Melville's broad analysis of the war is, for instance, a mixed one, ascribing evil to both sides: it emphasizes (along with heroism in both armies) needless death, mistaken strategy, the atrocities during the draft riots (in the poem "The House-top"), huge battle losses, stiff-neckedness in the winner, nobility in the loser. And if Melville's tragic sense of history is repugnant to American optimism, his religious nihilism, also present in *Battle-Pieces*, is even more so. It is certain that our literary history has not yet fully absorbed Melville's lyrics into its picture of nineteenth-century culture.

As we look at Melville's poetic works, admitting their documentary and historical relevance, we are bound to ask about his poetry's claims to greatness. The most evident claim is the depth of reflective thought in them; in some 1862 notes, he listed "the greatest number of the greatest ideas" as desirable for an artist. If one wishes to be sure of grasping Melville's ironies, the most gnarled and compressed of the "Battle-Pieces" demand rereading. An unusual structural principle, too, makes his historical poetry difficult. It is typical of Melville to reverse the usual manner in which lyric poems unfold. While the normative lyric presents at its beginning a first-person narrative with its accompanying feelings (and only secondarily, when plot and emotion have been exposed and clarified, turns to philosophical generalization), Melville tends, by contrast, to offer first an impersonal philosophical conclusion, next the narrative that has produced it, and last the lyric feelings accompanying it. This is the most original method Melville discovered by which he could fold the epic matter of history into lyric, and it is this and other strategies in his Civil War lyrics that I want to examine in some detail.

Melville's most famous poem, "The March into Virginia," is composed in the back-to-front fashion I have just mentioned. The poem was occasioned by the disastrous Union losses in the first and second battles of Bull Run (1861), fought on the plain of Manassas. The newly recruited federal troops marching toward First Manassas had no idea of the carnage they were to experience in battle. Were the poem to begin not with line 1 but with line 16, offering Melville's narrative of the uninitiated troops soon to be sacrificed to the god Moloch, the reader would have a story to grasp, one about blithe young soldiers:

> The banners play, the bugles call,
> The air is blue and prodigal.
>   No berrying party, pleasure-wooed,
> No picnic party in the May,
> Ever went less loth than they
>   Into that leafy neighborhood.
> In Bacchic glee they file toward Fate,
> Moloch's uninitiate;
> Expectancy, and glad surmise
> Of battle's unknown mysteries.

Melville's spectatorial observation—"Moloch's uninitiate"—full of historical and prophetic irony, reveals to the reader the boys' eventual fate.

But Melville refuses to begin his poem with this straightforward narrative. The passage just quoted is preceded by fifteen lines of grim brooding on youth's wish *not* to know what lies ahead (which would foreclose all surprise) and by the poet's sardonic appreciation that all wars need the ardors of ignorant youth as "Preparatives of fate." This philosophic overture would make perfect sense if one had already read the narrative of the naive boys off to battle, but as the first statement offered to the reader, it perplexes. One opens *Battle-Pieces* and reads:

Did all the lets and bars appear
    To every just or larger end,
Whence should come the trust and cheer?
    Youth must its ignorant impulse lend—
Age finds place in the rear.
    All wars are boyish, and are fought by boys,
The champions and enthusiasts of the state:
    Turbid ardors and vain joys
    Not barrenly abate—
Stimulants to the power mature,
    Preparatives of fate.

The reader accustomed to a lyric "I" will wonder where the speaker of these opening generalizations is hiding. The speaker is Melville as omniscient narrator—a personage not often found in nonballad lyric, though regularly present in epic. The storyteller of a ballad, however, does not philosophize like Melville's persona. And instead of retelling his own emotions, as the usual lyric speaker does, Melville's narrator focuses on the feelings of the young soldiers—first, as they go into battle ("a rapture sharp, though transitory"); second, as some of them die in battle ("enlightened by the vollied glare"); and third, as some of them survive First Manassas and, as the shamed and defeated successors of their slaughtered companions, fight the second battle of Manassas:

But some who this blithe mood present,
    As on in lightsome files they fare,

Shall die experienced ere three days are spent—
    Perish, enlightened by the vollied glare;
Or shame survive, and, like to adamant,
    The throe of Second Manassas share.

The theoretical phrase in the poem, revealing its implicit poetics, is "like to adamant." The response of the experienced survivors to their humiliating defeat and their traumatic knowledge is to harden themselves to adamant, to take on the stony posture of one who knows all—historically, metaphysically, and ethically—that it is possible to know about life's evil. This is Melville's posture, too, in his poetry: he knows the volcano below the crust, the storm that wrecks the ship, the estrangement that ends the friendship. He will, at all cost, write the poetry of the enlightened, not of the innocent. Therefore what takes first priority in "The March into Virginia" is the philosophic and political knowledge that a historical experience has produced. After the announcement of philosophical conclusions, and only then, will he offer the primal narrative. And only after that can he allow the lyric feelings of the soldiers—first rapture, then enlightenment, then shame—to take their place in the poem. It is this reversal of the usual order of lyric—the way he goes "backwards" from generalization to originating feelings—that makes Melville's best poetry both so oblique and so formally exciting.

Even the most topical of Melville's history poems tend to begin somewhere other than their actual locale. "The Battle for the Mississippi" (April, 1862) starts, for instance, not at the Mississippi but at Migdol, with the Israelites of Exodus 14, as Melville invokes typological precedent:

When Israel camped by Migdol hoar,
    Down at her feet her shawm she threw,
But Moses sung and timbrels rung
    For Pharaoh's stranded crew.

So God appears in apt events—
The Lord is a man of war!

Yet if the reader persists through the indirect and intriguing opening, a Melville poem often hurls itself into thrilling realist description, as this one does:

The shock of ships, the jar of walls,
The rush through thick and thin—
The flaring fire-rafts, glare and gloom—
Eddies, and shells that spin—
The boom-chain burst, the hulks dislodged,
The jam of gun-boats driven,
Or fired, or sunk—made up a war
Like Michael's waged with leven.

Many balladeers on the winning side might have written such a stanza; but they would neither have begun typologically nor have proceeded to Melville's mournful conclusion, which focuses on the slain: "The living shall unmoor and sail,/ But Death's dark anchor secret deeps detain." Melville risks incoherence by letting triumph end in elegy, and at least one critic has found a comparable poem, "The Battle for the Bay," a failure on that account. The latter poem, about Farragut's victory at the Bay of Mobile, first pays philosophical homage to the knowledge of the sea that comes from long experience, that perennial

. . . mystery of noble hearts,
To whom mysterious seas have been
In midnight watches, lonely calm and storm,
A stern, sad discipline. . . .

The poem continues with the narrative of the sea fight at Mobile, cast as a battle between Good and Evil. On the Union side,

No sprightly fife as in the field,
    The decks were hushed like fanes in prayer;
Behind each man a holy angel stood—
    He stood, though none was 'ware.

And "The Battle for the Bay" concludes with an elegy for the Union vessel *Tecumseh*, the leader of the fleet, sunk when it hit a Confederate mine. The poem, in short, follows the same plan as "The March into Virginia"—philosophical reflection, brisk narrative, and closing grief. But according to Stanton Garner, the most serious commentator on Melville's Civil War pieces, "The Battle for the Bay" is "a long, disunified, ultimately incomprehensible poem":

> The three sections . . . are essentially immiscible. . . . On what note, then, could the poem close, a reaffirmation of the educative powers of the sea or a crescendo of God-on-the-side-of-the-Union hokum? Both are abandoned when, unaccountably, the poem shifts its focus to the stricken [*Tecumseh*]. . . . Precisely why a ship that—on the periphery of the poem—had the misfortune to detonate a mine should be thought of as having earned a glory that will thrill the timbers and the cannon of navies throughout eternity is left to the reader's perplexed imagination.
>
> The poem is more about a poet in creative difficulty than it is about a battle. Confused about the point of the action, perhaps, in attempting to write one poem, Herman wrote fragments of three—one about moral maturity, one about moral and divine values in conflict, and one about the men of the *Tecumseh*, who . . . have been carried down to the bottom of war's waters. Had he focused on any one of the three, the poem might have succeeded.

But Melville can never focus on one aspect, is never content to be singleminded: the cost borne by the brave men drowned in the *Tecumseh* must haunt the close of Melville's victory-narrative, just as the college colonel, in the brilliant poem of that name, cannot forget, as he leads his exhausted but victorious regiment home, the unspeakable truth that came to him in battle. And just as "The March into Virginia" began not with epic narrative but with reflection, and closed not with narrative but with the tragic knowledge gained both by those who perished and those who lived to fight another day, so "The Battle for the Bay" begins in wisdom, continues with narrative, and ends in the tragedy that must qualify every deeply felt battle-song, even one of victory.

Melville has attempted to invent a lyric genre adequate to the complex feelings generated by the epic event of battle—a genre that was still, forty years later, being reinvented in a more desperate form by Wilfred Owen. Besides showing formal innovation in his battle poetry—as he makes a hybrid of the paean, the narrative, and the elegy—Melville displays in his poetry, as in his novels, an instinctive recourse to many forms of symbolic expression. These include, in *Battle-Pieces*, various staples of lyric writing: typology, analogy, personification, myth, allegory, refrain, allusion, proper name, synecdoche, and so on. Some of these devices, however familiar in theory, are striking in Melville's practice, such as his frequent allusive analogies of American events to civil wars in Rome and England: "Not Rome o'ercome by Roman arms we sing,/ As on Pharsalia's day," he remarks in "The Surrender at Appomattox"; and he claims, through an English spokesperson in "Battle of Stone River, Tennessee," that "In North and South still beats the vein/ Of Yorkist and Lancastrian." By such large historical reference, the American conflict is swept into Melville's panoptic view of the perennial eruption of human aggression: "War yet shall be, and to the end" ("A Utilitarian View"). On the other hand, Melville was vividly aware that though the substance of war might be forever the same, its means had changed from spears and chain mail to ironclad ships; and though the epic impulse to record might be a recurrent one, the function of the bard was now being fulfilled by the newspaper reporter. These technological changes were ones he reflected on, and found formal equivalents for. The armored ships require, he sees, a new sort of language and rhyme. In "A Utilitarian View of the Monitor's Fight," he advocates a plain style devoid of "fans/ Of banners" and "the gaud/ Of glory," and offers rhyme in only two lines out of six:

> Plain be the phrase, yet apt the verse,
> More ponderous than nimble;
> For since grimed War here laid aside
> His Orient pomp, 'twould ill befit
> Overmuch to ply
> The rhyme's barbaric cymbal.

And the poet aligns himself, not with the past feudal celebrant singing his lord's victory, but rather with the contemporary journalist sending daily dispatches that are scanned by worried civilians. Melville retells the story of the Union siege of Fort Donelson in Tennessee through the reporter's fluctuating and not always reliable messages, posted on a bulletin board:

> About the bulletin-board a band
> Of eager, anxious people met,
> And every wakeful heart was set
> On latest news from West or South.
> "No seeing here," cries one—"don't crowd"—
> "You tall man, pray you, read aloud."

After this genre scene, resembling so many nineteenth-century paintings, comes the first tacked-up bulletin:

IMPORTANT.

We learn that General Grant,
Marching from Henry overland,
And joined by a force up the Cumberland sent
(Some thirty thousand the command),
On Wednesday a good position won—
Began the siege of Donelson.

Melville imitates even the time headings of the bulletins ("1 P.M."; "3 P.M."), and lets them break into headlines—but Melville's headlines repeatedly (if inconspicuously) rhyme:

GLORIOUS VICTORY OF THE FLEET!

FRIDAY'S GREAT EVENT!

THE ENEMY'S WATER-BATTERIES BEAT!

WE SILENCED EVERY GUN!

THE OLD COMMODORE'S COMPLIMENTS SENT PLUMP INTO DONELSON!

Such experiments in the plain style and in new lyric genres fitted to the new technologies of war show Melville's unwillingness to settle (as did many Civil War poets) for a rousing, thoughtless ballad or a victory narrative in the old style. The fallibility and interruptedness of the daily newspaper bulletin becomes, in Melville's hands, a symbol of the unknowability of war; modern battles are always too complex to be fully grasped. The successive headlines become a symbol of modern epic discontinuity.

Melville was acutely conscious of the broad sweep of troop movements, and of the difficulty of getting that epic panorama into the lyric. He frequently places his observer at a vantage point from which the whole course of an event can be followed, as he does General Grant in "Chattanooga":

> Grant stood on cliffs whence all was plain. . . .
>
> He, from the brink,
> Looks far along the breadth of slope,
> And sees two miles of dark dots creep.

The many poems of far focus serve as nerve centers for *Battle-Pieces*: they gather large social disturbances into the X-ray vision of the watcher, who analyzes the intricate vectors of a many-faceted action. One such episode was the New York draft riots of 1863, which erupted after the Enrollment Act for conscription became law. Since the well-off could hire a substitute or pay a commutation fee to avoid being drafted, the law was in effect discriminatory; riots broke out in July, and before they were put down by the police and the army, more than a hundred people had been killed. Melville's speaker looks out from a housetop; he is scornful of the actions of the mob as he hears "the Atheist roar of riot" and sees "red Arson—there—and there": "The Town is taken by its rats—ship-rats/ And rats of the wharves." Yet the speaker is equally disillusioned by the actions of the government, which orders out cannon to disperse the mob:

> Wise Draco comes, deep in the midnight roll
> Of black artillery; . . .
> He comes, nor parlies; and the Town, redeemed,
> Gives thanks devout; nor, being thankful, heeds
> The grimy slur on the Republic's faith implied,
> Which holds that Man is naturally good,
> And—more—is Nature's Roman, never to be scourged.

Because Melville's speaker can see—from his high circumspection—all sides of a question, he is ironic toward all: toward the republic's faith in man, which has been disturbed by the sudden violence of the riots; toward the Draconian actions of the state, which have betrayed the faith on which the republic is founded; and toward the persistence in America, under republican pieties, of the pessimistic aristocratic "code corroborating Calvin's creed/ And cynic tyrannies of honest kings." (As a nod to the epic nature of his subject, Melville closes "The House-top" with a Virgilian hexameter alluding to the rights of Roman citizens.) All through *Battle-Pieces*, far-focus viewing is one of Melville's ways of inserting, into short lyrics, factional complexity of grand proportions. Yet he mistrusted any vantage that claimed to explain the whole: he said of the battles in the Virginia Wilderness,

None can narrate that strife in the pines,
A seal is on it—Sabaean lore!
Obscure as the wood, the entangled rhyme
But hints at the maze of war—
Vivid glimpses or livid through peopled gloom,
And fires which creep and char—
A riddle of death, of which the slain
Sole solvers are.

These doubts about anyone's ability to convey the persisting enigma and riddle of war suggest why, to Melville, the single grim detail, seen up close, can be as explanatory as the high vantage point and far focus of the roof-perch. If the distanced view gives the map of events, the detail relates their pang:

A path down the mountain winds to the glade
Where the dead of the Moonlight Fight lie low;
A hand reaches out of the thin-laid mould
As begging help which none can bestow.
("The Armies of the Wilderness")

The detail is often, as here, severed from the whole that it explains. Out of the earth extends an upraised hand—but whose?

Though the poems of far focus represent Melville's most significant attempt to encompass epic breadth in lyric form, poems of the single detail represent the aspect of his genius that yearned to condense reality into epigram, or—carried to the utmost reach—to a single word. Melville hopes that by emphasizing proper names in his lyrics—names of battles, of generals, of ships—he can finally enclose within a single word an entire "aspect" of the war. "The Cumberland," concerning a sunken Union sailing ship, begins,

> Some names there are of telling sound,
>   Whose voweled syllables free
> Are pledge that they shall ever live renowned;
>   Such seems to be
> A Frigate's name (by present glory spanned)
>   The Cumberland.

Each stanza closes with a rhyme on "Cumberland," and separating the stanzas is a three-line refrain, four times repeated (with slight variations): "Sounding name as ere was sung, / Long they'll roll it on the tongue—/ Cumberland! Cumberland!"

The aura that names can carry in legend is of course a part of popular lyric transmission, and here Melville is imitating refrain poetry, like the hymn that repeats "Maryland, my Maryland." Many other poems in *Battle-Pieces*, such as "The Stone Fleet" and "Donelson," exhibit a comparable faith in the single word or name as a powerful repository of epic memory. But condensation into a name is, I think, less successful as a technique of detail (perhaps because it is essentially a choral response) than Melville's use of the lone upraised hand or, in "A Utilitarian View," a single attribute of the warrior's dress. In commenting that technology has replaced earlier forms of warfare, Melville gestures toward those vanished forms with two antithetical details, severed from the bodies of their wearers—the lace of the feudal coat, the feather of the Indian brave—and a supplementary word, "singe," represents their imminent erasure:

War shall yet be, and to the end;
　　But war-paint shows the streaks of weather;
War yet shall be, but warriors
Are now but operatives; War's made
　　　　Less grand than Peace,
　　And a singe runs through lace and feather.

Arresting as the use of lace and feather may be, the true Melvillian detail—the one with the pang in it—comes in the words "a singe runs through": lace and feather are scorched not by battle but by what Frost would call "the slow smokeless burning of decay," an effacement by technological advance. As yet, lace and feather are neither entirely destroyed nor even uniformly discolored. Their end is forecast in their aesthetic unloveliness as the detail isolates it for our attention; the marring singe shows both lace and feather to be streaked like the earlier war-paint, on their way to obliteration.

I have emphasized the qualities in Melville's battle poetry that have made it unassimilable to his own epoch and to ours—his stoic irony, his steely view of warfare, his insistence on the ambivalence felt by any spectator, his refusal to pronounce easily on the whole, his invention of a species of epic lyric comprehensive enough to include metaphysics, narrative, panoramic tragedy, and individual pang. But I would not want to end without glimpses of the other, more tender, Melville. In "Time's Long Ago," the poet's memory of a tragic period of his past is now solace in a bleak present that can imagine no future. In the serenity of a backward look, even

> . . . Fates and Furies change their mien.
> Though strewn with wreckage be the shore
> The halcyon haunts it; all is green
> And wins the heart that hope can lure no more.

Beautiful though this is, taking as its presiding genius the bird who appears in calm weather, it is not so beautiful as Melville's late lyric absolving the hurt inflicted on him by life's four winds and bitter seas. Untypically, this seraphic poem begins with direct feeling:

> Healed of my hurt, I laud the inhuman Sea—
> Yea, bless the Angels Four that there convene;
> For healed I am even by their pitiless breath
> Distilled in wholesome dew named rosmarine.

The Stoic and Christian doctrine of the compensatory moral value of suffering is rephrased in a set of images that could have been invented only by Melville. The four winds shown at the corners of old maps (here transmuted to angels) replace the Holy Spirit as the breath of inspiration. The "wholesome dew" of sea-spray—Ovid's *ros maris*—replaces the baptismal water that obliterates sin. Though the ministers of experiential conflict are themselves inhuman and pitiless, the human mind can distill their assaults on the body into salutary healings of the soul. What it cost Melville to write this epigram, after all he had seen of personal tragedy and civil war, makes us pause, reading it. With *Clarel* and its companion poems—especially the epic-lyric *Battle-Pieces*—it is enough to win the poet Melville, in this century at least, what he prophetically named "the belated funeral flower of fame."

Dark Knowledge

Melville's Poems of the Civil War

Rosanna Warren

My subject is knowledge. In particular, the way in which several poems of Herman Melville dramatize the dawning of knowledge through struggle: in theme, the fratricidal national struggle of the American Civil War; in form, the inwrought, crabbed, ponderous, grimed verse through which Melville fought his way to private perception. *Battle-Pieces and Aspects of the War*, published in August 1866, involves us as modern readers in a more general struggle: the ever-renewed attempt by the present to envision or to evade the past. The Civil War represents, for citizens of the United States, a parental past which it is convenient to forget but which continues to work upon us and through us. As a nation we still suffer variously the aftershocks of slavery; and we are still, one hundred and thirty years after Lee's surrender at Appomattox, half-bewildered by the strains of being no longer an agricultural and maritime Jeffersonian democracy. We are, instead, an industrialized, militarized imperial nation whose dream has taken expansionist forms, as Melville foresaw, in

---

Reprinted by permission from *Raritan: A Quarterly Review* 19, no. 1 (summer 1999).

the poem "The Conflict of Convictions," observing the new iron dome on the Capitol:

> Power unanointed may come—
> Dominion (unsought by the free)
> And the Iron Dome,
> Stronger for stress and strain,
> Fling her huge shadow athwart the main;
> But the Founders' dream shall flee.

This project of looking at Melville's poems commits me to a particularly filial encounter. The Civil War, while largely forgotten in the North (though slavery is not), is still *the* war in the South, and I am the child of a Northern mother and a Southern father. Furthermore, my Southern father loved and edited the poems of Melville. For years I sought, with half my mind, to forget "my father's war" and the literature of that war: hadn't the elders sufficiently raked over those ashes? But the knowledge that counts most, I think, is tragic knowledge; so I find myself returning to those ancestral battlefields to try to understand where we have come from. All Americans are children of the Civil War whether we know it or not.

Melville, too, had an instinct for evasion. After the successes of his early books of travel adventures, *Moby-Dick* had met with incomprehension in 1851, and his successive works—the sprawling, haunted novel *Pierre; or, the Ambiguities*, *Israel Potter*, *The Piazza Tales*, and the bitter, self-cancelling *Confidence Man* in 1857—had flopped, leaving Melville with only family and friends for a reading public. Attempts at lecturing had failed as well. When in April 1860 the Democratic National Convention split into Northern and Southern factions at the meeting in Charleston, South Carolina, and a few weeks later the Republican Convention nominated Lincoln for president, Melville took flight, shipping out on 30 May on the clipper ship *The Meteor* of which his younger brother Tom was the captain. Stanton Garner has told this story well in *The Civil War World of Herman Melville*, documenting how closely connected to the war Melville would be through his large network of friends and family, including two cousins who took part in the fighting. *The Meteor* was bound around Cape Horn to San Francisco, a voyage of many months.

Leaving behind his wife and four children, a literary career in ruins, and a country on the verge of civil war, Melville was scudding south toward Cape Horn through ferocious storms. The Horn itself, when they rounded it, struck him as "Horrible snowy mountains—black, thundercloud woods—gorges—hell-landscape." A sailor fell from the main topsail yard, crashing to his death on the deck. In this oblique approach to the Civil War, Melville read Milton, Chapman's Homer, Schiller, the New Testament, and the Psalms. When *The Meteor* docked in San Francisco in October, Melville headed home, taking a steamer south to Panama City, a train across the isthmus, and another steamer north to arrive in New York City on 13 November. Lincoln had just been elected, and South Carolina had seceded.

Melville wrote *Battle-Pieces and Aspects of the War* in the last months of the conflict and after its conclusion. The book appeared in August 1866. Reviews ranged from polite to indignant; the *American Literary Gazette and Publisher's Circular* declared, "He has written too rapidly to avoid great crudities. His poetry runs into the epileptic. His rhymes are fearful." It is these crudities I want to examine. "The real war," wrote Whitman, who had nursed his brother and countless other wounded soldiers for three years in the war hospital in Washington D.C., "will never get in the books." It certainly did not get in the books through the patriotic, self-righteous, and popular regularities of John Greenleaf Whittier, whose ease of prosody carried the correspondingly easy freight of his abstractions and undisturbed convictions:

The storm-bell rings, the trumpet blows;
I know the sign and countersign;
Wherever Freedom's vanguard goes,
I know the place that should be mine.

Nor does the "real war" make much of an appearance in James Russell Lowell's elegy for the young white colonel Robert Gould Shaw who died leading the heroic black 54th Massachusetts Volunteer Infantry in their assault on Battery Wagner in Charleston, South Carolina, or in his "Ode Recited at the Harvard Commemoration, July 21, 1865," one of the most famous poems of the war. "Brave, good, and true,/I see him stand before me now," wrote Lowell of the young Shaw, but the reader sees neither the young man nor more than a glimpse of the action which killed and glorified him. The Harvard Commemoration Ode begins, "Weak-winged is song," quite true in this case; Lowell's praise of Lincoln is high-minded and well-meant, but doesn't bring the assassinated hero to life in the mind's eye: "The kindly-earnest, brave, foreseeing man,/Sagacious, patient, dreading praise, not blame,/New birth of our new soul, the first American."

While Whittier confidently and easily declared, "I know," Melville's *Battle-Pieces* labor for their knowledge, and engage the reader in that struggle. Poem after poem pursues its quarry of truth, casting off illusory knowledge along with conventional poetic solutions. The hunt after the white whale had prepared Melville for this probe into his country's nature and into human nature; Chapman's Homer had shown him a radiantly factual, unsentimental view of men at war, passion recorded with both supreme detachment and supreme detail of spear crunching through ligament and bone. The greatest art wars *against* illusion, as Simone Weil, one of the *Iliad*'s best readers, would write: "To love truth means to tolerate the void, and consequently to accept death. Truth is on the side of death." Melville's poems constitute such an art, an art that tolerates the void and accepts death.

It also accepts mystery. The introductory poem about the execution of John Brown, "The Portent," simultaneously reveals and veils. It gives no easy clue for the deciphering of its sign: "Hidden in the cap/Is the anguish none can draw;/So your future veils its face,/Shenandoah!/But the streaming beard is shown/(Weird John Brown),/The meteor of the war." God, in "The Conflict of Convictions," says neither "Yea" nor "Nay": "None was by/When He spread the sky;/Wisdom is vain, and prophesy." And how do civilians know a war? The long poem "Donelson" unfolds the progress of the three-day battle by Union forces to capture Fort Donelson on the Cumberland River in Tennessee, in February 1862, from the perspective of Northerners milling about the bulletin board in sleet to read the latest telegraphed news. "Washed by the storm, till the paper grew/Every shade of a streaky blue," the news changes shape through three days of rain until finally, after Grant's costly victory, "The death-list like a river flows/Down the pale sheet,/And there the whelming waters meet." "The House-top" ambiguously presents the New York City draft riots of July 1863, evoking both the vicious violence of the rioters, who lynched blacks and burned a black orphanage, and the viciousness of the force brought in to repress them. In "The Armies of the Wilderness," a long, ambitious poem drawing on the three battles fought (between 1863 and 1864) in that infernal wooded section of Virginia where the forest caught fire and burned hundreds of the wounded to death, the horror emerges through the splicing of lyric and narrative passages, but finally cannot be described.

None can narrate that strife in the pines,
    A seal is on it—Sabaean lore!
Obscure as the wood, the entangled rhyme
    But hints at the maze of war—
Vivid glimpses or livid through peopled gloom,
    And fires which creep and char—
A riddle of death, of which the slain
    Sole solvers are.

Because Melville's poems look to the outer void, they brave the inner depth as well. Whereas Emerson, in "Grace," thanks his "preventing God" for the defenses (against his own inner darkness) of "example, custom, fear, occasion slow," and confesses, "I dare not peep over this parapet/To gauge the roaring gulf below," Melville—who had savaged Emerson as Mark Winsome, "more a metaphysical merman than a feeling man," in *The Confidence Man*—could never resist a parapet. One such poem, " 'The Coming Storm,' " meditates upon a lowering landscape painting of that title by S. R. Gifford, exhibited in Washington in April 1865. The fulfilling impulse to the poem rises not from the landscape itself, but from the fact of its ownership by Edwin Booth, the famous Shakespearean actor whose brother, John Wilkes Booth, had just shot Lincoln: "No utter surprise can come to him/Who reaches Shakespeare's core;/That which we seek and shun is there—/Man's final lore." For a fratricidal war, a poem of dread fraternal acknowledgment.

I want now to look in detail at several of the poems, considering them as modes of action precipitating a provisional but tragic knowledge. The whole book, *Battle-Pieces and Aspects of the War*, can in a sense be regarded as one sustained action, a chronological sequence responding to significant points in the war; but the poems were, for the most part, written after the events they describe. They were not versified reports from the front like Henry Howard Brownell's popular *Lyrics of a Day: Newspaper Poems by a Volunteer in the U.S. Service*, published in 1864. The dates affixed to each of Melville's poems refer not to composition, but to the place of narrated events within the unfolding drama of the war. The introductory poem, isolated in italics at the outset and not included in the table of contents, throws down the initial challenge of vision and interpretation.

The Portent.
(1859.)

Hanging from the beam
Slowly swaying (such the law)
Gaunt the shadow on your green,
Shenandoah!
The cut is on the crown
(Lo, John Brown),
And the stabs shall heal no more.

Hidden in the cap
Is the anguish none can draw;
So your future veils its face,
Shenandoah!
But the streaming beard is shown
(Weird John Brown),
The meteor of the war.

Where to start? With the action the poem contemplates, or the action the poem *is*? In the poem itself, they fuse: historical event becomes event in the mind of the reader through the event in language. The brute data: on 16 October 1859, the abolitionist John Brown—already guilty of the murder of five proslavery settlers in Kansas—attacked the federal arsenal at Harper's Ferry, Virginia, with a band of followers. As is well known, he hoped his act would stir up a slave revolt. As is also well known, Colonel Robert E. Lee led the company of Marines who recaptured the arsenal and wounded and arrested Brown. Brown's hanging in Charleston, Virginia, on 2 December 1859, contributed to the passions, in both North and South, that would erupt into war: Union soldiers would march into battle singing, "John Brown's body lies amouldering in the grave. . . ."

But there all certainty stops. For a figure who assumed mythic proportions, Brown provoked wildly varying reactions, even among Northerners. Emerson was quoted as saying his execution would "make the gallows as glorious as the Cross"; Hawthorne responded, in his essay "Chiefly about War Matters, by a Peaceable Man," "Nobody was more justly hanged. He won his martyrdom fairly, and took it firmly." Melville's poem takes shape and life in the gap between these two statements. Anyone seeking clear-cut approbation or condemnation of Brown will leave "The Portent" baffled.

How does the poem behave? Look, first, at the obvious: its shape. Two symmetrical chunks. A central division. Presentation, and complication? And the meter: it's not revolutionary; it's far more irregular than Longfellow or James Russell Lowell, but this kind of varying line length within the stanza was standard within the lyric tradition in English. Its most startling move, metrically, is the elimination of all unstressed syllables in the penultimate line of each stanza: "(Lo, John Brown)"; "(Weird John Brown)." I'll have more to say about those parentheses and those three-beat, all-stress lines: it's not often that a poem names its main subject only in parenthesis. On the other hand, the parentheses and the stress focus the reader's attention on the deferred subject—"(Lo, John Brown)"—and so, like the poem as a whole, simultaneously conceal and reveal the heart of the matter.

Consider for a moment the meter and prosody. The poem observes a rigorous symmetry. First line of each stanza: trochaic trimeter catalectic. That is to say, three trochees, the last not having a fit but simply missing its last, unstressed syllable:

Hāng iňg/frōm thĕ/beām

....

Hīd dĕn/ĭn thĕ/cāp

Both ear and eye are working intensely here. First word and first stress: Hanging. Something—we don't yet know it is a corpse—is hanging. Last word of the first line, stressed: Beam. There we have the elemental scene: action and noun. Second line in each stanza: trochaic tetrameter catalectic. Our poet is sticking with trochees, but he's lengthening his breath to four beats. He still ends on a strong stress, however. What is he showing us now?

Slōw ly̆/swāy in̆g/(sūch thĕ/lāw)

It's the action of hanging these trochees are suffering: one feels the sway. But physical action observed and participated in gives rise to a parenthetical abstraction, a declaration that brooks no disagreement and concludes in one powerful, stressed monosyllable: Law. Alliteration seems to bind the physical motion of what we do not yet know is a corpse to the legal enforcement: "Slowly swaying (such the law.)" What law? It is the law of gravity that suspended bodies, under stimulus, swing like pendulums; it was the law of the United States—and certainly of the state of Virginia—in 1859 that murder and insurrection be punished by death. Meter, too, is a law, and enforces its argument.

The first sentence has not yet concluded, and we still don't know *what* is hanging. Third line: "Gaunt the shadow on your green": more trochees, another tetrameter, also catalectic; this hanging meter is becoming insistent. So is the alliteration, with *g* this time. Often in poetry when sound enforces a likeness, the deeper sense vibrates with significant difference, and that is the case here: the suggestions of starvation and death in "Gaunt" collide with the fertility implicit in "green." In the "shadow"—squarely placed in the center of the line—we seem to have discovered the subject of the sentence, though not of the poem. But what kind of subject is this: not the thing itself, but its projection, its dark two-dimensional image? Phonetically, "shadow" generates the whole fourth line, echoed symmetrically in the next stanza: "Shenandoah." The subliminal suggestion of "valley" in relation to "Shenandoah," combined with "shadow" and the ominous implications of the poem thus far, may call to mind "the valley of the shadow of death" from Psalm 23. The echo provokes ironic dissonance, not consolation. Still trochees, but contracted from four feet to two, from tetrameter to dimeter. And since the poet addresses the valley directly—"your green"—and concludes his first sentence here with an exclamation, we feel a corresponding quickening of dramatic interest. Still, the major point is that the poem continues to conceal its ostensible subject.

Line 5 comes as a jolt: a rapid shift from trochees to iambs—

Thĕ cūt/ĭs ōn/thĕ crōwn

—with the harshness of the alliterated *c* in the powerful nouns: cut/crown. Still mysterious. What cut? Whose crown? Is there a king here? Line 6, as noted before, appears to resolve the mystery: "(Lo, John Brown)." It has eliminated all unstressed syllables, and in keeping with the visual logic of the poem seems to point a finger at its subject: "Lo." The rhyme of "Brown" with "crown" appears to confer the crown of martyrdom upon the insurrectionary (Edmund Wilson in *Patriotic Gore* reminds us that Emerson was not alone in regarding Brown as a Christ figure). The sentence, however, has still not concluded. The last line of the stanza, an anapestic/iambic trimeter, rhymes with nothing in this stanza; it must await its sinister partner in the last line of the poem, and match "shall heal no more" with "war": "And the stabs shall heal no more."

The last three lines of stanza 1 provide a superficial and misleading clarity. The trimeter, basically iambic, seems consolingly familiar. But the images delivered in elemental monosyllables—cut/crown/John/Brown/stabs—are more troublesome the more one ponders them. In some loose symbolic manner the poem invites us to see in John Brown the conventional figure of abolitionist martyr; though hanged, he was in fact, during his capture, slashed by a sword on the head as on the symbolic kingly headgear betokening his martyr's station. Melville leaves the crown, however, unspecified, and since the poem is addressed to the green and fertile Shenandoah Valley, the reader's imagination is free to wander. The cut, perhaps, is on the crown of peace? Of the Union? And what about those "stabs"? Melville has introduced a grisly historical literalism which immensely complicates the reading of martyrdom. For the stabs associated with John Brown are not only the gashes he suffered from Lieutenant Green's sword at Harpers Ferry; the gashes are also those he and his two sons and henchmen inflicted in May 1856 in Pottawatomie Creek, Kansas, when they dragged out of bed, shot, stabbed in the face, and hacked off the fingers and arms of five illiterate poor whites from Tennessee—three men and two boys—who owned no slaves. Brown executed his massacre as retaliation for the murder of five freesoilers, two days before, by a proslavery gang in the melee of Bleeding Kansas. Behind that violence, implicit in the poem, looms the still greater violence of slavery itself. The hanging in "The Portent" has been preceded by many stabs, none of them innocent.

The second stanza reproduces the metrical pattern of the first, with minor substitutions. How does it contribute, however, to the slowly emerging image of John Brown? Stanza 1 had at least come around to naming the figure who cast the shadow over the green Shenandoah, soon to become a battlefield. Stanza 2, which like the first seems to contemplate a picture of the hanging, rebels against the visual medium and begins by insisting that the truth cannot be represented: "Hidden in the cap/Is the anguish none can draw." Metrical symmetry, syntactical parallelism, and alliteration insist on the kinship of "Hanging" and "Hidden." But more than the hanged man's individual face is hidden behind the cap. Once again the poem addresses the valley, which seems to expand so as to include the whole land in its illusion of prewar innocence: "So your future veils its face,/Shenandoah!" The poem exploits its privilege of tragic hindsight: to the eyes of 1859, the future did veil its face. The last three lines break from concealment to revelation. Unwilling to make a simple moralizing pronouncement, the poem instead enacts a startling metamorphosis. Prompted by the visual detail of the beard, the relatively small object which we saw as passive in stanza 1—the hanging corpse—becomes a heavenly body of terrifying scale, motion, and power: a meteor. This meteor may in turn call upon demonic energies if we remember, as Melville surely did, Satan's great banner streaming in *Paradise Lost*: "The imperial ensign, which, full high advanced/Shone like a meteor streaming to the wind." "Weird" brings to the transformation its etymological force, meaning not merely "strange," but, as Melville knew from the Weird Sisters of *Macbeth*, "having the power to control the fate or destiny of men," and "claiming the supernatural power of dealing with fate or destiny" (*O.E.D.*). While the poem does not presume to explicate Brown's moral nature, his role as portent is clear in the last, fatal monosyllable: war.

We are dealing, on the evidence of "The Portent," with a concentrated, elliptical art, which instead of delivering a ready-made judgment, forces readers to participate in the chiaroscuro process of arriving at judgment. In "The Portent," the reader may be induced to share, as a sensation of sound, in the rhythm of hanging. This is also an art of isolated visual details and shadows—Brown's shadow across the Shenandoah Valley, the shadow of the iron dome across the Potomac—rather than direct description. But Melville was creating himself as a poet in the course of writing these poems, experimenting with still other ways to dramatize the act of knowing.

The Civil War was for the United States a bloody ceremony of coming of age. It provided that experience for thousands of young soldiers from North and South, and Melville—who like Stephen Crane did not fight in the war—was fascinated by their transition from innocence to experience. A number of his poems focus on this testing of youth: "The March into Virginia, Ending in the First Manassas," "Ball's Bluff," "The College Colonel," "On the Slain Collegians." "All wars are boyish, and are fought by boys," is his compact, aphoristic pentameter in "The March into Virginia," and these poems—composed by a forty-six-year-old noncombatant, a man of physical strength who suffered from rheumatism and neuralgia—are haunted by the figure of the sacrificed Boy. Melville does not take either side in his grief; these lines from "On the Slain Collegians" have a bitterness one might expect from Blake:

> What could they else—North or South?
> Each went forth with blessings given
> By priests and mothers in the name of Heaven;
> And Honor in both was chief.
> Warred one for Right, and one for Wrong?
> So be it; but they both were young—
> Each grape to his cluster clung,
> All their elegies are sung.

Reading these poems as dramas of initiation, I reach out to clasp my father by his spectral hand. For that is how he read them, especially "The March into Virginia," which he loved. To read them in the light of his love is something of an initiation in itself: I come to them, no longer so young, with the line ringing in my ear, "Youth must its ignorant impulse lend." I will not try to improve on, or rehearse, my father's description of the rhythmical shifts in the poem's three sections—from gnomic abstraction, to the frolicking tetrameters of ignorance, to the lengthened, "experienced" pentameters of the conclusion; I will mention but not dwell on his remarking the pun on "berrying party" ("burying party") in line 18. But here is the poem:

The March into Virginia,
Ending in the First Manassas.
(JULY, 1861.)

Did all the lets and bars appear
To every just or larger end,
Whence should come the trust and cheer?
Youth must its ignorant impulse lend—
Age finds place in the rear.
All wars are boyish, and are fought by boys,
The champions and enthusiasts of the state:
Turbid ardors and vain joys
Not barrenly abate—
Stimulants to the power mature,
Preparatives of fate.

Who here forecasteth the event?
What heart but spurns at precedent
And warnings of the wise,
Contemned foreclosures of surprise?
The banners play, the bugles call,
The air is blue and prodigal.
No berrying party, pleasure-wooed,
No picnic party in the May,
Ever went less loth than they
Into that leafy neighborhood.
In Bacchic glee they file toward Fate,
Moloch's uninitiate;
Expectancy, and glad surmise
Of battle's unknown mysteries.
All they feel is this: 'tis glory,
A rapture sharp, though transitory,
Yet lasting in belaureled story.
So they gayly go to fight,
Chatting left and laughing right.

But some who this blithe mood present,
　　As on in lightsome files they fare,
Shall die experienced ere three days are spent—
Perish, enlightened by the vollied glare;
Or shame survive, and, like to adamant,
　　The throe of Second Manassas share.

The Battle of Bull Run, which this poem commemorates, delivered the first shock to Union confidence. On 21 July 1861, the Federal army, 35,000 strong under General McDowell, marched from Washington, D.C., to attack the Confederates who had 31,000 men under the generals Beauregard and Johnston at Manassas Junction, Virginia. So convinced were the Union troops and their officers of their superiority that spectators from Washington accompanied them with picnic baskets to delight in the victory. The advantage swayed back and forth sickeningly on the murderous field, but General Thomas J. Jackson, standing like a "stonewall" to earn his nickname, broke the Union army's resolve and sent it scrambling back to the Capitol. Six months later, Hawthorne visited Washington and recounted: "all of us were looking towards the terrible and mysterious Manassas, with the idea that somewhere in its neighborhood lay a ghastly battlefield, yet to be fought, but foredoomed of old to be bloodier than the one where we had reaped such shame. Of all haunted places, methinks such a destined field should be thickest thronged with ugly phantoms, ominous of mischief through ages beforehand." Whitman, who was not present at the battle, described the retreat with a journalist's vigor in *Specimen Days*:

> The defeated troops commenced pouring into Washington over the Long Bridge at daylight on Monday, 22nd—day drizzling all through with rain. The Saturday and Sunday of the battle (20th, 21st) had been parched and hot to an extreme—the dust, the grime and smoke, in layers, sweated in, follow'd by other layers again sweated in, absorb'd by those excited souls—

> their clothes all saturated with the clay-powder filling the air—stirr'd up everywhere on the dry roads and trodden fields by the regiments, swarming wagons, artillery, &c.—all the men with this coating of murk and sweat and rain, now recoiling back, pouring over the Long Bridge—a horrible march of twenty miles, returning to Washington baffled, humiliated, panic-struck. Where are the vaunts, and the proud boasts with which you went forth? Where are your banners, and your bands of music, and your ropes to bring back your prisoners? Well, there isn't a band playing—and there isn't a flag but clings ashamed and lank to its staff.

Like "The Portent," Melville's "The March into Virginia" is a poem of grim retrospective knowledge. It proceeds through the interplay of questions ("Whence should come the trust and cheer?" "Who here forecasteth the event?"), glimpses of description, and declaration; it moves also from a reflective present tense, to the past tense of narrative, to the suspended narrative present of innocence ("So they gayly go to fight"), to give birth to a future tense of futile enlightenment: "Shall die experienced . . ." We should notice certain currents of sound and the burden of imagery and thought they bear, to see (and hear) how the poem acts out its enlightenment.

Take the letter *b*. Along with the obvious pattern of rhyme at line ends, modulating from interlaced rhymes to couplets and back again, an alliterative pattern of *b*s guides us through the poem like a nerve: bars (as in hindrances to youth's impulsiveness); boyish; boys; turbid; not barrenly abate; banners; bugles; blue; berrying; neighborhood; Bacchic; battle; belaureled; but; blithe. That tells just part of the story, but an important part: the boyish, exuberant part. "Turbid ardors," a phrase that can scarcely be imagined in James Russell Lowell, swells with a sexual suggestiveness in the vicinity of "not barrenly abate"; the confused erotic energy of youth turns out, surprisingly, not to be "barren," but to have a sinister fertility: it fuels the war, "Stimulants to the power mature,/Preparatives of fate." Melville liked this word "abate"; it adhered in his mind to boyishness, as in the description of the slain collegians: "Each bloomed and died an unabated Boy." In both cases, a mortal irony attends the negative formula of "abate"; the boys have died; it is their boyish energy, translated into myth and memory, that does not "abate." The fertility they sow is a prodigality of death: "Not barrenly. . . ."

"Bacchic" concentrates and elevates this erotic energy. But "prodigal" prompts a pause and a detour. From *prodigus* in Latin, meaning "extravagant," the word awakens in English hearers immediately the image of another boy, the wastrel, the biblical son returned and redeemed. Two lines earlier the poem has hinted, in legal parlance, that redemption will be "foreclosed" for these young soldiers who have spurned "at precedent/And warnings of the wise,/Contemned foreclosures of surprise." For the moment, it's the air, not the boys, that's blue and prodigal, but the word has subliminally raised the question: Will these sons return home?

Returning to the trail of *b*s, we should consider "leafy neighborhood." This is the Edenic wood, unillumined by experience; the very word, "neighborhood," carries connotations of fraternal play, vicinity, and intimacy. For a brotherly war—Bull Run was just twenty miles from Washington—"neighborhood" has a fatal appropriateness. The boyhood woods of "The March into Virginia" give way later in the sequence to ghastly metaphysical versions of wilderness in which men discover their bestial selves and brothers, signally in the poems "The Armies of the Wilderness" and "The Scout toward Aldie." "The March into Virginia," however, concerns itself only with the revelation of the first Battle of Bull Run, the knowledge that springs on the poem in a traplike rhyme: "In Bacchic glee they file toward Fate,/Moloch's uninitiate."

"Fate," in lower case, had already slipped into the poem at the end of stanza 1, rhyming with "not barrenly abate." Now the rhyme with "fate" acts out the destiny of the boys; unwittingly, they rhyme with their own deaths as they pass from the sphere of a celebratory god to a god worshipped in the immolation of children: Moloch's uninitiate. The negative, as always in Melville, acts stressfully. Moloch breaks into the poem, inducing a horrible prescience in the reader, and perhaps, too, a retrospective Miltonic shudder at the thought of Satan's fierce companion in arms from *Paradise Lost*; but the boys, still *un*initiate, retard the discovery, so this blocklike, multisyllabic line—just two words holding the whole tetrameter fort—quivers with the contradiction of knowledge proposed and resisted.

The adversative "But," starting the third stanza, swings the poem from Bacchus to Moloch, from innocence to experience, from life to death. The blue air and "lightsome files" give way to the enlightenment of "the vollied glare;" the *b*s surrender to a new but insistent pattern of sound, the *sh* of "shall," "perish," "shame," and "share." Even in Melville's crossed-out manuscript versions of the last line, the *sh* dominates: "Thy after-shock, Manassas, share"; "Thy second shock, Manassas, share." But the elemental story had already been told by the key words; "shock," as Melville decided, was both too obvious thematically to be stated, and an overblowing of the alliteration. The deep instruction of defeat—one Melville knew well—was, for the survivors, to outlive shame and to define tempered forms of shared experience.

Only poetry of the highest order weaves its strands of sound so complexly into its semantic and syntactic orders, converting the arbitrary into the provisionally significant. What, then, about Melville's "crudities"? Why were his rhymes considered "epileptic"? He was not the only nineteenth-century American poet to fall afoul of a reading public accustomed to the confirmations of regularity. It is not insignificant that in 1855 Whittier threw his copy of *Leaves of Grass* into the fire; that the book sold poorly; that one reviewer called it "a gathering of muck . . . entirely destitute of wit," and another described Whitman as "this arrogant young man . . . who roots like a pig among the rotten garbage of licentious thoughts." Whitman rebelled: in the poem "1861," he declared, "No dainty rhymes or sentimental love verses for you terrible year,/Not you as some pale poetling seated at a desk lisping cadenzas piano." In the midcentury in the United States the genteel and expert mellifluousness of Longfellow and Lowell held sway. In the work of Jones Very, a devotional poet of urgent simplicity and intensity, or in the intimate, slightly irregular sonnets of Frederick Goddard Tuckerman, the inherited versification could find its own peculiar and forceful realization and reach a modest audience; but the expressive irregularities in rhythm, diction, and syntax with which Whitman, Melville, and Dickinson responded to the strongest promptings in English had almost no purchase on the minds of contemporary readers.

But new truths, inwardly felt, demand new forms. The American Civil War, with its massive industrialization in the manufacture and distribution of weapons, its development of repeating rifles and ironclad warships, and (with Sherman) its total assault on the means of sustaining life, was immediately recognized as a novel kind of conflict by military specialists abroad and at home. Melville, Hawthorne, and Mark Twain, among others in the broader public at home, saw that the Romantic era had passed in literature as in warfare. Like the poets of a later modern war, Wilfred Owen, Isaac Rosenberg, Ivor Gurney, and David Jones, Melville found himself writing poems of undeception ("What like a bullet can undeceive!"), not so much jettisoning poetic decorum as insisting on a new standard of fitting language to fact. In such terms Melville salutes the retiring *Temeraire*, the wooden warship in the British fleet famous from the Battle of Trafalgar:

A pigmy steam-tug tows you,
    Gigantic, to the shore—
Dismantled of your guns and spars,
    And sweeping wings of war.
The rivets clinch the iron-clads,
    Men learn a deadlier lore . . .

In another poem responding to the fight between the ironclad ships in March 1862, "A Utilitarian View of the Monitor's Fight," Melville faces head on the challenge of readjusting poetic convention: it may have been his rhyming "heroic" with "caloric" that so distressed the reviewer at the *American Literary Gazette and Publisher's Circular*. The poem runs:

Plain be the phrase, yet apt the verse,
    More ponderous than nimble;
For since grimed War here laid aside
His Orient pomp, 'twould ill befit
        Overmuch to ply
    The rhyme's barbaric cymbal.

Hail to victory without the gaud
    Of glory; zeal that needs no fans
Of banners; plain mechanic power
Plied cogently in War now placed—
        Where War belongs—
    Among the trades and artisans.

Yet this was battle, and intense—
    Beyond the strife of fleets heroic;
Deadlier, closer, calm 'mid storm;
No passion; all went on by crank,
        Pivot, and screw,
    And calculations of caloric.

Needless to dwell; the story's known.
    The ringing of those plates on plates
Still ringeth round the world—
The clangor of that blacksmiths' fray.
        The anvil-din
    Resounds this message from the Fates:

War shall yet be, and to the end;
    But war-paint shows the streaks of weather;
War yet shall be, but warriors
Are now but operatives; War's made
        Less grand than Peace,
    And a singe runs through lace and feather.

"Plain be the phrase," indeed. The poem achieves itself not merely by intruding an industrial vocabulary upon a diction inherited from Scott ("plain mechanic power"; "crank,/Pivot, and screw"; "plates on plates") but, more dynamically, by using its few rhymes to rivet the argument. Contrast the rhymes of Lowell's Commemoration Ode with those of Melville's "A Utilitarian View." In Lowell's first stanza, what Pope had called "the sure returns of still-expected rhymes" ferry the song along its untroubled current of feeling: song/height/light/wrong/hearse/verse/come/drum/desire/fire/strong/save/grave /throng. Melville, not wanting "Overmuch to ply/The rhyme's barbaric cymbal," reduces his rhymes to the second and sixth lines of each stanza, relying on meter to discipline his lines. With the exception of nimble/cymbal in the first stanza (which associates the action of verse with the action of the ship), each rhyme registers the collision between romance and realism: fans/artisans, heroic/caloric, plates/fates, weather/feather. This new, deadlier mechanical warfare continued to develop through our own century's wars and has culminated in the smart bombs and video game warfare that have so transfixed the American public since the Gulf War. More than the shot for liberty heard round the world in Emerson's "Concord Hymn," Melville ironically predicts, "The ringing of those plates on plates/Still ringeth round the world."

We have been speaking of the Civil War, and of different kinds of knowledge born of that war in Melville's poems. One crucial truth was born for the nation as a whole only imperfectly and through the agony of the conflict itself, and that was the real purpose of the war. Even now, people disagree about that purpose. Lincoln in his First Inaugural Address stated, "I have no purpose, directly or indirectly, to interfere with the institution of slavery in the states where it exists. I believe I have no lawful right to do so, and I have no inclination to do so." Many white Southerners seceded, less to protect slavery, than to insist on the principle of states' rights; the majority of white Northerners supported the war for the preservation of the Union, not for the abolition of slavery; when Lincoln signed the Emancipation Proclamation on 1 January 1863, many white Northern soldiers simply quit. But by the Second Inaugural Address, Lincoln admitted that slavery "constituted a peculiar and powerful interest. All knew that this interest was, somehow, the cause of the war." For many Northern whites, including abolitionists, it was difficult not to turn black people into abstractions; the difficulty of keeping their human reality in focus—by no means entirely outgrown in our time—is evident in the treatment of black and other nonwhite figures in the works of Melville, Whitman, and Hawthorne.

For these writers—even for Melville, who felt much less racial animosity toward nonwhites than Whitman did, as his portrayal of Queequeg suggests—the black stands as a haunting enigma, at times seen hopefully as benign, at times as murderous and vengeful. After his trip to the war zone around the Capitol in January 1862, Hawthorne described a party of escaped slaves:

> So rudely were they attired,—as if their garb had grown upon them spontaneously,—so picturesquely natural in manner, and wearing such a crust of primeval simplicity (which is quite polished away from the Northern black man), that they seemed a kind of creature by themselves, not altogether human, but perhaps quite as good, and akin to the fauns and rustic deities of olden times. . . . At all events, I felt most kindly towards these poor fugitives, but knew not precisely what to wish in their behalf, nor in the least how to help them. For the sake of the manhood which is latent in them, I would not have them

> turned back; but I should have felt almost as reluctant, on their own account, to hasten them forward to the stranger's land; and I think my prevalent idea was, that, whoever may be benefited by the results of this war, it will not be the present generation of negroes, the childhood of whose race is now gone forever, and who must henceforth fight a hard battle with the world, on very unequal terms.

Whitman and Melville both interrogate the sibylline figure of an old black woman, and leave us with a portrait not of her, but of their own estrangement and bewilderment: "Who are you dusky woman, so ancient hardly human,/With your woolly-white and turbann'd head, and bare bony feet?" asks Whitman in "Ethiopia Saluting the Colors." Melville, reflecting on the portrait *Formerly a Slave* by Elihu Vedder, in a poem of the same title, tries to see hope in the suffering face of Jane Jackson: "Her dusky face is lit with sober light,/Sibylline, yet benign." John Hollander, in *The Gazer's Spirit*, has acutely observed the various senses of "light" and the play of retrospection and prophecy in Melville's poem, which seems to have influenced later work by the painter. But in other works Melville allows for a far more troubled apprehension. In "The Swamp Angel," the great cannon of that name used to bombard the city of Charleston, South Carolina, in August 1863, is associated explicitly with the justified vengeance of former slaves:

> There is a coal-black Angel
>   With a thick Afric lip,
> And he dwells (like the hunted and harried)
>   In a swamp where the green frogs dip,
> But his face is against a City
>   Which is over a bay of the sea,
> And he breathes with a breath that is blastment,
>   And dooms by a far decree.

As he had a few years earlier in the tale "Benito Cereno," the story of a ferocious revolt on board a slave ship and of an amiable white visiting captain who cannot for the whole length of the tale read the signs, Melville apprehends in "The Swamp Angel" the violence of revenge, the complex layerings of guilt, and the motion of the soul toward the kind of forgiveness that can emerge only from an encounter with truth:

Who weeps for the woeful City
    Let him weep for our guilty kind;
Who joys at her wild despairing—
    Christ, the Forgiver, convert his mind.

I want to conclude on this note of chastened forgiveness. It is the note on which Lincoln closed his Second Inaugural Address just weeks before his death: "with malice toward none; with charity for all." It is the deepest knowledge born of Melville's *Battle-Pieces*, when the delusions of partisanship fall away in the face of shared suffering and death:

Shiloh.
A Requiem.
(April, 1862.)

Skimming lightly, wheeling still,
    The swallows fly low
Over the field in clouded days,
    The forest-field of Shiloh—
Over the field where April rain
Solaced the parched ones stretched in pain
Through the pause of night
That followed the Sunday fight
    Around the church of Shiloh—
The church so lone, the log-built one,
That echoed to many a parting groan

And natural prayer
Of dying foemen mingled there—
Foemen at morn, but friends at eve—
Fame or country least their care:
(What like a bullet can undeceive!)
But now they lie low,
While over them the swallows skim,
And all is hushed at Shiloh.

The hush with which Melville concludes his poem, in the mysterious, prolonged syllables of Shiloh (where dwelt the house of the Lord for the kingless and divided Israelites in Judges 18), grants tragic silence and recognition, but not absolution. In his refusal of facile comfort, Melville shows how art points the way to the life of conscience, however fitfully illuminated. In establishing his silence, he educates our speech. Perhaps in that hush we can hear the dead speak.

"A Careful Disorderliness"

The Organization of Battle-Pieces

Richard H. Cox

> There are some enterprises in which a careful disorderliness is the true method.
>
> Ishmael, *Moby-Dick*, chapter 82

Melville does not make it easy to see the order—let alone what I shall show to be the meaningful disorder—in *Battle-Pieces*. Initially, in fact, he baffles his reader about how he put the book together. He prefaces the whole with an opaque comment on organization, for his poems, he says, were "composed without reference to collective arrangement, but, being brought together in review, naturally fall into the order assumed" [v]. What this means is unclear. What is more, in the subsequent table of contents Melville at once gives the titles of many poems, but supplies no general title for the first rather long group. Later in the contents, he inserts a single title, "Verses Inscriptive and Memorial," which appears to characterize the remaining smaller group.

Despite these baffling qualities which characterize the surface of Melville's book, at least some readers do sense that it has a certain organization. One example may suffice: In the recent *Cambridge Companion to Herman Melville*, Lawrence Buell, of Harvard, claims the poems are "grouped into two sections: a longer sequence featuring particular episodes (mostly battles, with emphasis on aftermath, result, stock-taking) and personalities (mostly officers) and a shorter sequence featuring elegies, epitaphs, and requiems"; and he adds about the order of poems: "they follow the sequence of major events from John Brown's Harpers Ferry raid in November 1859 to the interrogation of Confederate Commander-in-Chief Robert E. Lee before the Reconstruction Committee of Congress in April 1866" (138–39).[1]

While there are indeed parts and a certain use of chronology in Melville's book, Buell's statement nonetheless is not completely accurate. In presenting what I believe to be a more accurate account, I will begin with an overview of the book. I then will analyze two of the ways in which Melville orders his poems: first, he divides the poems into four discernible parts, notwithstanding the general lack of overall titles for all but the third of the four parts; and second, he makes intricate use of chronology both orderly and disorderly. Throughout my voyage, I shall take my bearings from that student of cetology, Ishmael, who speaks the epigram above. That is, I will argue not simply that Melville's book has an order, but more importantly, that this order is the context within which a "careful disorderliness" contains the poet's teaching.

Overview of the Structure of *Battle-Pieces*

Melville's 1866 version of *Battle-Pieces* falls into the following six parts: (1) prose dedication to the 300,000 Union dead (1 page); (2) untitled brief prose statement on the composition and nature of the poems (1 page); (3) contents, listing titles of poems (4 pages); (4) seventy-two poems (233 pages); (5) twenty-four prose Notes to the poems (9 pages); and (6) prose "Supplement" (14 pages).

Thus Melville's book, when viewed as a whole and on its surface, proves to consist of two pairs of prose bookends, one fore and very brief, one aft and considerably longer, framing a substantial poetic center. How these prose bookends are related to each other, and they, in turn, to the poetic center, is by no means apparent. For example, between fore and aft prose statements there are certain troubling tensions. Thus, although the dedication to the 300,000 Union dead (1) and silence about the roughly equal number of Confederate dead suggests Melville writes simply as a Union partisan, nonetheless the prose "Supplement" (6) suggests that Melville stands above such partisanship. Again, although the untitled prose preface (2) speaks of Melville as a singer of verse inspired by he knows not what and certainly not in conscious control of his poetry, the notes (5) make clear that Melville was scrupulously conscious of what he wrote, leaving certain possibly inflammatory sentiments in his poetry only upon careful reflection and perhaps taking other sentiments out after similar thought. How to resolve such conflicts would take me beyond both the space at my disposal as well as my current understanding of Melville's book. As for the relationship of the prose bookends—above all, that of the "Supplement"—to the poems at the center, that will be treated in Paul Dowling's interpretive essay. My more limited concern here is with the ordering of the poems (4) situated in between these prose bookends.

The Groupings into Parts of the Poems in *Battle-Pieces*

Only gradually upon rereading does one begin to discern that Melville's seventy-two poems fall into parts, parts the reader is largely obliged to discover by patiently working through the book. The first, but quite unapparent, part is that of "The Portent," which stands apart from the rest of the poems, indeed as the ruling part. As Rosanna Warren observes, this initial poem of but fourteen lines constitutes the only poem completely in italics—a typographical feature Melville uses with great care throughout his book. Furthermore, it is the only poem not included in Melville's table of contents. I consider this brief poem on the hanging of John Brown to be intended as a kind of epigraph to the rest of the poems, as that historical event itself was a kind of meteor prognosticating the beginning of the Civil War.

With the blindfolded, mute, swaying body of John Brown and his flowing beard metamorphosed as meteor lingering in his mind, the reader is at once led into the main body of the poetry. These seventy-one poems prove to fall (I shall argue) into three parts. The first part, which has no general title, contains fifty-two poems; the second part, titled by Melville himself "Verses Inscriptive and Memorial," contains sixteen poems; and the third part, which, like the first, has no general title, contains three poems.

At first glance, the initial, untitled part of fifty-two poems seems to fit the title of the whole volume. Here are battles, officers, and military events. Here are Donelson, Gettysburg, and Richmond; here are Stonewall Jackson, General McPherson, and General Sheridan; here finally are marches into Virginia and to the sea, along with the surrender at Appomattox. And all these seem to follow a vaguely perceived chronology. Here, in short, is the Civil War we know.

But there is much more to this grouping. For as one reads and then rereads the fifty-two poems, certain organizing features are discerned. Thus, it becomes evident that within this first part, beginning and ending poems are substantially related. The first poem, "Misgivings (1860)," speaks unequivocally in the voice of a Northern patriot who muses "upon my country's ills"; who characterizes America as "the world's' fairest hope linked with man's foulest crime," the crime of enslavement of Negroes; and who, in contemplating the emergent political and military storm, reflects that "Nature's dark side is heeded now—(Ah! optimist-cheer disheartened flown)—" [13]. The fifty-second and last poem in the first part is titled "America." It thus marks a return to the theme of "my country" in "Misgivings." This poem speaks in a voice which seems to be that of a patriot, yet not now the Northern patriot of "Misgivings," but one who transcends the fundamental division into North and South. This new patriot, aware of the pit into which America has sunk, reflects on the course of the war; on America as a mother who "speechless stood,/ Pale at the fury of her brood"; and on the fact that at "her feet" lies "a shivered yoke" cast off from the enslaved. But this new patriot ends with an ominous thought: America now comes to view as a triumphant figure, "Law on her brow and empire in her eyes" [160–62]. What that possibly portends is deeply troubling regarding the nature of the American Republic in an uncertain future following the Civil War.

Between these two framing poems of the first part are lyric poems of widely varying lengths, spoken by many different voices, and presented within a complex and interacting set of three perspectives. The first perspective is a dialectic which frames the military dimension of the war within the political dimension. The first main part begins with a subpart of three poems—"Misgivings" is the first—which articulate the increasingly hate-filled political atmosphere in America leading up to the outbreak of hostilities at Fort Sumter. The whole part ends with a subpart of thirteen poems—"America" is the last—which feature a variety of voices reflecting upon various facets of the war in the aftermath of Robert E. Lee's surrender to Ulysses S. Grant at Appomatox. Among these is one called "The Martyr"; it is an evocation of the passion of "the people" in the North which was unleashed by the assassination of Abraham Lincoln. At the center of the thirteen is one called "The Released Rebel Prisoner"; it is a sympathetic evocation of a Southern soldier, released from imprisonment, moving through New York City on his way to his devastated "home," under the gaze of "the Foe"—who are also called "His cousins and his countrymen" [150–52]. Thus the entire first part opens and closes with complex reflections on the nature of the Civil War, in particular on its political dimensions and consequences, and these reflections frame a long central section of thirty-six poems, the majority of which treat specific battles of the war and the remainder treat themes closely related to but distinct from the specifically military dimension of the struggle.

The second perspective in this opening part—this interlocking of battles and related topics—thus proves to be intertwined with the first, and to be reflective of the two themes announced in the title of Melville's book. The first theme is "battle-pieces." These poems treat an astonishingly small handful of the over ten thousand military engagements of the Civil War and include poems on crucial and famous battles such as Donelson, Shiloh, and Gettysburg.[2] The principles informing Melville's selection of battles are difficult to grasp, but a beginning has been made in the table at the end of this essay, a table schematizing Melville's use of chronology in *Battle-Pieces*. Futhermore, Paul Dowling, in his essay, shows, as one example of Melville's rhetorical strategy, good reason why the poet almost certainly deliberately omits a poem explicitly on Grant's great victory at Vicksburg. Such a poem ought, by rights, at once to follow that on Gettysburg, especially since the surrender at Vicksburg took place on July 4, 1863, the day Lee began his retreat from his defeat at Gettysburg, the day of celebrating the Declaration of Independence.

The second theme is "aspects." This theme characterizes poems treating highly various subjects: "The Housetop," on the draft riots in New York City in July 1863; "The Swamp Angel," on a huge black mortar used over many months in the siege of Charleston, a mortar likened to "a thick Afric lip" and set in vivid symbolic tension with the "white man's seraph," St. Michael's Church; and A "Dirge for McPherson," on the military funeral of General James McPherson, the highest-ranking Northern officer to be killed in battle, struck down by a Confederate bullet before Atlanta. The interplay between the "battle-pieces" and the "aspects" of the war is thus one of the most challenging dimensions of Melville's book, one which I do not pretend yet fully to have understood.

The third perspective which comes to light within the first part is a sketchy chronology of the war. This is most readily visible where Melville has added a date to the title of a poem. At first, it is simply a year (1859); in later poems, it is a month and year (May 1863); and for one and only one poem, that which treats the death of Lincoln, Melville sees fit to append the exact date, April 15, 1865. Melville's deliberate, subtle, and rigorously accurate attention to chronology—rigorously accurate, that is, with two remarkably revealing exceptions—is a complex subject, the details of which may be found in the argument set forth in the next section of this essay.

The third part of the poems has, as we noted, the general title "Verses Inscriptive and Memorial." Nearly all of these sixteen lyrics poetically anticipate a thought uttered in the "Supplement": "the glory of the war falls short of its pathos—a pathos which now at last ought to disarm all animosity" [265]. The poems which convey this pathos, this suffering, are nearly all elegiac: they are mourning songs. As such, they are quieter, simpler, and nearly all are shorter than those in the first part. Though they sometimes allude to specific battles—such as Pea Ridge, Arkansas (a Northern victory) and Chickamauga, Tennessee (a stinging Northern defeat)—the perspective, the emphasis, is not on the battle activity as such, nor on who was victorious or who was defeated. Rather, it is on those who suffered and died, or who suffered and lived on, fated to meditate on that suffering: soldier, parent, brother, widow, orphaned child. And here, though Melville again employs different voices—soldiers who were slain speaking from the grave to the living, or a commemorative speaker standing at a grave—it is often impossible to tell whether the scene is in the North or in the South, or whether the speaker is from either part of the now problematically reunited Republic. Suffering, deep human suffering, in a war that was "an upheaval affecting the basis of things" [259] has joined even foes, in North and South alike, in a way that transcends political boundaries and, in a sense, obliterates them. Such at least is the possibility delicately conveyed by the poetry.

Though thus predominantly elegiac, this third part comes to a seemingly fitting conclusion in two poems which portray victorious Northern soldiers in their transition from war to peace, first in a public, then in a private setting. The penultimate one, "Presentation to the Authorities, by Privates, of Colors captured in Battles ending in the Surrender of Lee," portrays Northern soldiers laying surrendered Confederate battle flags on "the altar which of right claims all—/Our Country," then turning toward "waiting homes with vindicated laws" [182]. The ultimate one, "The Returned Volunteer to his Rifle," portrays a Northern volunteer, from the Hudson Valley region of New York, soliloquizing as he in fact returns to his "hearth—my father's seat." The soldier's apostrophe to his rifle includes the last evocation of a specific battle in this third part of the poems:

> How oft I told thee of this scene—
> The Highlands blue—the river's narrowing sheen.
> Little at Gettysburg we thought
> To find such haven; but God kept it green.
> Long rest! with belt, and bayonet, and canteen. [183]

With this poetic apostrophe, one might think that Melville's poetry on the Civil War should come to a close: the war is ended, peace is restored, the soldier is home. But it is troubling to realize that, although in the elegiac poems of the third part the boundaries between North and South are largely obliterated by shared pathos, yet here at the very end there is no poem treating the return home of a Southern soldier. Furthermore, by the deft device of making the Northern soldier remember but one battle, his survival at the slaughter at Gettysburg, the poet also calls attention to the high point of the Confederacy's assault on the North, and more galling to Southern sensibility, to Lee's defeat, which was sealed by the devastation of Pickett's division in what is perhaps the best-known and most disastrous maneuver of the entire war. Is this not to rub salt in Southern wounds still raw from utter defeat in battle? Is this a proper way to make the transition from war to peace? Has the poet forgotten that the end of war is peace?

What we find, in fact, is that the poetry does not end with the transition from war to peace. Instead, the reader is confronted at once with a fourth and final part of the poems. This part has three poems. It has no general title. And it at once thrusts the reader back into the war. For the first poem of this final part proves to be another "battle-piece," one which seems properly to belong in the second part. This jolting poetic return to war takes place in a poem titled "The Scout toward Aldie." It is set off from the preceding elegaic poems and from the poem itself by a separate title page, with the title set in bold-faced type. It is by far the longest poem in Melville's book with 798 lines; in fact, it seems like a novella placed within a novel. It is a ballad rather than in the lyric form of the rest of the poetry.

"The Scout toward Aldie" narrates a Northern cavalry raid into northern Virginia, not far from Washington—indeed, within sight of the Dome of the Capitol [188]. The raid is directed against the formidable—almost mythic—Confederate Colonel John S. Mosby, who leads a skillful and tenacious group of guerilla rangers in repeated attacks on Northern forces. The Northern commander of the raid is an audacious young colonel of cavalry, a bridegroom, who leaves his bride in his tent as he goes to capture or kill Mosby. The raid is a disaster. The colonel is killed and Mosby and his men escape. At the end, the poet evokes the grief of still one more widow, whose heart "no more shall spring:/To Mosby-land the dirges cling" [225].

One must wonder if Melville's poetic art has failed him in so ordering his book. Why does he make a lengthy and manifestly disorderly poetic return to the agonies of battle of the war that has but so recently ended? Why at the least is not "The Scout toward Aldie" where it belongs—among the "battle-pieces" set within the chronological unfolding of the war within the second main part? And why does the poet rekindle the pathos of the third part of the poems by compelling the reader once again, at the end, to witness and share in the grief of still one more young widow—thus reminding the reader of poems in the third part, such as "An Epitaph"?

In reflecting on these questions, we are moved to recur, first, to my epigraph from *Moby-Dick*, and second, to a poem within the second part of *Battle-Pieces*, a poem that speaks of the poet's art. At the beginning of a chapter titled "The Honor and Glory of Whaling," Ishmael makes this striking pronouncement: "There are some enterprises in which a careful disorderliness is the true method" (ch. 82, 361). Such a paradox is unintelligible unless one thinks through what "careful disorderliness" may mean, and why it is, in a given "enterprise," the "true method." Ishmael's thought is poetically figured forth, I suggest, in the poem titled "Dupont's Round Fight (November, 1861)." It portrays a sea battle at Port Royal, South Carolina: Northern steam-propelled warships move repeatedly around a perfect geometric course, a broad ellipse, to unleash devastating broadsides against Southern land batteries. Prefacing the two-stanza poetic narrative of the naval maneuver and its effects is a single stanza concerning Art:

> In time and measure perfect moves
> All Art whose aim is sure;
> Evolving rhyme and stars divine
> Have rules and they endure. [30]

This first stanza is itself an exemplar of the principle it states: perfect measure in each and every line—that is, perfect iambic feet, four to each odd- and three to each even-numbered line. Thus Hennig Cohen observes that in this poem "Melville adheres to a degree of regularity of form remarkable for him. This regularity is appropriate in a poem which has as its theme the necessity for 'rules' " (Cohen, 215). All the more striking, then, is the momentary irregularity that suddenly appears in the second line of the third and final stanza:

> The rebel at Port Royal felt
> *The Unity overawe*,
> And rued the spell. A type was here,
> And victory of law. (Emphasis added)

The third-to-last line, and it alone, momentarily breaks the otherwise perfect measure of iambics with the anapestic foot in "o-ver-awe," and, paradoxically, thus undermines the very unity it expresses. The broken line is a clue to the meaning of the whole.

That sudden poetic disorderliness within a larger framework of strict orderliness, a disorderliness itself rooted in a sense of what true Art ultimately requires, underlies Melville's placement of "The Scout toward Aldie." For as we shall now see, that seemingly disorderly reopening of warfare in the third-to-last poem of his book, a structural disorderliness anticipated by the poetic disorderliness of the third-to-last line of "Dupont's Round Fight," is itself a poetic reflection of Melville's concern that the war may not truly be over.

Melville's concern is shown, first, by the fact that only in "The Scout toward Aldie" does he ever depict guerilla warfare. That warfare is vividly and terribly portrayed as one in which the combatants on both sides are reduced to a Hobbesian state of nature, a war that is conducted seemingly endlessly by small bands of determined combatants operating utterly on their own in no-man's-land. It is warfare in which even the most minimal laws of war are ignored: those captured on either side are often not treated as legitimate prisoners of war under the law of nations but are peremptorily hung from the nearest tree. This is a fearfully barbaric action which Melville powerfully evokes when he causes a Union officer somberly to refer to the hangings as "that vile jerk and drop" from the "gallows-bough" of a tree in the forest [198] The image of the swaying body of legally executed John Brown, which opens Melville's book, is now replaced by the image of the swaying bodies of lynched victims of guerrilla warfare of the most savage kind.

Melville's concern that the war may not in fact be over is shown, second, in "Lee in the Capitol," the poem that immediately follows "The Scout toward Aldie." In this the central poem of the fourth part, Melville turns at once from battle to politics; what is more, it is the only time in his book he poetically treats an actual political event: the compulsory testimony of Robert E. Lee before a Joint Committee of Congress in February 1866. The crux of the inquiry directed to Lee is a series of questions concerning the bona fides of the Southern surrender, including, in particular, the question whether "should we our arm withdraw,/Would that betray" the newly emancipated blacks [232]? Lee is made to reply as best he can, a reply which comes to a climax in his delivery of a noble, albeit wholly fabricated speech, given to him by Melville. But the senators remain unconvinced as Lee concludes. Not even the eloquence of Melville speaking through the persona of General Lee is able to move these stern men of the North.

Melville's concern that the war may not be over is shown, third, by a remarkable passage in the "Supplement." Emphasizing that there remain great and troubling "doubts" and "fears" as to what will be the course of events a year or so after the war has ended, Melville poses these pregnant questions:

> Why is not the cessation of war now at length attended with the settled calm of peace? Wherefore in a clear sky do we still turn our eyes toward the South, as the Neapolitan, months after the eruption, turns toward Vesuvius? Do we dread lest the repose may be deceptive? In the recent convulsion has the

> crater shifted? Let us revere that sacred uncertainty which forever impends over men and nations. [267–68]

In the event, "that sacred uncertainty" proves, mercifully, not to have opened in the direction of prolonged savage guerrilla warfare, as the gruesome aftermath of full-scale massed battles, but in the direction of an uneasy peace called "reconstruction." And, of course, the long-term aftermath of that war remains with us, as in our debates about the status of African Americans in the American polity, about the propriety of displaying the Confederate flag, and, indeed, about the nature of the war itself: A "civil war"? A "war between the states"?

In this sense, Melville's foreboding proved true. As Rosanna Warren remarks, "All Americans are children of the Civil War whether we know it or not." Similarly T. S. Eliot noted (speaking of the persistence in Milton criticism of controversies regarding the English civil war): "The Civil War is not ended: I question whether any serious civil war ever does end."[3]

But although the war may not end, Melville makes a final poetic effort to moderate its hostile passions. Thus, his last poem makes a return to elegy, to the poetic mode of the central part of the three main parts of his Civil War poetry, in the hope, it seems, that it may be the final such poetic rendering required by his Art. It is most fitting that his very last poem is called "A Meditation." It alone of all the poems has a lengthy subtitle, one much worthy of that meditation—that deep and searching contemplation—to which the title calls us: "ATTRIBUTED TO A NORTHERNER AFTER ATTENDING THE LAST OF TWO FUNERALS FROM THE SAME HOMESTEAD—THOSE OF A NATIONAL AND A CONFEDERATE OFFICER (BROTHERS) HIS KINSMEN, WHO HAD DIED FROM THE EFFECTS OF WOUNDS RECEIVED IN THE CLOSING BATTLES" [238].

The American Civil War at its darkest reaches was indeed at times one of brother against brother. It is awesome to contemplate that the unnatural act of fratricide proved to be a rough and ugly stone in a new foundation of the American Republic; and it is worth noting, in this connection, that the only political philosopher to be named in *Battle-Pieces* is Machiavelli [267], whose *Discourses on Livy* presents the most searching treatment ever written of the tradition of the fratricidal origins of ancient Rome. As Ishmael says in *Moby-Dick:* "To produce a mighty book, you must choose a mighty theme" (ch. 104, 456). Certainly in choosing America's Civil War Melville chose a mighty theme, and, I think, produced a mighty book. That it is a *book*, not simply a collection, is embedded, I think, in that enigmatic early pronouncement by the poet regarding the separate elements of the whole: "being brought together, *in review*, [they] naturally fall into the order assumed" (emphasis added). In what precedes, I do not pretend fully to have grasped the ordering of the book into parts, but to have made a tolerable beginning—one reinforced by a consideration, now, of Melville's use of chronology.

On the Use Of Chronology and Abraham Lincoln

Having considered the whole, the order of all the poems in their parts and their occasional disorder within order, let us now return to the first poems, those from "The Portent" to "America." As mentioned above, when the reader turns from the contents page to the body of the book, he finds that Melville has placed "The Portent (1859)," depicting the executed body of John Brown, prior to "Misgivings" but has not listed it in the contents; and he also finds that Melville has appended the year, 1859, to the title. By the first action, Melville at once reorders the structure of the book that is indicated in the contents: "The Portent" becomes an epigraph to all the other poems.

By the second action—to come to my subject—Melville adds an element which is also not visible in the contents—the element of historical time for the poetically event depicted, but only to the extent of placing it within a year—1859. The significance of this unobtrusive addition is by no means apparent. A survey of all the poems as they appear in the body of the book—a summary of this survey is presented in the table at the end of this essay—shows these features of the use of chronology: First, Melville appends dates to the titles of thirty-eight of the seventy-two poems, which is to say that nearly half refer to events which do not appear to have any date at all. On the other hand, thirty-seven of the first fifty-three poems (or about three-fourths) are dated. Second, the use of dates begins with a single event dated only as 1859; the use of dates then moves through a series of events for every year from 1860 through 1865; and it ends with a single event dated as April, 1866. Third, at first, Melville appends only a year (1859), or two years (1860–1). But beginning with "The March into Virginia," the first poem to treat a battle of the war—First Manassas (or Bull Run)—Melville now adds a month: (July, 1861). This mode of dating—by both month and year—is then the dominant one throughout the rest of the book, but with one notable exception: "The Martyr," a poem on the "passion of the people" on the day Lincoln died. Here, for the only time in his book, Melville uses a date of a specific day: April 15, 1865.

This pattern of Melville's use of chronology prompts more questions than I can answer. Why, in the case of "The Portent," does not Melville at least indicate the month of the execution of John Brown, which is to say, December? And if by the month as well as year, why not date the event still more exactly, by the specific day it took place—December 2, 1859? And so on. Is Melville concerned with such chronological precision? And, more generally, if he proves to be, what has that dimension of his presentation of the Civil War to do—indeed, has it anything to do—with the purpose of his book?

The singularity of the precision with which Melville dates one and only event—the passion of the people on the day Lincoln dies—suggests both that Lincoln's death is of the utmost significance, and also that Melville was perfectly capable of exactly the same precision for other poems which treat events that occurred on a single day: For example, November 7, 1861, the date of the naval battle depicted in "Dupont's Round Fight," or April 9, 1865, the date of the surrender of Lee to Grant in "The Surrender at Appomatox." In fact, however, he does not so proceed. The result is a curious mixture of chronological precision with chronological imprecision, a mode of orderliness joined to or containing a possibly revelatory disorderliness.

Three related questions then are these: First, what evidence is there that Melville had access to and used documentary sources for the construction of his chronology? Second, how accurate is that construction, especially as tested by extraneous sources? Third, how is a reader to construe departures from accuracy, if and when they are found?

In a note to "Rebel Color Bearers at Shiloh," Melville himself points the way toward answers to the first two questions. For in that note Melville alludes to a specific documentary source: "The incident on which this piece is based is narrated in a newspaper account of the battle to be found in the 'Rebellion Record.' " Melville then quotes part of the newspaper account [252]. Twentieth-century researchers, including Frank Day in particular, followed this clue to discover that Melville made extensive use of the documentary volumes titled *The Rebellion Record* as source material for at least twenty poems in his book.[4] In some cases—especially "Donelson (February, 1862)"—Melville's use of *The Rebellion Record* is both subtle and complex, as Paul Dowling shows in his essay. More generally, the evidence mounted by Day and others shows conclusively that Melville made detailed use of at least seven of the twelve volumes of *The Rebellion Record*. These volumes, which average eight hundred pages in length, were published by Van Nostrand, in New York, from 1861–1868. Most volumes contain a "Diary" section, which chronicles events of the war, virtually day by day; a large "Documents" section, which contains official reports on battles, speeches, legislative actions, newspaper accounts, and other detailed material on the war; and finally, a section of miscellany titled "Poetry, Rumors and Incidents." Day's analysis shows that Melville at times made use of material from each section of these documentary volumes. What is more, the chronological order of the poems with dates exactly follows the chronology of events set forth in the relevant volumes of *The Rebellion Record*. In short, Melville, in constructing the order of his poems which date the event depicted, was remarkably attentive to chronological exactitude and had detailed documentary materials allowing him so to proceed.

Nor is that chronological exactitude confined to the poems with datings. In the "Comments" column of the table appended to this essay I show the remarkable chronological orderliness of the events Melville treats, whether in poems which are dated or in those which are not. Thus, for example, he places "The Cumberland" just before "In the Turret"; when one turns to the historical record, whether in *The Rebellion Record*, or in *The Civil War Day by Day*, by E. B. Long and Barbara Long, one finds that these poems refer to events on March 8 and March 9, 1862, precisely the order of the two poems as they are presented by Melville. Thus, for example, having treated the two Battles in the Wilderness—one of May 1–4, 1863 and one of May 5–8, 1864—in a single poem, "The Armies of the Wilderness (1863–4)," Melville allusively indicates in the immediately following poem, "On the Photograph of a Corps Commander," that it concerns General Hancock. The historical materials show that Hancock was a corps commander at the battle of Spotsylvania, May 28, 1864; thus this poem also falls into its correct chronological place. Finally, to cite just one more example: Melville places "The Martyr"—the only poem, as we have noticed, to specify an exact date—just before "The Coming Storm," which must be intended to follow the poem on Lincoln's assassination because its text alludes to that terrible event.

These pieces of evidence that Melville strove to be both

orderly and accurate in the chronology of the events he depicts stand in contrast to the surface sense of the work, which suggests that the book is a mere loose collection in which there is a but a rough chronological dimension. But let us return to a revision of our third question above: What is Melville's purpose in obscuring the dating of certain events while making manifest that of others? Are there no datings which undermine the hypothesis of great exactitude? And if so, what do they indicate?

As it happens, there are, so far as I have been able to perceive, exactly two such datings, and both prove to be remarkably revealing once they are brought to light and interpreted. The first problematic use of chronological ordering is in a note appended to a line in the text of "Gettysburg: The Check (July, 1863)." The second is in the specification of the month of April in the parentheses appended to "Lee in the Capitol (April, 1866)." Both of these misdatings prove to be obliquely connected to Abraham Lincoln and, in particular, to aspects of his speeches.

In the last stanza of his dense, thirty-six-line poem on the battle which marked the turning point of the Civil War, Melville causes his narrator to speak of an obscure event—one when a "warrior-monument, crashed in fight." To that line, he appends a note, where he now speaks for himself, when he says: "On the 4th of July, 1865, the Gettysburg National Cemetery, on the same height with the original burial ground, was consecrated, and the corner-stone laid of a commemorative pile" (249).

What can Melville mean? Is he oblivious of the fact that the official dedication of the cemetery at Gettysburg took place on November 19, 1863, and that the event was widely celebrated in pamphlets and other publications? One such booklet gives extensive details of the ceremony and prints, among other materials, Lincoln's speech, perhaps the single most famous speech in the English language. Or has Melville simply made a gross blunder? I think that, far from being oblivious or grossly blundering, he acted with great deliberation and political perspicacity.

We start from the fact that Melville transposes what he calls the "consecration" of the most famous cemetery of the Civil War from its true historical date to the date of the first celebration of our national independence after the carnage of the Civil War had at last ended. The fundamental premise of the Declaration of Independence, the "self-evident truth" that "all men are created equal," had on this date finally been acted upon by virtue of the war's irreversible emancipation of millions of Negro slaves. In seeking by this rhetorical device of transposing dates to direct such close attention to the significance of the Fourth of July, 1865, and to the principles embedded in the fundamental document which gives that date its deepest meaning, Melville exercises what he will in a note later call "poetical liberty." What is more, it is poetic liberty with political import, for it is commemorative of, and, I suggest, consciously rooted in, a single wonderful sentence in Lincoln's Gettysburg Address: "But, in a larger sense, we cannot dedicate—we cannot *consecrate*—we cannot hallow this ground" (emphasis added). Melville's choice of Lincoln's central verb, *consecrate*, to refer to the public ceremony at which Lincoln spoke seems utterly fitting. Nor is this all. Melville causes his narrator to imitate the terse poetic profundity of Lincoln's speech by the immense poetic compression of the poem on the immense battle at Gettysburg. In so doing, Melville pays a tribute to Lincoln that is as remarkable as it is oblique and subtle. It is a tribute which indicates a concern by Melville for the part Abraham Lincoln played both in the articulation of the ultimate issue of the Civil War, and in the fighting of the war, however unevident that concern is on the surface of his book. It is poetic teaching by a master poet who knows how to indicate more than he directly says.

The second problematic dating by Melville comes to light in the central poem of the last part of the poems: "Lee in the Capitol (April, 1866)." But in addition to the problematic dating , also problematic here are two other features of the poem: first, a speech which Melville invents for Lee to deliver; second, the way Melville designates Lee's interlocutors in the poem.

I begin with the last of these anomalies. The text of the poem depicts Robert E. Lee's appearance before a group of what the narrator calls "Senators," who have summoned Lee to testify within the Capitol of the United States. In historical fact, the Joint Committee to which Lee gave testimony was comprised of both Representatives and Senators. In restricting the interlocutors to "Senators," Melville, while violating strict historical accuracy, seems to intend to focus on poetic truth: that Senators are traditionally understood, both in America and in ancient polities, as the wisest of the representatives of the people. They, if any among the North's spokesman—now that Lincoln is in his grave—might be expected to respond wisely. Whether they do so is a large question.

After Lee tersely responds to several questions, the Senators ask him if he wishes to add anything. The narrator next portrays an internal struggle in Lee's soul. That struggle focuses on this troubling question: Who, if not he, will speak for "the brave [Southern dead],/ Who else no voice or proxy have . . ."? His struggle ended, Lee then gives a long and eloquent speech, which begins: "My word is given—it ties my sword . . ." [233]. It is by far the longest speech in Melville's book; it is uttered in the Capitol of the United States; and it is entrusted to the most revered general of the Confederacy.

Helpful in clarifying his intentions in so proceeding in this remarkable penultimate poem of his mighty book is a note Melville appends to the title of the poem. The note is divided into three paragraphs. In the first, Melville states that Lee was among those summoned to appear, "during the spring just passed," before the "Reconstruction Committee of Congress," and recapitulates the gist of the questioning set forth in the poem. This is the central paragraph:

> In the verse, a poetical liberty has been ventured. Lee is not only represented as responding to the invitation, but also as at last renouncing his cold reserve, doubtless the cloak to feelings

> more or less poignant. If for such freedom warrant be necessary, the speeches in ancient histories, not to speak of Shakespeare's historic plays, may not unfitly perhaps be cited. [255]

Finally, in the third paragraph, Melville tersely treats the probable cause of Lee's speaking as he does: Lee feels deep concern for the kind of treatment the South is likely to receive from the Congress of the victorious North.

My contention that Melville engages in poetic liberty in his treatment of July 4, 1865, in the note to his poem on Gettysburg, is now reinforced by his own explicit admission, in the note on Lee, that he has engaged in "a poetical liberty" in giving Robert E. Lee a speech that never in historical fact was ever delivered. That admission compels the reader, we suggest, to look carefully at another aspect of the poem on Lee and at the note appended to it.

Concerning Melville's dating, Hennig Cohen has this to say:

> The date in the subtitle is incorrect. The fact that Melville was accurate in his dating in all previous subtitles suggests that the error may have been deliberate. If it is indeed not simply due to inadvertence, the cause may be that Melville attached a value to the first anniversary of the surrender and changed the date accordingly, or else that he wished to make his book appear as timely as possible. . . . Lee arrived in Washington on February 16, 1866 and left on February 20. . . . (Cohen, 291–92)

I go further than Cohen. I suggest that Melville quite deliberately transposed the setting of his poem on Lee from February to April 1866, and did so in order to make it fall in that month of "spring," April, when the Civil War began and ended, and, what is more, in the month which marks the first anniversary of the assassination of Abraham Lincoln. In so proceeding, Melville manages, in the course of his book, to combine remarkable historical accuracy with even more remarkable poetic orderings. What is more, in citing the authority of "ancient histories"—

Thucydides and Livy surely come to mind—and "Shakespeare's historic plays," Melville indicates a supreme standard of excellence against which his own book is meant to be appraised, both as to "history" and "poetic truth." Still further, by this second transposing of dates, he reminds us of the earlier transposing of dates: parallel to the transposing of Lee's fictitious, poetical truth-telling speech from February to April of 1865, is the transposing of Lincoln's actual, poetical truth-telling speech from November 1863 to July 4, 1865.

Following from these observations about the transposed dating from February to April of the last dated poem I derive one further, particularly revealing one: Melville's overall plan for the structure of the poems features precisely eight poems with datings in the month of April: "Shiloh. A Requiem" (1862), "The Battle for the Mississippi" (1862), "Running the Batteries" (1863), "The Fall of Richmond" (1865), "The Surrender at Appomatox" (1865), "The Martyr" (1865), "The Coming Storm" (1865), and "Lee in the Capitol" (1866). But given the transposition of Lee's speech from February 1866 to April 1866, as the consequence of employing "poetical liberty," Melville falsifies the otherwise impeccable historical record. That falsification, in turn, reduces the number of poems historically and accurately, as opposed to poetically, placed in April to seven. It thus falls out that the central poem placed in April is "The Fall of Richmond."

That placement proves to square exactly with the significance attributed to that event in Melville's little untitled preface: "With few exceptions, the Pieces in this volume originated in an impulse imparted by the fall of Richmond." In bringing this great event, of April 1865, to the literal center of all the events in April that he has chosen to be dated, Melville also focuses attention on the most *politically* significant event of the Civil War. It is the fall of the seat of the Confederate government, which, from beginning to end, was the political main-spring of the military attempt to destroy the Union. Melville may well have known, in fact, of a remarkable statement made by Jefferson Davis, who had moved the capital to Danville, Virginia, in a last desperate attempt to evade the destruction of the Confederate cause. Davis said: "It would be unwise, even if it were possible, to conceal the great moral, as well as material injury to our cause that must result from the occupation of Richmond by the enemy."[5] The Confederate Constitution, although largely modeled on the Federal Constitution of 1789, boldly made the enslavement of the Negro constitutional.

With the fall of Richmond, and shortly after, of the government itself, that attempt to make the enslavement of Negroes a constitutional right, in a modern republic, was finally defeated, albeit at enormous cost to citizens in both North and South, as well as to both free and enslaved Negroes. The fundamental conflict between the natural right to equality of the Declaration of Independence and the ambiguous, disputed, yet actual protection of slavery in the Constitution had at last ended. Lincoln's somber, bold contention, in June 1858, that " 'A house divided against itself cannot stand.' I believe that this government cannot endure, permanently half *slave* and half *free*" had at last proved to be prophetic.

Given the centrality of this constitutional conflict, it seems fitting that lurking in the background of *Battle-Pieces*, even—or rather, perhaps most particularly—in its apparent mistakes about chronology, is the figure of Abraham Lincoln. Or rather, what there lurks are Lincoln's extraordinary speeches to the American people about the intrinsic connection between the principle of the natural right to equality, in the Declaration, and the principle of the equal protection of the laws, in the Constitution—the ultimate "organic law" of the American Republic. This connection may explain the shift in dates from November to July (for the speech consecrating the Gettysburg cemetery) and from February to April (for Lee's remarkably Lincolnian speech before "Senators"). Melville seems to construe his own book as a poetic substitute for the great speeches of the magnanimous president whose voice had been silenced by a bullet fired by hate-inspired John

Wilkes Booth. As it were, the fallen standard of democratic rhetoric, held so high by the statesman before and during the war, is now picked up and sustained by the patriotic poet, who goes so far as to give the noblest speech in his book to Robert E. Lee.

Conclusion

I have sought in this brief essay to move from an overview of the surface of Melville's *Battle-Pieces* to a closer and closer look at some of its significant features—above all, features limning the peculiarly Melvillean fusing of poetry with politics. Informing that movement and the analysis which it sets forth is the underlying conviction that Melville's *Battle-Pieces and Aspects of the War* is a book of remarkable density, complexity, and subtlety. I reached that conviction only after repeated ventures into the text, often emerging more perplexed than when I entered. At first and for some time the perplexity was discouraging. But after many such ventures, I came to realize that the perplexity itself was a form of the good: it suggested questions and difficulties which I had to tackle, willy nilly, if I was to try to make sense of the whole. And throughout, in spite of my perplexities, I was guided by the sense that a writer capable of the subtleties of *Moby-Dick* and *Benito Cereno* could not plausibly have lost his art in constructing a book on the mighty theme of the Civil War. Rosanna Warren has aptly characterized some of the poems in *Battle-Pieces* as containing "dark knowledge"—as works which "dramatize the dawning of knowledge through struggle." It now seems to me, after many ventures, apt to say that her characterization properly applies to the whole of Melville's book.

It also seems to me apt to say that Melville's book is a kind of extended ode to magnanimity—a rare, a difficult virtue, a virtue profoundly opposed to the vices of resentment, hatred, and the inclination to severity of punishment, a virtue which is problematically teachable. Only thrice in his book does our poet use the word "magnanimity." The first is in the title to the third-to-last poem in the second part of the poems, which is to say in the context of the subpart of poems that treat "aspects" of the Civil War after the fighting mercifully has at last ended. The title of the poem is "Magnanimity Baffled." It portrays an encounter between a victor and a vanquished after a hard-fought battle. The victor—who seems to be a Northern soldier, though that is not certain—speaks to the vanquished, who lies, apparently wounded, on a cot. He praises the vanquished for having striven "stoutly," says "I honor you,/ Man honors man" and "Brave one! I here implore your hand." Hearing no response to all his speeches, the victor impetuously seizes the hand of the vanquished—only to discover that "it was dead," the poem stunningly ends [156]. The occasion for acting as well as speaking magnanimously has been seized by the victor, but as to having it recognized, that possibility has been forever cut off by death. It has been left to the poet to cause the striking encounter to be remembered as an "aspect" of the war—and to cause the thoughtful reader to ponder whether magnanimity is destined, as such, to be "baffled." That question, I shall now argue, underlies two further statements on magnanimity in Melville's mighty book.

The second use of "magnanimity" is given by Melville to Lee in Lee's Lincolnian speech to the "Senators." Lee says, in commenting on the dangers that may arise from hubristic Northern flaunting of the triumph against the South: "Where various hazards meet the eyes,/ To elect in magnanimity is wise" [235]. Surely this part of Lee's speech is in perfect harmony with the spirit of the last paragraph of Lincoln's "Second Inaugural": "With malice toward none, with charity for all . . . [let us] do all which may achieve and cherish a just and lasting peace, among ourselves and with all nations."

The third and final use of "magnanimity" Melville gives to himself in his closing prose "Supplement." Counseling his fellow

Northerners to act as Lee had counseled the "Senators" to act, Melville says: "Some revisionary legislation and adaptive is indispensable; but with this should harmoniously work another kind of prudence, not unallied with entire magnanimity. Benevolence and policy—Christianity and Machiavelli—dissuade from penal severities toward the subdued" (266–67).

Poet, statesman, and general—Melville, Lincoln, and Lee—praise magnanimity, urge its practice, exhibit it in deeds and words, yet possess but limited ability to effectuate its practice in policy. Each is mortal, each is therefore destined to die, as had the vanquished soldier in "Magnanimity Baffled," and as Lincoln already had done by the time Melville composed his book. But the speeches of all three men live on in published works—Lincoln's and Melville's composed by themselves, Lee's composed for him by our poet. Whether we as citizens of the American Republic seek to be instructed by their magnanimity depends decisively on whether we are willing to venture into those speeches and to let our perplexity be our guide—whether, to recur once more to Rosanna Warren's splendid formulation, we are courageous and tenacious enough to pursue "knowledge through struggle."

Notes

1. "Melville the Poet," *The Cambridge Companion*, ed. Robert S. Levine (New York: Cambridge University Press, 1998), 138, 139. From the first appearance of Melville's book until the present, however, the dominant perception of commentators is that it is simply a collection, which is to say a loose assemblage of poems treating various battles and other aspects of the Civil War and loosely joined to some prose elements. Hennig Cohen and some few others go further, to argue that the book does manage to achieve a certain coherence. Cohen says that "The central theme of *Battle-Pieces* is one of opposition and reconciliation"; that Melville's "choice" of certain material "contributed to the thematic and structural unity of his book"; and that the variety and range of the "verse

forms" is "perhaps a formal principle, intended to show unity in diversity, and to reflect the 'varied amplitude of the war" (Cohen, 19–22). For similar statements, see Stanton Garner, *The Civil War World of Herman Melville* (Lawrence: University of Kansas Press, 1993), 33–34.

I think this appraisal of Melville's book is more just than that which views the book simply as a collection. But even it does not reach the question whether Melville intends his volume to be understood as a *book* in the most emphatic sense—that is, as a whole in which the constitutent parts have been chosen with great care and combined to set forth a teaching. A book in this emphatic sense would be Plato's *The Republic*, Shakespeare's *The Tragedy of King Lear*, or Montaigne's *Essais*, all books Melville knew and held in high regard. I think, as the argument in the text seeks to show, that Melville did intend for *Battle-Pieces* to be perceived as a book in the emphatic sense.

2. An indispensable book to accompany the study of *Battle-Pieces* is E. B. Long with Barbara Long, *The Civil War Day by Day: An Almanac 1861–1865* (New York: Da Capo Press, Inc., A Da Capo Paperback, n.d.).

3. T. S. Eliot, "Milton II," in *On Poetry and Poets* (New York: Noonday Press, 1961), 168.

4. Frank L. Day, *Herman Melville's Use of* The Rebellion Record *in His Poetry* (Thesis, University of Tennessee, 1959).

5. Long and Long, *The Civil War Day by Day*, 666.

TABLE. CHRONOLOGY OF POEMS: NUMBERS 1–47 AND NUMBER 71

POEM	MELVILLE'S DATE	COMMENTS
1859		
1. The Portent	(1859)	Dec. 2, 1859: John Brown hanged.
1860		
2. Misgivings	(1860)	Late autumn 1860 ("late autumn brown").
3. Conflict of Convictions	(1860–1)	"the early part of the winter 1860–1" Melville note.
4. Apathy and Enthusiasm	(1860)	"cold November," 1860, to Easter, 1861, and then April, "Hearing Sumter's cannon."
1861		
5. March Into Virginia	(July, 1861)	July 21, 1861.
6. Lyon	(August, 1861)	August 10, 1861.
7. Ball's Bluff	(October, 1861)	October 21, 1861.
8. Dupont's Round Fight	(November, 1861)	November 7,1861.
9. Stone Fleet	(December, 1861)	December 20, 1861.
1862		
10. Donelson	(February, 1862)	February 13–16, 1862.
11. Cumberland	(March, 1862)	March 8, 1862.
12. In the Turret	(March, 1862)	March 9, 1862.
13. Temeraire		[same time as 11 and 12, because same theme of ships & technology]
14. Utilitarian/Monitor		[same time because same theme as above]
15. Shiloh	(April, 1862)	April 6–7, 1862.
16. Battle for Mississippi	(April, 1862)	April 24–25, 1862.
17. Malvern Hill	(July, 1862)	July 1, 1862.
18. Victor of Antietam	(1862)	Battle of Antietam: September 17, 1862.
1863		
19. Battle of Stone River	(January, 1863)	December 31, 1862–January 3, 1863.
20. Running the Batteries	(April, 1863)	April 16,1863.
21. Stonewall Jackson	(May, 1863)	May 2, Jackson wounded; May 10, died. This and the next poem treat Jackson in retrospect after the end of the war, though the date in the subtitle accurately focuses on the wounding and death.
22. Stonewall Jackson		
23. Gettysburg	(July, 1863)	July 1–3, 1863. In a note to the poem, Melville transposes the date of the "consecration" of the military cemetery at Gettysburg from November 19, 1863 to July 4, 1865. See, also, the "comments" section for "Lee in the Capitol."
24. House-top	(July, 1863)	July 13–16, 1863.
25. Look-out Mountain	(November, 1863)	November 24, 1863.
26. Chattanooga	(November, 1863)	November 23–25, 1863.
27. Armies of Wilderness	(1863–4)	Winter 1863 through Spring 1864.

1864		
28. On Photo Commander		Reference to Spotsylvania, May 28, 1864.
29. Swamp Angel		Intermittent use of Parrott gun assumed.
30. Battle for Bay	(August, 1864)	August 5, 1864.
31. Sheridan: Cedar Creek	(October, 1864)	October 17–19, 1864.
32. In the Prison Den	(1864)	
33. College Colonel		
34. Eagle of Blue		
35. Dirge for McPherson	(July, 1864)	July 22, 1864, killed; funeral in October assumed?
36. At Cannon's Mouth	(October, 1864)	October 27, 1864.
37. March to the Sea	(December, 1864)	March begins November 15, ends December 21.
1865		
38. Frenzy in the Wake	(February, 1865)	Sherman's advance through Carolinas.
39. Fall of Richmond	(April, 1865)	April 2–3, 1865.
40. Surrender–Appomatox	(April, 1865)	April 9, 1865.
41 A Canticle		Between April 9 and April 15, 1865.
42. The Martyr	(April 15, 1865)	Only date specified by day: Lincoln dies on Easter Saturday.
43. Coming Storm	(April, 1865)	[after April 15, for it alludes to assassination]
44. Rebel Color Bearers at Shiloh		[after April 15, for it alludes to assassination]
45. The Muster	(May, 1865)	Parade celebrating victory, but in shadow of assassination.
46. Aurora-Borealis	(May, 1865)	Beginning of dissolution of "Armies of the Peace."
47. Released Rebel Prisoner	(June, 1865)	Last poem to which Melville gives a date within Part II of his book.
		NB: Melville appends no dates to poems in Part III.
1866		
71. Lee in the Capitol	(April, 1866)	Lee's testimony to a Joint Committee of Congress took place on February 17, 1866. This is the only instance where Melville, in a sub-title to a poem, exercises "poetical liberty" by transposing the date of an actual event. See "comments" section, above, to the poem on Gettysburg.

Melville's Quarrel with Poetry

Paul M. Dowling

> It is impossible, in view of what
> Mr. Melville has done and of his intention
> in his present book, not to read his "*Battle-Pieces*" with
> a certain melancholy.
> Nature did not make him a poet.
> —Charles Eliot Norton, *The Nation*, September 6, 1866

Battle-Pieces disappoints readers. Despite its martial subject, the book eschews grand passion. Writing about the great tragedy of the Civil War, Melville is a poet of moderation. Instead of participating in the passions the war, he seems to stand back in order to study it. Frustration with this restraint breaks out in some of the poet's best critics. Consider the fine review by William Dean Howells in an 1867 *Atlantic Monthly*. Howells says, "Mr. Melville's skill is so great that we fear he has not often *felt* the things of which he writes, since with all his skill he fails to *move* us" (Kaplan ed., xlii; emphasis added). And in the same review he adds:

> Is it possible—you ask yourself, after running over all these celebrative, inscriptive, and memorial verses—that there has really been a great war, with battles fought by men and bewailed by women? Or is it only that Mr. Melville's inner consciousness

> has been perturbed, and filled with the phantasms of enlistments, marches, fights in the air, parenthetic bulletin-boards, and tortured humanity shedding, *not words and blood*, but words alone? (xli; emphasis added).

Howells's assumption is that successful poetry, especially war poetry, is supposed to be emotionally evocative: it moves us to share in the passionate turmoil of the war's participants. This is the convention known to good critics. Hence also Edmund Wilson censured *Battle-Pieces* as "versified journalism; a chronicle of the patriotic feelings of an anxious, middle-aged non-combatant as, day by day, he reads the bulletins from the front."[1] To the distress of these critics, Melville is a poet of emotional distance.

On this point of emotional distance, I agree with Melville's critics. However, I differ with them about the source—the etiology—of Melville's temperateness. Where they see natural inability, I see deliberate choice. Where they see weakness, I perceive strength. This disagreement is pivotal; upon it everything hinges. For if Melville purposefully chose moderation, we need to ask why he so chose. Instead of concluding that the book avoids tragic passion, we need to begin here, to use this as a starting point for speculation. This I shall attempt. The following argument falls into two parts: first, an attempt to show that Melville deliberately chose moderation on political grounds; and second to show that this choice rests also on poetical ones.

The Political Choice: Responding to Lincoln

Battle-Pieces was composed retrospectively in two senses: first, Melville wrote at the end of the war; second, he reshaped that war to meet the needs of postwar Reconstruction. The first sense can be documented immediately; the second is the argument of this section.

In the preface Melville claims both that he recollected "the strife as a memory" and that most of the poems "originated in an impulse imparted by the fall of Richmond," which is to say, the fall of the Confederate government and thereby the harbinger of war's end. Also, more than a third of the poems treat events after Appomattox. But it is Melville's reshaping of the Civil War, that second sense of retrospect, which will concern us now.

To understand it, we shall take our bearings by the prose "Supplement" at the end of *Battle-Pieces*, first by explicating its teaching; then by showing how the argument for moderation in the "Supplement" reshapes or poetically refashions the Civil War. By taking our bearings from the "Supplement," we imitate Melville: as he read the war from the perspective of its end, so we shall read his book.

The subject of the "Supplement" is post–Civil War Reconstruction. Addressed to the victorious North, its purpose is to plead for generosity toward the defeated South in order to restore the Union. But the defeated South means the white South and such generosity involves temporarily subordinating the black freedmen to the goal of reuniting the country.

Where, then, does such an argument fit on the political spectrum of that time? Hennig Cohen locates Melville's politics this way: "[Melville] inclined in his political sympathies toward the Democrats and the moderate wing of the Republican party, and one of the few reviews of any length devoted to *Battle-Pieces* was in a newspaper of this persuasion (*New York Herald*, September 3, 1866)" (294). Cohen, of course, limits himself to living political forces. But in so doing he neglects the towering figure of Abraham Lincoln. This may be like trying to understand Shakespeare's *Hamlet* by ignoring the Ghost who sets the plot in motion. In fact, as I shall argue, certain of the poet's core political sympathies approximate those of President Abraham Lincoln: generosity toward the defeated South coupled with temporary subordination of the needs of the freedmen.

This is the Lincoln who, toward war's end, claimed that our task extended beyond final surrender: "With malice toward none; with firmness in the right, as God gives us to see the right, let us strive on to finish the work we are in; to bind up the nation's wounds; to care for him who shall have borne the battle, and for his widow, and his orphan—to do all which may achieve and cherish a just, and a lasting peace, among ourselves, and with all nations."[2] This is the Lincoln who is reported by Lord Charnwood to have rejected harsh treatment of Confederate leaders:

> Lastly, there was talk of the treatment of rebels and of the demand that had been heard for "persecution" and "bloody work" "No one need expect me," said Lincoln, "to take any part in hanging or killing these men, even the worst of them. Frighten them out of the country, open the gates, let down the bars, scare them off." "Shoo," he added, throwing up his large hands like a man scaring sheep. "We must extinguish our resentments if we expect harmony and union."[3]

This is finally the Lincoln who, in his last public address, delineated a policy on Reconstruction magnanimous to the South. The date was April 11, 1865, after both the fall of Richmond and the surrender of Lee at Appomattox. In the following passages from that address, the president enunciates the general principle of Reconstruction and then illustrates with the proposed new state government for Louisiana:

> We all agree that the seceded States, so called, are out of their proper practical relation with the Union; and that the sole object of the government, civil and military, in regard to those States is to again get them into that proper practical relation. . . . The amount of constituency, so to to [sic] speak, on which the new Louisiana government rests, would be more satisfactory to all, if it contained fifty, thirty, or even twenty thousand, instead of only about twelve thousand, as it does. It is also

> unsatisfactory to some that the elective franchise is not given to the colored man. I would myself prefer that it were now conferred on the very intelligent, and on those who serve our cause as soldiers. Still, the question is not whether the Louisiana government, as it stands, is quite all that is desirable. The question is "Will it be wiser to take it as it is, and help improve it; or to reject, and disperse it?" "Can Louisiana be brought into proper practical relation with the Union *sooner* by *sustaining*, or by *discarding* her new State Government?" . . . Concede that the new government of Louisiana is only to what it should be as the egg is to the fowl, we shall sooner have the fowl by hatching the egg than by smashing it? . . . What has been said of Louisiana will apply generally to other States. (Basler ed., vol. 8, 403–404)

Before his own assassination, then, Abraham Lincoln sketched a Reconstruction policy resembling that of Herman Melville.

Nonetheless, between the president and the poet, there are differences concerning means to the end of harmonious Reconstruction. Perhaps most fittingly for a poet, in contrast to Lincoln, Melville ignores details of legislation and concentrates on the sentiments needed to support laws.[4] The poet thus recalls the teaching of Plato and Rousseau: laws by themselves are weak; to be effective, they require support in the mores. Especially is this true after a civil war, where laws have failed and arms have destroyed so much. As Melville says, "the pacification . . . which lovers of their country yearn for, and which our triumphant arms . . . did not bring about, and which law-making never by itself can achieve, may yet be largely aided by generosity of sentiment, public and private" [266]. Questions the poet finds appropriate are about manners: ". . . true reconciliation seldom follows a violent quarrel; but . . . nice observances and mutual are indispensable to prevention of a new rupture" [270].

The manners of interest to the poet, of course, are primarily those of the North: "Rightly will more forbearance be required from the North than the South, for the North is victor" [271]. Furthermore, this forbearance is directed toward white Southerners. Blacks are to be considered, of course, but in a subordinate position. "In our natural solicitude to confirm the benefit of liberty to the blacks," writes Melville, "let us forbear from measures of dubious constitutional rightfulness toward our white countrymen—measures of a nature to provoke, among other the last evils, exterminating hatred of race toward race" [268]. The poet is well aware of dangers lurking in such a policy toward blacks, but he hopes for future remedies to these: "Something may well be left to the graduated care of future legislation, and to heaven."[5]

As Melville's "Supplement" shows, however, generosity toward white Southerners and subordination of freedmen ran against the grain of Northern feelings. Northerners after the war felt bitter, triumphant, and censorious. Bitterness is mentioned three times. Melville worries lest he contribute to "a bitterness which every sensible American must wish at an end"; he aborts a line of thought which "leads toward those waters of bitterness from which one can only turn aside and be silent"; he breaks off another theme "with resentments so close as to be almost domestic in their bitterness" [263, 269, 272]. Such bitterness finds causes. One is the "clinging reproach" of "the systematic degradation of man," this "curse of slavery" [261, 266].

So Melville's "Supplement" challenges Northern public opinion in pleading for generosity to the South and for subordination of the freedmen. But I began by claiming that the argument in the "Supplement" poetically refashions Melville's Civil War. So let us turn now to the poetry in order to read Melville's book retrospectively. Melville's poems (I shall show) portray the war in such a manner as to temper extremes of passion. This poetic refashioning is achieved by omission and by commission, by avoiding certain inflammatory things and emphasizing or even fabricating other irenic ones. The key to these choices is found in the "Supplement": Melville wants "to modify or do away" with those feelings and opinions "of a less temperate and charitable cast" [265,

260]. Everything must be done with a view, not to historical accuracy but to facilitate "the pacification . . . lovers of their country yearn for" [266].

This reshaping of history can be illustrated by the poetic treatment of three leaders of the war: Abraham Lincoln, Ulysses Grant, and Robert E. Lee.[6] Lincoln's is a particularly telling case in view of the agreement between president and poet as to the goal of Reconstruction. Nonetheless, there are differences as to the means to that goal. Strikingly enough, Lincoln and his speeches all but disappear from the poetic part of *Battle-Pieces*. In seventy-two poems about the Civil War, the following words never appear: Abraham Lincoln, slavery, and the Declaration of Independence. "The Martyr," a poem about Lincoln's assassination, never mentions the president by name; and in fact its true focus, suggested by its subtitle, is "the passion of the people on the 15th of April, 1865" [141]. Mention is made of "The Abrahamic rivers" in "The Muster," a poem about the final postwar review of the Northern troops at Washington [145, 146]. But this phrase is ambiguous, since in context it could also refer to either the biblical patriarch or the Mississippi River. The omission of Lincoln's name is best explained in one of Melville's notes: "Few need be reminded that, by the less intelligent classes of the South, Abraham Lincoln . . . was regarded as a monster wantonly warring upon liberty. He stood for the personification of tyrannic power. Each Union soldier was called a Lincolnite" [251]. The disappearance of Lincoln's name from the poems, even from the poem devoted to his assassination, is a training of Northern restraint.

If Lincoln's name is hardly mentioned, his speeches fare even worse. In his Second Inaugural Address, Lincoln claimed slavery was the root of the conflict: "All knew that this interest was, somehow, the cause of the war" (Basler ed., vol. 8, 332). For his own purposes of moderating postwar hostilities, however, this is a claim Melville downplays. The word "slavery" itself never appears in the poems. And there is but one mention of "slaves," in a poem about Northern general Sherman's "March to the Sea": as Union troops march through the South, "And the banners brightly blooming/The slaves by thousands drew,/ And they marched besides the drumming,/ And they joined the armies blue" [130].

There is, however, a poem titled "Formerly a Slave," a poem which suggests Melville's ambivalence toward the freedmen. Although hinting at dangers for the blacks, this poem reiterates the need to subordinate their immediate interest to reconciliation among whites. One hint of peril is the placement of this poem within a group of poems set just after the war, poems where troubling events suggest the passions of the conflict have not died and, indeed, will not easily die. In the first of this small subgroup, a released Southern prisoner of war, stopping at New York ("the Nineveh of the North"; "The City of the Foe"), cannot stop thinking of the war. In the second, Southern guns, buried in a Virginia cemetery, suggest Southerners' desire to continue the war. In the fourth, "The Apparition" describes a volcanic eruption desolating an idyllic pastoral scene, a desolation recalling the war. The fifth, "Magnanimity Baffled," finds a Northerner trying to befriend a Southern soldier who, he discovers, is already dead.

Into the numerical center of this foreboding context Melville inserts "Formerly a Slave," describing a painting of a black woman freed from slavery. Its beginning is ominous: "The sufferance of her race is shown" [154]. The allusion may be to Shakespeare's *Merchant of Venice* where the Jewish Shylock remarks to his Christian enemy Antonio, "In the Rialto you have rated me/ About my moneys and my usances./ Still I have borne it with a patient shrug,/ For sufferance is the badge of all our tribe."[7] Shortly thereafter, the two enemies enter into a bond or contract which leads to both Antonio's near loss of life and Shylock's unjust ruin. Thus Melville's beginning is unsettling, suggesting hatred between different races and creeds as well as unjust treatment of minorities. Nonetheless, much of the poem bespeaks the argument of the "Supplement," with its hope for the future of the black race in America. Although the woman in the portrait suffers, nonetheless "Her children's children they shall know/ The good withheld from her;/ And so her reverie takes prophetic cheer." The final line speaks of her face as "Sibylline, yet benign," prophetic of future good.

These ambivalent poetic sentiments are consistent with the prose "Supplement." The poet, on the one hand, is touched by the plight of the freedmen. "The blacks, in their infant pupilage to freedom, appeal to the sympathies of every humane mind." Nonetheless he argues, while we are rightly concerned for the future of the blacks, "the future of the whole country, involving the future of the blacks, urges a paramount claim upon our anxiety" [267]. While we rejoice at the downfall of slavery as an abhorred "atheistical iniquity," yet "the coexistence of the two races in the South . . . seems (even as it did to Abraham Lincoln) a grave evil." With such the poet counsels moderate hope; for "with certain evils men must be more or less patient" [269].

Finally, there is the Declaration of Independence. Central to Lincoln's indictment of slavery was this document's equality clause: "We hold these truths to be self-evident, that all men are created equal." For Abraham Lincoln, this clause not only revealed the injustice of slavery; it also unified our nation of immigrants. As Lincoln explained in an 1858 speech, not all Americans are descendants of Englishmen.

> We have besides these [English descendants] among us perhaps half our people who are not descendants at all of these men, they are men who have come from Europe—German, Irish, French and Scandinavian—men that have come from Europe themselves, or whose ancestors have come hither and settled here, finding themselves our equals in all things. If they look back through this history to trace their connection with those days by blood, they find they have none, they cannot carry themselves back into that glorious epoch and make themselves feel that they are part of us, but when they look through that old Declaration of Independence they find that those old men

> say that "We hold these truths to be self-evident, that all men are created equal," and then they feel that that moral sentiment taught in that day evidences their relation to those men, that it is the father of all moral principle in them, and that they have a right to claim it as though they were blood of the blood, and flesh of the flesh of the men who wrote that Declaration and so they are. That is the electric cord in that Declaration that links the hearts of patriotic and liberty-loving men together. . . . (Basler ed., vol. 2, 499–500)

And it was this "electric cord in that Declaration" which Lincoln, in his 1863 Gettysburg Address, made both the purpose to which the country dedicated itself at its birth ("Four score and seven years ago our fathers brought forth on this continent a new nation . . . dedicated to the proposition that all men are created equal") and for which it fought the Civil War: "Now we are engaged in a great civil war, testing whether that nation . . . can long endure."

Melville reverses Lincoln. In place of the equality clause from the Declaration the poet reinstates the common English ancestry of Americans. Hence the battle of Fort Donelson becomes a "perverted Bunker Hill"; the narrator in one poem observes "In North and South still beats the vein,/ Of Yorkist and Lancastrian"; another searches the lineage of a Northern commander:

> Trace back his lineage, and his sires,
> Yeoman or noble, you shall find
> Enrolled with men of Agincourt,
> Heroes who shared great Harry's mind. [105]

Finally, Melville himself in the "Supplement" distinguishes the blacks from Southern whites by speaking of the latter as "having a like origin with ourselves" and "nearer to us in nature" [44, 73–74, 151, 266, 267].

This emphasis on common ancestry conduces to pacification; it also turns the war itself into fratricidal slaughter and reconciliation into family harmonizing after the war. Hence just before the war the narrator of "Apathy and Enthusiasm" speaks of "The appealings of the mother to brother and to brother,/ Not in hatred so to part"; the Wilderness in Virginia, where two fratricidal battles were fought, resembles "the plain/ Tramped like the cindery beach of the damned—/ A site for the city of Cain." As opposed armies warily wait for battle on the same field, a chorus warns, "*Picket, Take heed—take heed of thy brother!*" [96]. The final "Meditation" is narrated by a Northerner after attending two funerals of brothers on opposites sides; it recalls moments during the war when brothers and kinsmen felt a sympathy toward the other side, when "something of a strange remorse/ Rebelled against the sanctioned sin of blood,/ And Christian wars of natural brotherhood." And this same narrator, surveying the fratricide, asks. "Can Africa pay back this blood/ Spilt on Potomac's shore?" [97, 13, 241, 242].

So both Lincoln's name and his speeches about slavery and citizenship are replaced by poetry attempting different means to fulfill Lincoln's goal, "to bind up the nation's wounds." In contrast to Lincoln's unobtrusiveness, the two military leaders of the war figure prominently in these poems about "the wars of Grant and Lee" [137]. Grant is mentioned twenty-two times (in eight poems as well as the notes and the "Supplement"); Lee appears seventeen times (in five poems and the notes).[8] Yet the portraits of both have also been artfully remodeled to fit postwar needs.

Grant, the war figure mentioned most often, receives considerable praise. What Helen Vendler calls his panoramic view at Chattanooga ("Grant stood on cliffs whence all was plain") suggests a statesmanly foresight like that of Melville himself.[9] A poem for the 1863 battle of "Chattanooga" speaks of Grant having a "plan"; one for the 1864 battle of the Wilderness mentions his "resolute scheme" [90, 101]. And at war's end in "The Fall of Richmond," his star is in the ascent:

Honor to Grant the brave,
Whose three stars now like Orion's rise
When wreck is on the wave—
Bless his glaive. [135]

Highly praised though he be, Grant is nonetheless sketched selectively. His praiseworthiness rests less on brilliantly conceived and ruthlessly fought battles than on magnanimous clemency after the fighting. The Northern general does not receive a poem celebrating his most brilliant triumph at Vicksburg, although this campaign is mentioned for purposes of reconciliation. Specifically, the surrender of the Southern forces is depicted in the final lines of the final poem in order to encourage not triumph but generous refusal to be triumphant:

When Vicksburg fell, and the moody files marched out,
Silent the victors stood, scorning to raise a shout. [243]

Grant is allowed a celebratory triumph in "The Surrender at Appomattox," but later, after a poem on the assassination of Lincoln, this surrender is mentioned in a poem whose subtitle reads: "A plea against the vindictive cry raised by civilians shortly after the surrender at Appomattox" and which ends thus:

Spare Spleen her ire,
And think how Grant met Lee. [145]

Furthermore, Grant's generalship is downplayed. In the second-longest poem, "Donelson," Grant's excellence is limited to a passive kind, such as observing the spirit which is already in his soldiers [47] and then restraining his soldiers from a night fight [50]. This passivity belies Melville's source. A newspaper account in *The Rebellion Record* praises Grant's generalship, such as his logistical sense of where a variety of men and material could be brought to bear upon this fort, as well as his immediate leadership at several crises in the battle.[10] Even on small points Grant's achievements are usurped by those of his men: it was Grant, not his men, who uttered the following:

> Our troops are full of spirits—say
> The siege won't prove a creeping one.
> They purpose not the lingering stay
> Of old beleaguerers; [34]

In fact, Donelson was the beginning of Grant's great strategic insight into the nature of this war: fight the enemy wherever you meet him; use Northern superiority in men and materiel; and demand unconditional surrender. But no mention is made of Grant's demand in this and subsequent battles for "unconditional surrender." Nor is mention made of his reputation as a "butcher" of men in battles including the Wilderness. In other words, instead of opposing Grant's generalship to that of Lee in ways which might rekindle wartime hate, Melville downplays military leadership and emphasizes Grant's noble restraint and magnanimity toward a fallen foe. However inaccurate to history, a General Grant so remodeled fits the "Supplement" policy of moderating the passions of war for the needs of Reconstruction.

Similar to the treatment of the Union general is that of his Confederate opponent. Like Grant, Lee does not receive a poem celebrating his most brilliant victory, that at Chancellorsville, although that battle is mentioned in connection with Stonewall Jackson's death. Nor is Lee's terrible defeat mentioned in the poem on Gettysburg. Thus Melville hews to a middle way, intending to rouse neither triumph nor resentment, for neither passion conduces to true pacification.

Lee, however, receives the honor of becoming the poet's spokesman. In the lengthy penultimate poem, "Lee in the Capitol," Melville invents for the now-retired Confederate general a speech to a congressional hearing, one which echoes crucial points of the "Supplement." Melville's note to this fabricated speech justifies his poetic license:

> In the verse, a poetical liberty has been ventured. Lee is not only represented as responding to the invitation [by the senators to speak], but also as at last renouncing his cold reserve, doubtless the cloak to feelings more or less poignant. If for such freedom warrant be necessary, the speeches in ancient histories, not to speak of those in Shakespeare's historic plays, may not unfitly perhaps be cited. [255]

In this fabricated speech, Lee tells the Northern congressmen what they must accept of Southern attitudes toward the war. Responding to questions by Northerners about the mind of the South, Lee goes beyond the questions to counsel Melvillian restraint and magnanimity:

> Push not your triumph; do not urge
> Submission beyond the verge. . . .
> Where various hazards meet the eyes,
> To elect in magnanimity is wise. [234–35]

Lee's poetic remarks echo Melville's "Supplement" in calling for Northern forbearance: "It is enough, for all practical purposes, if the South have been taught by the terrors of civil war to feel that Succession, like Slavery, is against Destiny; that both now lie buried in one grave; that her fate is linked with ours; and that together we comprise the Nation" [260]. That is, the South must only "feel" the inevitability of the war's outcome; we in the North ought not push the South beyond this to hypocritical statements of penitence for having waged the war. And we should exercise this restraint not simply out of realism, but also in the name of higher virtues. As Melville argues: "Some revisionary legislation and adaptive is indispensable; but with this should harmoniously work another kind of prudence, not unallied with entire magnanimity" [266–67].

Melville and his spokesman Lee not only counsel Northern restraint toward the South, but also Northern sympathy for the South's attachment to its own, to its war heroes, its kith and kin. As Melville writes in his own name, "The mourners who this summer bear flowers to the mounds of the Virginian and Georgian dead are, in their domestic bereavement and proud affection, as sacred in the eye of Heaven as are those who go with similar offerings of tender grief and love into the cemeteries of our Northern martyrs" [263].

A similar sympathy for Southern love of its own is conveyed by means of a little tale or parable Lee tells of a Moorish maid. After she converted to Christianity, the priests demand the maid prove her Christian faith by leaving her Moorish father and even by hating her kin. To this request she responds in moving terms:

> Then will I never quit my sire,
> But here with him through every trial go,
> Nor leave him though in flames below—
> God help me in his fire! [236]

And Lee uses this appeal to natural love of one's own in order to urge a certain restraint by the North, especially by Northern lawmakers.

In short, Melville's political choice was for restraint or moderation. The poet reshapes the Civil War so as to temper those of its extreme passions inhibiting Reconstruction. Melville's political intention was perceived by William Dean Howells, who concludes his essay by saying: "If the Rebels were as pleasingly impalpable as those the poet portrays, we could forgive them without a pang, and admit them to Congress without a test-oath of any kind" (xliv). Or, as Abraham Lincoln said, in a previously quoted remark, "We must extinguish our resentments if we expect harmony and union" (Charnwood, 450).

The Poetic Choice: Responding to Plato

As we have seen, Melville's political reason for writing moderately was to dampen the Civil War passions during Reconstruction. But besides this civic reason for that time period of Reconstruction, there is a poetical reason, one which places Melville on a stage older and larger than postwar America. Indeed, to elucidate Melville's thinking requires some understanding of a disagreement between poets and philosophers as understood by Plato and Shakespeare.

Melville himself justifies this departure from the American context. *Battle-Pieces* abounds in references to Shakespeare and Milton, to Plato and Homer. These are not mere decorative erudition; they indicate bench marks by which our poet ambitioned to be judged. For Melville is an American writer who sees his writing on a world stage. And so he should.

This aspiration was sensed by the poet and critic Robert Penn Warren. While finding Melville deficient in the craft of poetry, Warren claims that his ambition was of a higher order than his more successful contemporaries:

> It must be admitted that Melville did not learn his craft. But the point is that the craft he did not learn was not the same craft which some of his more highly advertised contemporaries did learn with such glibness of tongue and complacency of spirit. Even behind some of Melville's failures we catch the shadow of the poem which might have been. And if his poetry is, on the whole, a poetry of shreds and patches, many of the patches are of a massy and kingly fabric—no product of the local cotton mills.[11]

Following the lead of Warren, I shall argue that Melville's "kingly fabric" ought to be judged by the height of his aspirations, not the lowly success of his contemporaries. Melville aspires to a place in company with the world's great writers.

This claim, of course, requires explanation. Melville views poetic greatness set off against poetic convention, a convention he alludes to twice in *Battle-Pieces*. But his remarks are so brief and elusive we are apt to miss his precision. One is in "On Sherman's Men: who fell in the Assault of Kenesaw Mountain, Georgia." Here the narrator remarks, "battle can heroes and bards restore" [174]. This is the convention: poets need heroes in battle. And in the "Supplement" Melville enlarges upon poetic convention, while allowing space for his unconventional poetry: "Zeal is not of necessity religion," he writes, "neither is it always of the same essence with poetry or patriotism" [264]. He speaks precisely when he says "Zeal is *not* . . . *always* of the same essence with poetry. . . ." One can almost hear Melville add, however, "not always" but "almost always." Which is to say, Melville insinuates that poetry is often about warriors and is almost always zealous. The prototypical poetic subject is wrathful Achilles of Homer's *Iliad*. But this is a convention, as we have shown, Melville eschews. His is war poetry neither heroic nor zealous.

To grasp Melville's poetic reason for challenging this convention we need to consider those great poets and philosophers Melville mentions and their sense of the quarrel. To begin our excursus, consider first that friendly critic of poets, Plato's Socrates. In the *Republic*, he claims "there is an old quarrel between philosophy and poetry" (10.607B). In this quarrel philosophers charge poets with flattering the dominant passions of their audiences. They are entertainers unconcerned with truth. This accusation is leveled at poets in two of Plato's dialogues, *Ion* and *Symposium*. Speaking in the former to the rhapsodist or dramatic reader Ion, Socrates criticizes poets and performers who manipulate the passions of audiences: "Shall we assert that this man is then in his right mind who, adorned with rich raiment and golden crowns, cries in the midst of sacrifices and festivals, although he has lost none of these things, or who is frightened while standing before twenty thousand friendly human beings, although no one is stripping or harming him?"[12] Nonplused by this critique of his profession, the foolish rhapsodist blurts out that moving the audience is for him the real business of poetry:

> I look down on [the audience] each time from the platform above as they are crying, casting terrible looks and following with astonishment the things said. I must pay the very closest attention to them, since, if I set them to crying, I shall laugh myself because I am making money, but if they laugh, then I shall cry because of the money I am losing. (535E)

Socrates' case against the poets, then, is that they are mere entertainers for profit, unprincipled manipulators of human passion. This is a charge whose force more thoughtful poets than Ion have recognized. Hence in the *Symposium*, Socrates teases the popular tragic poet Agathon. Speaking with some irony of Agathon's mass appeal, Socrates says:

> My wisdom's a poor, dubious thing, but yours is brilliant and effusive. Why, just the day before yesterday you displayed your youthful brilliance and dazzled more than thirty thousand witnesses from all over Greece.

To this the somewhat nettled Agathon replies: "Don't be insolent, Socrates."[13] As self-aware poets like Agathon know, in order to remain popular, they must flatter their audience by glorifying the lively and intense passions. Otherwise stated, it is difficult for a wise or rational character to find an important role on a stage mirroring the life of its audience.

Difficult, but not impossible. For at the end of Plato's *Symposium*, Socrates suggests a way for poetry to overcome philosophy's criticism. He forces Agathon and Aristophanes, tragedian and comedian, to accept that "the writing of both tragedy and comedy is the job of the same man, and a skilled tragedian also knows how to write comedies" (223D). What Socrates means by arguing the skilled playwright should write both tragedy and comedy he does not make perfectly clear. Perhaps he means that by mixing the two kinds of poetry, that of tears and that of laughter, it is possible to present a rational character on stage. This is what the Platonic dialogues themselves do. But how is one to achieve this task on the popular stage? The Platonic dialogues are not, after all, popular with large audiences.

Our greatest poet and at the same time our most popular playwright, Shakespeare, exemplifies the possibility as well as the difficulty of finding a dramatic role for wisdom in this mixed mode.[14] Shakespeare's great tragedies, of course, foreground passionate heroes like Lear and Macbeth, with wiser souls like Edgar and Malcolm in the background. But in certain dramas other than the tragedies, Shakespeare attempts to place wisdom center stage. The best examples are plays written toward the end of his career in the so-called Romances, such as *The Tempest* dominated by the wise Prospero. Earlier in comedies often called "problem plays," wisdom has an important but less central role in such characters as the wise Portia in *Merchant of Venice*, the studious Duke in *Measure for Measure*, and the crafty Ulysses in *Troilus and Cressida.* But these "problem plays" receive criticisms similar to those of *Battle-Pieces*. Even *The Tempest* is so disparaged. Readers not charmed by the play's music and magic find its hero, Prospero, somewhat cold, calculating, and talkative. He never performs a passionate great deed. His great work of magic is to moderate the passions of those enemies he brings to his island and to reform their souls. At the height of his powers over his foes, he tempers his own anger and forgives:

> Though with their high wrongs I am struck to the quick,
> Yet with my nobler reason 'gainst my fury
> Do I take part: the rarer action is
> In virtue than in vengeance: they being penitent,
> The sole drift of my purpose doth extend
> Not a frown further. (5.1. 25–30)

Such rational restraint is not the stuff of popular drama, some would say. We want poetic heroes like the Othello who ends his life proclaiming to have loved "not wisely, but too well" (5.2.344) and then killing himself with his sword. That is what Howells wanted: "words and blood"—and words which flatter our passionate lives and do not remind us by contrast of our lack of wisdom.

Shakespeare's efforts to find dispassionate wisdom a dramatic role were understood by Melville, who calls himself "Shakespeare's pensive child. . . . Who reaches Shakespeare's core" in "The Coming Storm" [143]. According to Melville, Shakespeare's core is philosophy, albeit philosophy somewhat obscured by the trappings of popular plays. Such thoughtful perception Melville revealed both in a critical review and in his prose fiction. In his review "Hawthorne and His Mosses," he distinguishes Shakespeare as popularly appreciated entertainer from Shakespeare as comparatively unappreciated philosopher:

> For by philosophers Shakespeare is not adored as the great man of tragedy and comedy.—"Off with his head! so much for Buckingham!" this sort of rant, interlined by another hand, brings down the house,—those mistaken souls, who dream of Shakespeare as a mere man of Richard-the-Third humps, and Macbeth daggers. But it is those deep far-away things in him; those occasional flashings-forth of the intuitive Truth in him; those short, quick probings at the very axis of reality;—these are the things that make Shakespeare, Shakespeare. . . . But, as I said before, it is the least part of genius that attracts admiration. (*The Piazza Tales*, 244)

These comments focus on Shakespeare's tragedies, with truth tellers in the background; they ignore his late plays which put wise characters in major roles.

Not so restricted is Melville's prose fiction. Here he imitates the full rage of Shakespeare's responses to Plato. In *Moby-Dick* his response resembles the Bard's earlier plays, such as *Troilus and*

Cressida. Here he avoids the risk of wisdom on center stage: his main character, Ahab (like Shakespeare's Troilus), has the tragic passion and his detached narrator, Ishmael (like Shakespeare's Ulysses), has the wit. That great novel is antebellum and its separation of heart and head is not what Melville tries in postwar works. In fact, we might compare Melville's last work, *Billy Budd*, to *The Tempest*. In the former, the main character (Captain Vere) is judicious, somewhat like Prospero. But Vere is clearly not heroic; indeed, Melville contrasts him with the heroic Admiral Nelson who died at Trafalgar, the moment of his greatest naval victory. Nelson expired doing what heroes in poetry do: speak passionately and die passionately. As Melville writes about the heroic admiral in *Billy Budd:* "the poet but embodies in verse those exaltations of sentiment that a nature like Nelson, the opportunity being given, vitalizes into acts."[15] Captain Vere by contrast died in bed; and his greatest moment is not a deed but a speech before a Drum Head Court moderating between two extremists, Billy Budd and John Claggart.

As in *Billy Budd* so in *Battle-Pieces*, Melville frustrates our desire for the heroic, even while indicating awareness of our longing. Corresponding to the former novella's use of Lord Nelson is the latter's mention of two characters with tragic potential: weird John Brown in the first poem, "The Portent," and fanatic Edmund Ruffin in the "Supplement" [10 and 265]. Brown's deeds are widely known. The less well known secessionist Ruffin "fired the first shot of the Civil War at Sumter, and a little more than four years afterwards fired the last one into his own heart at Richmond." Melville's judgment on Ruffin could also be applied to Brown: "Noble was the gesture into which patriotic passion surprised the people in a utilitarian time and country." Which is to say, either of these passionate extremists could have been the hero of a Homeric tragedy of the Civil War. But a stirring rendition of the war keeps the warlike passions alive. So, instead of choosing such a hero, Melville picks as his spokesman and thus main character

Robert E. Lee. And as if to emphasize the anomaly of this choice, Melville describes the now retired Confederate general recently appointed president of Washington College with understated irony as a "quiet seminary's head" [229]. Can a college administrator be the centerpiece of poetry about "the terrible historic tragedy of our time" [272]?

Merely to state this question is to catch sight of the great risk Melville took in imitating Shakespeare. Nonetheless, this "quiet seminary's head" is the poet's spokesman, as we have seen, in a speech appealing to nature and to magnanimity. But, as we shall now see, Lee is Melville's spokesman even in his silence. Indeed, Lee is made by Melville to exhibit a heroic restraint from speech. Traveling from Washington College through the war-ravaged South, he passes his now confiscated estate of Arlington:

> And—last—seat no more his own,
> But Honor's; patriot grave-yards fill
> The forfeit slopes of that patrician hill,
> And fling a shroud on Arlington.
> The oaks ancestral all are low;
> No more from the porch his glance shall go
> Ranging the varied landscape o'er,
> Far as the looming Dome—no more.

After a pause, Lee exhibits an antipoetic self-possession: "the burst, the bitterness was spent,/ The heart-burst bitterly turbulent, /And on he fared" [230]. Dutifully he wends his way to the halls of Congress where he is to testify. When the senators ask if he has anything to say after answering their questions, his first instinct is to vigorously defend his own soldiers:

> Speak out? Ay, speak, and for the brave,
> Who else no voice or proxy have;
> Frankly their spokesman here become,
> And the flushed North from her own victory save.

That inspiration overrode—
Hardly it quelled the galling load
Of Personal ill. The inner feud
He, self-contained, a while withstood; [233]

Finally, however, he delivers his speech unpoetically counseling a moderating of Northern desire for vengeance. And so pleading, Lee serves Melville's dual purposes of both modifying the passions of the Civil War and responding to Plato's criticism of the poets.

So I close by returning to Melville's critics. As we noted earlier, Edmund Wilson censured *Battle-Pieces* as "a chronicle of the patriotic feelings of an anxious, middle-aged non-combatant" (479). Wilson of course meant that Melville was not a combatant in the American Civil War. But this point, while true, disregards a combat considerably older than the wars of Grant and Lee. For the poet of *Battle-Pieces* was a belligerent in Socrates' "old quarrel of philosophy and poetry." And as what might be called a traitor siding in this combat with philosophy, Melville knew his restraint would be viewed by many as poetic deficiency. But what was loss in popular appeal was gain elsewhere, in patriotic duty and in poetic ambition. If Melville's "kingly fabric" of poetry is not yet Shakespeare's –and I do not claim this book is as successful as *The Tempest*—it is already something to be able to compare the two without embarrassment. One can hardly do so with most American writers. If nature did not make Melville a poet in the conventional sense—as Charles Eliot Norton claims in my epigraph—nature and education made him something rarer. *Battle-Pieces* disappoints readers because Herman Melville subordinated commercial popularity to his love of country and his love of wisdom.

Notes

1. Edmund Wilson, *Patriotic Gore* (New York: Oxford University Press, 1962), 479.

2. *The Collected Works of Abraham Lincoln*, ed. Roy Basler, vol. 8 (New Brunswick, N.J.: Rutgers University, 1953), 333. Subsequent quotations annotated in text by parenthesis (Basler ed., volume number in Roman, page numbers in Arabic).

3. Lord Charnwood, *Abraham Lincoln* (New York: Henry Holt and Company, 1917), 450. Subsequent annotations in text in parenthesis (Charnwood, page numbers).

4. Plato, *The Laws of Plato*, trans. Thomas L. Pangle (New York: BasicBooks, 1980), 788A–835B; and in the same volume, Pangle, "Interpretive Essay," 477–78. Rousseau, *Letter to M. d'Alembert on the Theatre*, trans. Allan Bloom (Glencoe, Ill.: Free Press, 1960), 65–75.

Melville could have learned of Plato's teaching about mores supporting written laws from John Milton's *Areopagitica*, where the English poet speaks of "those unwritten, or at least unconstraining laws of virtuous education, religious and civil nurture, which Plato there mentions [in his *Laws*], as the bonds and ligaments of the Commonwealth, the pillars and sustainers of every written Statute" (*Complete Prose Works of John Milton*, ed. Don M. Wolfe et al. [New Haven: Yale University Press, 1953–73] II, 526). For an explanation of Milton's Platonism in this work, see Paul M. Dowling, *Polite Wisdom: Heathen Rhetoric in Milton's Areopagitica* (Lanham, Md.: Rowman & Littlefield, 1995), 53–54.

5. [269]. Some critics call Melville inconsistent for defending the Negro before the Civil War in *Benito Cereno*, and then after the war subordinating the freedmen's interest. See for instance Lawrence Buell, "Melville the Poet," *The Cambridge Companion to Herman Melville*, ed. Robert S. Levine (Cambridge: Cambridge University Press, 1998), 153–54.

But consistency in political matters does not require saying the same thing in changed historical circumstances. For a thoughtful treatment of this issue, see Herbert Storing's "Frederick Douglass." The changed circumstances for blacks from before the war to after was sufficient to moderate the speech of even so vehement a critic as the black leader Frederick Douglass. ("Frederick Douglass," *American Political Thought*, ed. Morton J. Frisch and Richard G. Stevens [New York: Charles Scribner's Sons, 1971], 153–54.) See also Winston S. Churchill, "Consistency in Politics," *Thoughts and Adventures* (London: Macmillan & Co., 1942), 39–47.

6. For an extended form of this argument, see Richard H. Cox and Paul M. Dowling, "Herman Melville's Civil War: Lincolnian Prudence in Poetry," *Political Science Reviewer* 29 (2000): 241–60.

7. 1.3.111. All quotations from Shakespeare found in *The Riverside Shakespeare* (Boston: Houghton Mifflin Co., 1974). Subsequent quotations annotated in text in parenthesis (by act, scene, line).

8. These and other word counts were aided by the "Concordance of Great Books," William A. Williams Jr.'s site on the Internet.

9. Helen Vendler, "Melville and the Lyric of History," 263–64 in this volume.

10. *The Rebellion Record: A Diary of American Events* (New York: D. Van Nostrand, Publisher, 1861–68), volumes I-XII; IV, 170–85. Subsequent annotation to this volume in text in parenthesis (volume in Roman, pages in Arabic).

11. "Melville the Poet," in *Melville: A Collection of Critical Essays* (Englewood Cliffs, N.J.: Prentice-Hall, Inc., 1962), 148.

12. Thomas L. Pangle, ed., *The Roots of Political Philosophy: Ten Forgotten Socratic Dialogues*, trans. Allan Bloom (Ithaca, N.Y.: Cornell University Press, 1987), 535D. Subsequent annotation in main text in parentheses.

13. "The Symposium," *The Symposium and The Phaedo*, trans. Raymond Larson (Arlington Heights, Ill.: Harlan Davidson, Inc., 1980), 175E.

14. For this understanding of both Shakespeare's mixed mode and of Plato's *Symposium*, I am indebted to Allan Bloom, *Love and Friendship* (New York: Simon & Schuster, 1993), 274, 348, 394–95.

15. *Billy Budd, Sailor and Other Stories*, ed. Harold Beaver (New York: Penguin Books, 1982), 336. I am indebted for this point about *Billy Budd* to James R. Hurtgen, "*Billy Budd* and the Context of Political Rule," in *Critical Essays on Billy Budd*, ed. Robert Milder (New York: G. K. Hall & Co., 1989), 173–85, esp. 180–81.

Selected Bibliography

EDITIONS

Battle-Pieces and Aspects of the War. New York: Harper & Row Publishers, 1866. 272 pages.

The Battle-Pieces of Herman Meville. Edited with Introduction and Notes, by Hennig Cohen. New York: Thomas Yoseloff, 1963. 302 pages. Cohen's numerous annotations about points linguistic, literary, and historical are indispensable for a study of Melville's poems.

Battle-Pieces and Aspects of the War. Edited with an Introduction by Sidney Kaplan. Amherst: University of Massachusetts Press, 1972. Pages v–xliv, and 272. Kaplan reprints a number of the first reviews of Melville's book. He also includes a number of Melville's emendations of the text, which generally are minor.

Battle-Pieces and Aspects of the War. New Introduction by Lee Rust Brown. New York: Da Capo Press, 1995. Pages iii–xvi, and 272.

GENERAL BACKGROUND

Garner, Stanton. *The Civil War World of Herman Melville.* Lawrence: University Press of Kansas, 1993. This study contains the single most extensive bibliography of works which treat the background to and interpretations of Melville's *Battle-Pieces*. See pp. 513–24.

Long, E. B., with Barbara Long. *The Civil War Day by Day: An Almanac*

1861–1865. New York, Da Capo Press, n.d. As the title suggests, this volume treats events—especially military and political events—of the Civil War literally day by day.

McPherson, James M. *Battle Cry of Freedom. The Civil War Era*. New York and Oxford: Oxford University Press, 1988.

The Rebellion Record: A Diary of American Events. New York: D. Van Nostrand, Publisher, 1861–68. Volumes I–XII. Melville made extensive use of several of these volumes, especially in poems about some battles.

The Atlas of the Civil War. Edited by James M. McPherson. New York: Macmillan, 1994.

Commentary

There is no book-length study exclusively devoted to an analysis and interpretation of Melville's *Battle-Pieces*. But some essay-length commentaries and interpretations are to be found in the following publications. Briefer treatments are cited in the biblographies to Hennig Cohen's edition of *Battle-Pieces* and Stanton Garner's *The Civil War World of Herman Melville*.

Brown, Lee Rust. "Introduction" (pp. iii–xvi) of the Da Capo edition of *Battle-Pieces*.

Buell, Lawrence. "Melville the Poet," *The Cambridge Companion to Herman Melville*. Edited by Robert S. Levine. Cambridge and New York: Cambridge University Press, 1998, pp. 135–56.

Cohen, Hennig. "Introduction" (pp. 11–28), and "Notes" (pp. 203–95), of the Yoseloff edition of *Battle-Pieces*.

Cox, Richard H., and Paul Dowling. "Herman Melville's Civil War: Lincolnian Prudence in Poetry." *Political Science Reviewer* 29 (2000): 192–295.

Day, Frank L. *Herman Melville's Use of* The Rebellion Record *in His Poetry*. University of Tennessee thesis, 1959.

Garner, Stanton. "*Battle-Pieces*, 1865–1866." In Garner, *The Civil War World of Herman Melville*, chapter 9, pp. 388–439.

Kaplan, Sidney. "Introduction" (pp. v–xliv) of the University of Massachusetts edition of *Battle-Pieces*.

Warren, Robert Penn. "Melville the Poet." *Kenyon Review* 8 (1946): 208–23.

———. *Selected Poems of Herman Melville: A Reader's Edition*. Edited with an introduction by Robert Penn Warren. New York: Random House, 1970. Especially valuable are Warren's "Introduction" (pp. 8–35) and his "Notes" (pp. 351–85) to thirty-one poems from *Battle-Pieces* selected for this volume.

———. *American Literature: The Makers and the Making*. Book B. 1826 to 1861. Cleanth Brooks, R. W. B. Lewis, and Robert Penn Warren. New York: St. Martin's Press, 1974. Warren wrote the general introduction to the selections from Melville (pp. 809–33) and the headnotes to several of the poems from *Battle-Pieces* (pp. 917–24).

Vendler, Helen. "Melville and the Lyric of History." *Southern Review* 35, no. 3 (summer 1999): 579–94.

Warren, Rosanna. "Dark Knowledge: Melville's Poems of the Civil War." *Raritan* 19, no. 1 (summer 1999): 100–21.

Contributors

RICHARD H. COX is professor emeritus of political science at the State University of New York (Buffalo). He has published works on Thucydides, Aristotle, Machiavelli, Shakespeare, Locke, and Camus, as well as on American Constitutionalism. His most recent publications are "Herman Melville's Civil War: Lincolnian Prudence in Poetry," coauthored with Paul Dowling for the *Political Science Reviewer* (2000); and *Four Pillars of Constitutionalism: The Organic Laws of the United States* (Prometheus Books, 1998).

PAUL DOWLING is Professor of English at Canisius College, Buffalo, New York. He has published *Polite Wisdom: Heathen Rhetoric in Milton's Areopagitica* (Rowman and Littlefield, 1995).

JAMES M. MCPHERSON is George Henry Davis '86 Professor of American History at Princeton University, where he has taught since 1962. He is the author or editor of nearly two dozen books, mostly on the Civil War era, including *Battle Cry of Freedom* (1988), which won the Pulitzer Prize for history in 1989, and *For Cause and Comrades: Why Men Fought in the Civil War* (1997), which won the Lincoln Prize in 1998.

HELEN VENDLER is the A. Kingsley Porter University Professor at Harvard. She has written books on Yeats, Stevens, Herbert, Keats, Shakespeare, and Heaney, and her essays and reviews appear in three volumes: *Part of Nature, Part of Us*; *The Music of What Happens*; and *Soul Says*. Her Eliot Lectures have been collected as *The Given and the Made*, and her Ellmann Lectures as *The Breaking of Style*. She is a frequent reviewer of contemporary poetry in such journals as the *New York Review of Books*, the *London Review of Books*, and the *New Republic*.

ROSANNA WARREN teaches comparative literature at Boston University. Her most recent volume of poems is *Stained Glass*. Her most recent book is a verse translation of Euripides' *Suppliant Women* (with Stephen Scully).

LEE COUNTY LIBRARY SYSTEM